D1162889

BATMAN®

ARCHIVES ▼ VOLUME 4

BOB KANE

ARCHIVE  EDITIONS

DC COMICS

BATMAN ARCHIVES
VOLUME FOUR

ISBN 1-56389-414-9

PUBLISHED BY DC COMICS

DC COMICS
1700 BROADWAY
NEW YORK, NY 10019

A DIVISION OF WARNER BROS. -
A TIME WARNER ENTERTAINMENT COMPANY
PRINTED AND BOUND IN CANADA.
FIRST PRINTING.

THE DC ARCHIVE EDITIONS

COVER ILLUSTRATION BY DICK SPRANG.
COVER COLOR BY RICK TAYLOR.
SEPARATIONS BY ROB SCHWAGER.

SERIES DESIGN BY ALEX JAY/STUDIO J.

PUBLICATION DESIGN BY JASON LYONS.

BLACK-AND-WHITE RECONSTRUCTION
BY RICK KEENE.

COLOR RECONSTRUCTION BY BOB LE ROSE.

TABLE OF CONTENTS

TABLE OF CONTENTS

Art credits assembled by Joe Desris.
Writing credits assembled by Martin O'Hearn, Richard Morrissey and Joe Desris.

***Story originally untitled.**

FOREWORD

It was mid-1941, and Whitney Ellsworth, executive editor of National Comics Publications (later named DC Comics), was looking at the very first 13-page Batman story he had assigned me to pencil, ink and letter, and bring to him completed in sixteen days.

As a sprout of 26 years, I had been writing and illustrating Western pulp stories in New York since 1936, after I had quit a good newspaper job in the midwest. In these years of the Great Depression I was no stranger to hard work and hard-to-find work in my bracket of the creative arts. There was nothing I wanted to do more than dramatic illustration. But the pulps were dying. The comics were replacing them. It appeared my future lay in them.

Whitney Ellsworth looked at each 15" x 18" page, not slowly, not rapidly, squared them on his desk, picked up his phone and told the comptroller to cut me a check. A substantial check.

Thirteen pages, six panels each, seventy-eight illustrations, and no negative comment.

"Mr. Ellsworth," I said, "I've never turned in a work anywhere this complicated without being asked to make changes."

Whit shook his head and smiled. "If we need minor changes they'll be made by our staff artists in our bullpen. I'd like you to work for us on full-time Batman production."

"Gladly," I darn near shouted, "but why did you like my work on this story?"

"I like the way you interpret a script, and you got the work in on time."

The 1940s were the early years of comics, a new medium, not daily strips of four panels or lone Sunday pages, but long stories told in scores of panel illustrations all culminating in complete, unified adventure stories, some of which, entirely unimagined by us at the time, would five decades later be reprinted here to be read by collectors and fans.

Whitney Ellsworth had a vision. Quality comics were possible, and he would produce and publish them. The early work of Vince Sullivan, followed by Ellsworth teamed with Mort Weisinger and Jack Schiff, laid the solid foundation of today's DC Comics.

Whit never told me how to draw, what

to put in or leave out. He left script interpretation fully up to me. He liked the accuracy of my architecture, interiors, machinery, ships, weapons and costumes which are to some extent illustrated in my *Crime Between the Acts* story reprinted herein.

By giving me free rein, he accepted the risk of my fouling up, but it appears he figured I was the kind of animal that would realize the risk he was taking and do my best to eliminate it. He trusted me, and thus I honor him as my friend and as the man who built the Golden Age of comics. He carefully selected his writers and artists, and he let them write and draw as they saw their commitment. Who could ever want a better editor to work for?

My early stories, the several reprinted here, present some evidence of work to come as I grew into the medium. What I tried to pull off was making movies in frozen frame, drawn images that produced a recognition and feeling of dramatic movement, lighting and setting, cutting from close-up to long shot, bird's eye to ground-level view, and perspective untamed. All comic art pages are a collection of images. But how do you arrange them to establish danger, serenity, suspense, fear and humor; how do you interpret a script with gusto, liveliness, vigor and authentic substance? The working relationship between writers and artists is fascinating.

My influences were Alex Raymond, Hal Foster, Roy Crane, Milt Caniff, and the great N. C. Wyeth. But mainly, the influence that counted most was Whit Ellsworth. He gave me a great trip. According to comic-book historian Joe Desris, I drew 60 covers and 238 stories. If averaged to 11 pages each, the page total would be 2,618. At 6 panels per page, the result is 15,708 individual panels. Mike Shields has broken this figure down to "2.15 panels per day every day for twenty years."

My honored fans, thank you for your long support. Perhaps, in future Archives, we'll talk about technique and the special effects that can be created in drawing.

Dick

Dick Sprang

(A biography of Jerry Robinson appears on page 224.)

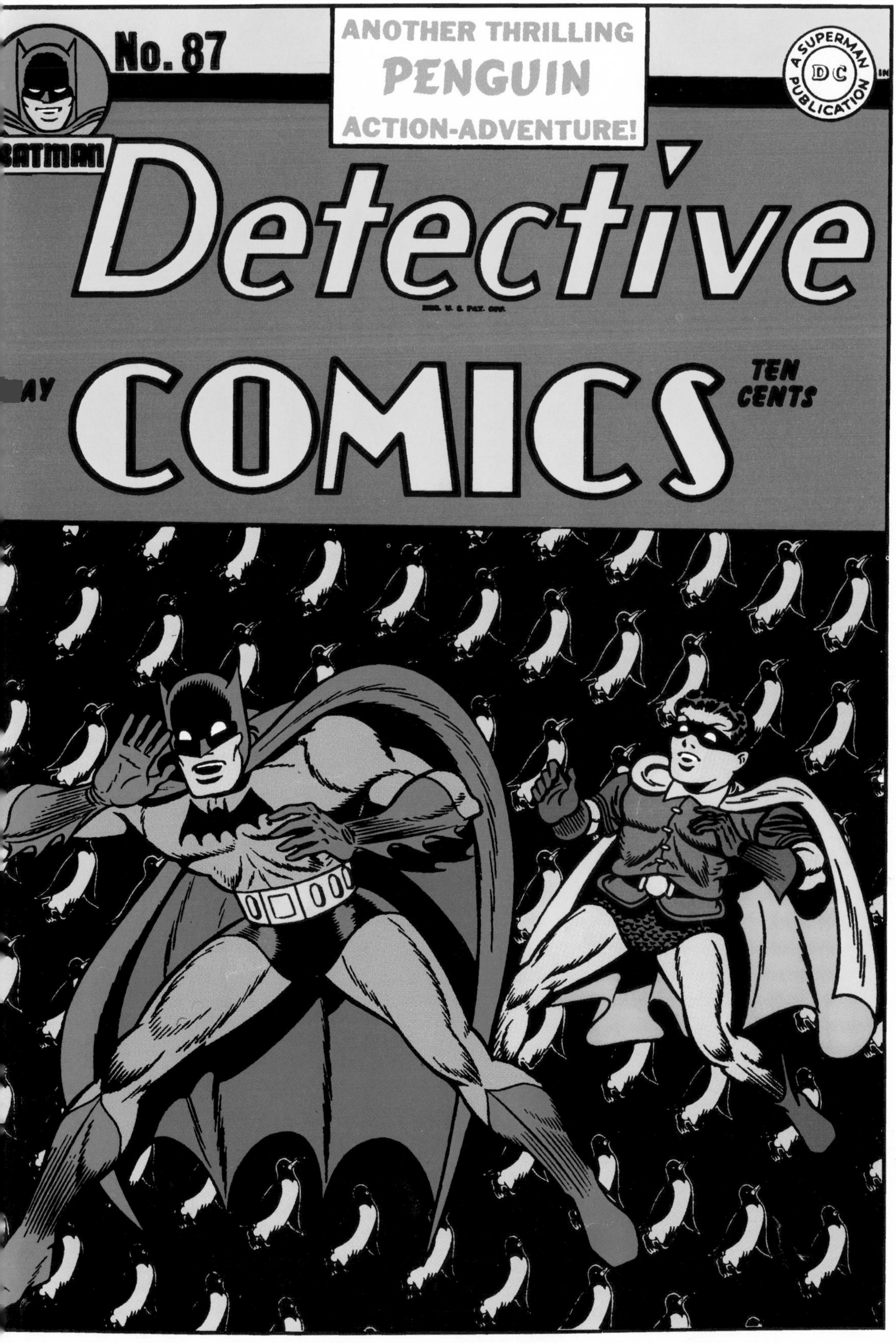

BATMAN

No. 87

ANOTHER THRILLING
PENGUIN
ACTION-ADVENTURE!

A SUPERMAN DC PUBLICATION

Detective

REG. U. S. PAT. OFF.

AY

COMICS

TEN CENTS

BATMAN
WITH
ROBIN
-THE BOY WONDER-
THERE'S NOTHING LIKE AN ORDINARY UMBRELLA FOR KEEPING DRY IN AN ORDINARY SHOWER...
BUT WHEN THAT BOLD BIRD OF BANDITRY, THE PENGUIN, UNLIMBERS HIS ARSENAL OF EXTRA-SUPER-SPECIAL UMBRELLAS--- THEN'S THE TIME TO LOOK OUT FOR SUCH A THUNDERSTORM OF VILLAINY AS ONLY THE RAZOR-EDGED WITS OF ONE OF THE WORLD'S SHREWDEST CRIMINALS CAN STIR UP!
IT IS IN SUCH A DEADLY DOWNPOUR THAT THE MIGHTY BATMAN AND THE DAREDEVIL ROBIN ARE CAUGHT WHEN THEY SWING INTO DAZZLING ACTION ONCE MORE AGAINST AN OLD ENEMY, MATCHING TRICK FOR TRICK WITH---
"THE MAN OF A THOUSAND UMBRELLAS"
BRUCE WAYNE, SOCIETY PLAYBOY, AND HIS YOUNG WARD, DICK GRAYSON, FIGHT A LOSING BATTLE WITH BOREDOM AT THE BEACH...
HO, HUM! THREE GUESSES, DICK--- WHAT DO ALL THOSE UMBRELLAS REMIND ME OF?
LET ME SEE... HO, HUM...

THAT I'M GOING TO GET SUNBURNED IF I DON'T TURN OVER?
NO!

THAT THOSE LITTLE CLOUDS LOOK LIKE RAIN?
NO!

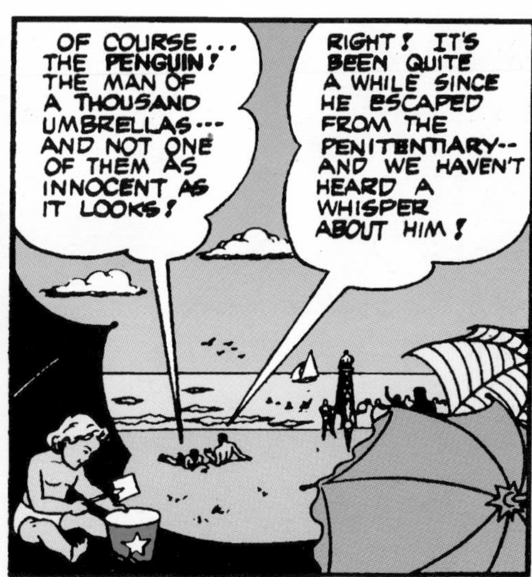
OF COURSE... THE PENGUIN! THE MAN OF A THOUSAND UMBRELLAS--- AND NOT ONE OF THEM AS INNOCENT AS IT LOOKS!
RIGHT! IT'S BEEN QUITE A WHILE SINCE HE ESCAPED FROM THE PENITENTIARY-- AND WE HAVEN'T HEARD A WHISPER ABOUT HIM!

THINGS HAVE BEEN TOO QUIET! I'M SO BORED, I'D WELCOME A GOOD, OLD-FASHIONED FIST FIGHT!
ME, TOO! THE BATMAN AND ROBIN WILL GET RUSTY IF THEY DON'T START SOMETHING SOON!

START SOMETHING? NOW YOU'RE TALKING! WHAT HAVE YOU GOT UP YOUR SLEEVE--- IF YOU HAD A SLEEVE!
ONLY AN IDEA!

HOW WOULD YOU LIKE TO SMOKE THE PENGUIN OUT OF HIDING?
HOW WOULD I LIKE IT? YIPPEE,--- LET'S GO!

BUT HOW'LL WE GO ABOUT FINDING A BIRD AS CAGEY AS HE IS?
I HAVE A PLAN....

IN ONE WORD--- WHAT?
IN ONE WORD--- UMBRELLAS!

SO IT HAPPENS THAT, TWO DAYS LATER, A CREAKING, WHEEZING WAGON PREPARES TO TOUR THE STREETS OF GOTHAM CITY...
UMBRELLAS EXPERTLY MENDED
YOU BREAK 'EM WE FIX 'EM
NOT EXACTLY HANDSOME--- BUT IT SAVES GAS AND TIRES!
AND THAT AIN'T HAY!
UM-BRELLAS MENDED! ANY UM-BRELLAS TODAY?
LOUDER!
UMBRELLA REPAIRS
I BENT THIS ONE OVER THE HEAD OF A BURGLAR--- CLIMBING THROUGH A WINDOW---ONLY HE TURNED OUT TO BE MY HUSBAND!
RECKON THE MOTHS MUSTA GOT INTO THIS!
YOU REALLY KNOW YOUR STUFF! WE COULD MAKE A GOOD LIVING AT THIS!
I CAN THINK OF WORSE WAYS!
WE'VE BEEN DRIVING ALL DAY--- AND NO PENGUIN!
IT'S A BIG CITY, DICK... BUT EVEN IF IT TAKES US WEEKS, IT'LL BE BETTER THAN LYING AROUND DOING NOTHING!
BUT THE PSEUDO-UMBRELLA-MENDERS ARE NEARER THE END OF THEIR SEARCH THAN THEY THINK---FOR NOT FAR AHEAD OF THEM WADDLES A FAMILIAR FIGURE...
SMOKED GLASSES ARE ENOUGH OF A DISGUISE TO FOOL THE STUPID POLICE! HMMM... NEARLY TIME FOR SHOPS TO CLOSE!
THE PENGUIN!
I KNOW IT'S CLOSING TIME, BUT I SIMPLY MUST HAVE THOSE MAGNIFICENT EMERALDS YOU HAD ON DISPLAY EARLIER!
WELL--- OF COURSE IF YOU WISH TO MAKE A PURCHASE THAT LARGE...
3

I AM THE MANAGER, SIR... WE HAVE LOCKED THE EMERALDS IN THE SAFE, BUT IF YOU WISH, I SHALL OPEN IT! ---
DON'T TROUBLE YOURSELF, MY GOOD MAN!
JEWELRY
DIAMONDS
WATCHES
RARE GEMS

... I ASSURE YOU, I AM QUITE CAPABLE OF OPENING IT MYSELF!
WHAT---? GAS! AAA-H-H-H!
A THIEF! OOOHH-H!

NOTHING LIKE AN UMBRELLA TO HELP A MAN PROVIDE FOR A RAINY DAY! IT'S A WEAPON, A BURGLAR TOOL ---

---AND A SAFE, UNSUSPICIOUS CARRY-ALL FOR LOOT!

ONLY A SINGLE SEEMINGLY MILD MISHAP MARS THE PENGUIN'S PERFECT ROBBERY--- BUT IT IS ONE THAT IS DESTINED TO GIVE HIM MORE TROUBLE THAN HE DREAMS...
UGH! STUPID FELLOW, LYING RIGHT IN MY WAY! WHY, I MIGHT HAVE SPILLED THE GEMS ALL OVER THE FLOOR!

HOW UNFORTUNATE! ONE OF MY FAVORITE UMBRELLAS--- AND IT'S THE FOURTH I'VE DAMAGED THIS WEEK!

MOMENTS LATER...
AHA--- AN UMBRELLA MENDER!... I WON'T RISK ACCOSTING HIM PERSONALLY, BUT--- HERE, BOY!
YA CALLIN' ME, MISTER?
JEWELRY
DIAMONDS
WATCHES
RARE GEMS

4

A MAN GIMME A QUARTER T' BRING YA DIS NOTE!
SOMEBODY NAMED FEATHER WANTS US TO CALL AT HIS HOUSE TOMORROW AFTERNOON TO MEND SOME UMBRELLAS!
BUSINESS IS TOO GOOD! HOW CAN WE CATCH THE PENGUIN THIS WAY?

NEXT DAY...
WE'RE THE UMBRELLA MENDERS MR. FEATHER SENT FOR!
OH, YEAH--- YOUSE CAN COME RIGHT IN!

DESE IS DEM!
SO I SEE--- HMMM....

MAYBE WE'VE FOUND SOMETHING! DID YOU GET THE BUTLER'S SING SING ACCENT?
YES... AND I'M ALSO LOOKING AT THE FINEST COLLECTION OF UMBRELLAS I'VE SEEN SINCE WE INVADED THE PENGUIN'S LAST HIDEOUT!

NIGHT---AND TWO MANTLED FIGURES CREEP THROUGH THE SHADOWS TOWARD "MR.FEATHERS" HOME...
WHAT A SURPRISE HE'S GOING TO GET!
WE HOPE!

IT'S THE PENGUIN, ALL RIGHT!
ANY UMBRELLAS NEAR HIM?

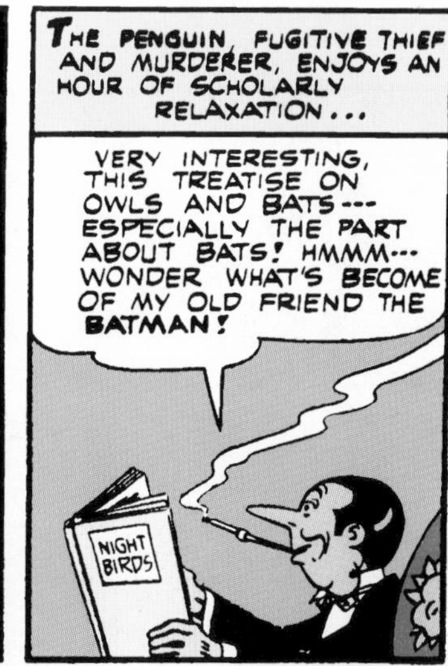

THE PENGUIN, FUGITIVE THIEF AND MURDERER, ENJOYS AN HOUR OF SCHOLARLY RELAXATION...
VERY INTERESTING, THIS TREATISE ON OWLS AND BATS---ESPECIALLY THE PART ABOUT BATS! HMMM---WONDER WHAT'S BECOME OF MY OLD FRIEND THE BATMAN!
NIGHT BIRDS

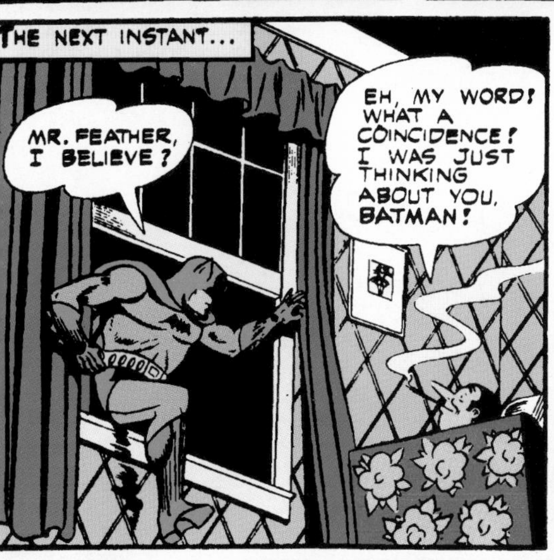

THE NEXT INSTANT...
MR. FEATHER, I BELIEVE?
EH, MY WORD! WHAT A COINCIDENCE! I WAS JUST THINKING ABOUT YOU, BATMAN!

BELIEVE ME, MY FRIENDS, YOU ARE A SIGHT FOR SORE EYES!
ALWAYS THE GENTLEMAN!
LOOK OUT, BATMAN, HE'S GOING TO PULL SOMETHING!
NIGHT BIRDS

ON THE CONTRARY, ROBIN, MY LITTLE MAN---I'M GOING TO PUSH SOMETHING! THIS BUTTON!
OH, NO YOU DON'T!

A SHEET OF THICK PLATE GLASS SHOOTS UPWARD, AND...
OW! WHAT HIT ME?
GLASS---INCHES THICK AND STRONG AS STEEL!
YOU SEE, I AM ALWAYS PREPARED TO RECEIVE UNEXPECTED VISITORS!

KNOWING HOW TENDERHEARTED I AM, YOU'LL UNDERSTAND MY RELUCTANCE TO REMAIN WHILE MY HOUSEHOLD STAFF PERFORMS A SLIGHTLY FATAL OPERATION UPON YOU... TOODLE-OO!

6

AS THE DOOR CLOSES UPON THE RESOURCEFUL ROGUE...
OH, OH--- THEY MEAN BUSINESS!
COITAINS FOR DE BATMAN! I BET MOST BUTLERS DON'T HAVE DIS MUCH FUN!

UGH! DID I SAY FUN?
I DON'T KNOW WHERE YOU GET YOUR TRAINING--- BUT ITS CUSTOMARY FOR A BUTLER TO BOW WHEN ENTERING A ROOM!

TAKE THE REST OF THE RUBBISH WITH YOU AS YOU PASS OUT!
MAYBE WE SHOULDA TOOK TH' LITTLE FELLA FOIST!

BUT THE LITTLE FELLA IS ALSO ENJOYING HIMSELF..
I SHOVE YOUR NOSE BACK, AND YOU JUST FOLLOW YOUR NOSE! SEE?
ALL I CAN SEE IS SKYROCKETS!

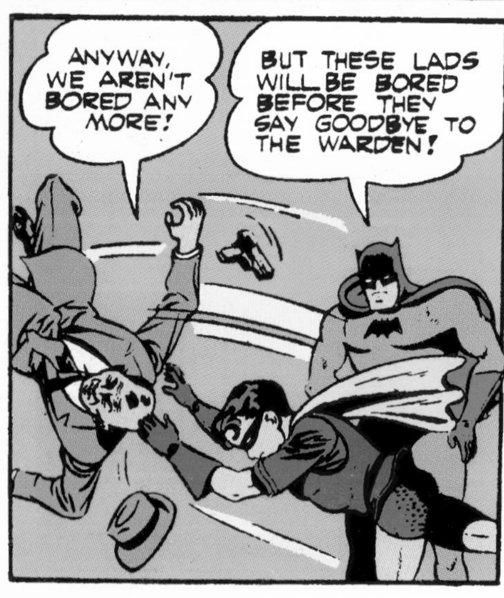
ANYWAY, WE AREN'T BORED ANY MORE!
BUT THESE LADS WILL BE BORED BEFORE THEY SAY GOODBYE TO THE WARDEN!

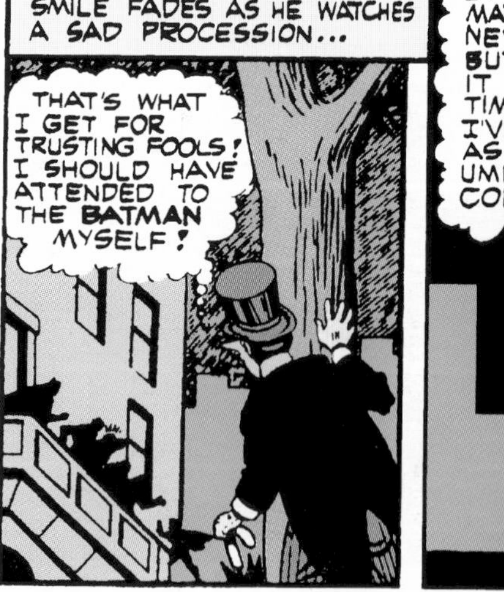
OUTSIDE, THE PENGUIN'S SMILE FADES AS HE WATCHES A SAD PROCESSION...
THAT'S WHAT I GET FOR TRUSTING FOOLS! I SHOULD HAVE ATTENDED TO THE BATMAN MYSELF!

IT WILL BE A SIMPLE MATTER TO FIND NEW QUARTERS--- BUT I'M AFRAID IT WILL BE A LONG TIME BEFORE I'VE GATHERED AS FINE AN UMBRELLA COLLECTION!
7

NEXT DAY IN THE BRUCE WAYNE HOME...
I FEEL LIKE AN IDIOT WHEN I THINK HOW WE LET HIM SLIP THROUGH OUR HANDS!
DON'T TAKE IT SO HARD... NEXT TIME WE'LL TURN THE TABLES!

IF THERE IS A NEXT TIME! BUT HE'LL BE EXTRA CAREFUL AND NEVER GO OUT WITHOUT A DISGUISE!
WELL, IF WE SEE A SHORT-LEGGED LITTLE MAN CARRYING AN UMBRELLA ON A SUNNY DAY, WE'LL TAKE A PEEK BEHIND THE FALSE WHISKERS!

TRUE, THE PENGUIN'S TRADE MARK IS AN UMBRELLA--BUT WHEN BRUCE AND DICK SCOUT THE CROWDED STREETS...
SEEMS TO ME I NEVER SAW SO MANY UMBRELLAS IN MY LIFE BEFORE WHEN THE SUN WAS SHINING!
YOU NEVER DID, DICK!
3rd AVE
42nd ST

SOMETHING TELLS ME THIS IS ONE OF THE CLEVEREST STUNTS THE PENGUIN HAS THOUGHT UP YET! AND I'M GOING TO GET TO THE BOTTOM OF IT!
LET'S INTERVIEW SOME OF THESE UMBRELLA-TOTERS!

AS IS THE CASE WITH MOST MYSTERIES, THE EXPLANATION IS SIMPLE ENOUGH WHEN TRACKED DOWN..

YOU SEE?
I THINK I DO!
UMBRELLAS
P.N. QUINN
UMBRELLAS FREE TODAY ONLY

AND SO SHALL WE SEE IF WE GLANCE INTO THE WORKSHOP BEHIND THE UMBRELLA STORE, WHERE A PUDGY MAN HUMS HAPPILY AT HIS FAVORITE OCCUPATION...
TA-DA-DE-DA... THIS IS PERFECT! WHY DIDN'T I THINK OF BUYING AN UMBRELLA SHOP BEFORE? AS FOR MY IDEA OF GIVING AWAY SAMPLES TO CONFUSE THE BATMAN--- IT'S SHEER GENIUS!

MERELY ONE OF MANY AMUSING AND USEFUL DEVICES I SHALL CREATE--- A RADIO UMBRELLA TO DIRECT MY MEN IN THEIR OPERATIONS! THE RIBS ACT AS AN AERIAL, AND THE PERSON HOLDING IT PROVIDES THE GROUND CONNECTION!
8

AS DARKNESS FALLS, A WEIRD VEHICLE GLIDES THROUGH THE QUIET STREETS---THE BATMOBILE!

THIS IS THE PLACE ... ALL SET FOR SOME EXCITEMENT!

AND HOW!

A PERISCOPIC VISION DEVICE WARNS THE PENGUIN ...

SO HE SAW THROUGH MY SCHEME OF GIVING AWAY UMBRELLAS! PERHAPS IT'S JUST AS WELL!

YOU'RE PRETTY GOOD AT PICKING THAT LOCK!

A MAN CAN'T CATCH CROOKS UNTIL HE HAS LEARNED ALL THEIR TRICKS!

THE BIRD HAS FLOWN!

I DOUBT IT ... THE DOOR IN THE BACK IS OPENING!..

THERE'S NO HIDING FROM YOU GENTLEMEN, IS THERE? STEP RIGHT INTO MY PARLOR!

KEEP YOUR HANDS AT YOUR SIDES AND DON'T REACH FOR ANY OF YOUR INFERNAL UMBRELLAS, PENGUIN!

PRIVATE

I PROMISE NOT TO LIFT A FINGER TO TRAP YOU! BUT IF YOU SHOULD BE SO UNFORTUNATE AS TO STEP ON A HIDDEN BUTTON ...
BATMAN--- LOOK OUT!

YOU SEE, YOU DID IT YOURSELVES! ONLY A BATMAN IN A GILDED CAGE!
THESE CAGES WON'T HOLD US LONG!
9

BECAUSE OF YOU, THEY WERE GOING TO KEEP ME IN JAIL FOR A LONG WHILE! NOW I AM ABOUT TO ENJOY THE EXQUISITE PLEASURE OF PUTTING YOU AWAY -- FOR GOOD!
DON'T DO ANYTHING YOU'LL BE SORRY FOR!

HIGH-VOLTAGE WIRES ARE HOOKED TO THOSE UMBRELLA STAYS THAT IMPRISON YOU, AND THERE IS A SWITCH INSIDE THE CLOCK! AT MIDNIGHT--- IN EXACTLY TEN MINUTES-- A LETHAL CURRENT WILL DISPOSE OF YOU!

I MUST LEAVE TO TEST A NEW UMBRELLA I HAVE INVENTED--- BUT I'LL RETURN TO DISPOSE OF YOUR BODIES!

LEFT ALONE, THE CRIME-CRUSHERS WATCH THE CREEPING HANDS OF THE CLOCK APPROACH THE HOUR OF DOOM...

I CAN'T EVEN BEND THESE STEEL RODS!
NEITHER CAN I! IF I HAD A LEVER OF SOME KIND...

IF I COULD ONLY REACH ONE OF THOSE UMBRELLAS ...
YOUR BELT, BATMAN!

ROBIN, IF THIS WORKS, I'LL GIVE YOU FULL CREDIT FOR SAVING BOTH OUR LIVES!

NEVER MIND THE CREDIT! DO SOMETHING BEFORE MIDNIGHT STRIKES!

LET'S HOPE THIS IS A STRONG UMBRELLA!
I'M HOPING--- AND THE CLOCK IS TICKING!

ANOTHER INCH AND I'LL BE FREE!
DON'T FORGET ME!
10

STEADY, ROBIN!
CAN I HELP IT IF I'M IMPATIENT!

SECONDS LATER...
HE WASN'T FOOLING!
NEITHER WILL WE BE WHEN HE RETURNS!

THAT'S IT... OPEN ALL OF THEM!
IF YOU SAY SO... BUT I DON'T SEE THE POINT!
PRIVATE

MEANWHILE, THE PENGUIN IS MAKING A BUSINESS CALL AT A LUXURIOUS PENTHOUSE...
DON'T WORRY, MRS VAN VOORT... I ASSURE YOU, YOU AND YOUR MAID WILL AWAKEN NONE THE WORSE FOR THIS WHIFF OF SLEEP-INDUCING VAPOR!
HELP!... AA-A-HH-H----

AH... THE FAMOUS VAN VOORT PEARLS! THEY'LL MAKE A SNUG NEST-EGG FOR THE PENGUIN!

A THUNDERSTORM IS COMING UP! I'D BETTER HURRY!

MY NEW GLIDER UMBRELLA WILL BE INVALUABLE IN MY PROFESSION! TOO BAD THE BATMAN CAN'T SEE ME NOW!

A SUCCESSFUL TEST FLIGHT INDEED!... BUT I MUST HASTEN TO AVOID THE STORM!
UMBRELLAS
P.N. QUINN

PRESENTLY...
SURPRISE!
YOU! HOW? WHAT---?
YOU'LL BURN YET! ... HUH? IT DOESN'T WORK!
NO LIQUID FIRE, PENGUIN! WE PERFORMED A SLIGHT OPERATION ON THAT UMBRELLA!
A COUPLE OF SWORD-THRUSTS, AND ---
WE HAD NOTHING ELSE TO DO, SO WE REMOVED THE BLADE!
AT LEAST, I CAN GET AWAY!
HEY !--WE MISSED THAT ONE, BATMAN!
ONE OF THESE DAYS I'LL FIX YOU FOR GOOD!
NOT IF I FIX YOU FIRST!
PUTT
PUTT
PUTT
BE CAREFUL! YOU MIGHT HURT ME!
OH, WE WOULDN'T DO ANYTHING LIKE THAT!
POOF
WHAT GOES UP MUST COME DOWN!
BUT HARDER!
12

THE PENGUIN MAKES A FINAL DESPERATE DASH FOR FREEDOM...
BY THE TIME YOU GET THIS DOOR OPEN, I'LL BE MILES AWAY!
WANT TO BET?

THIS WON'T TAKE LONG!
IT BETTER NOT...IT'S STARTING TO RAIN--- AND WE HAVEN'T AN UMBRELLA LEFT!

IN THE DARK STORE, THE PENGUIN DISCOVERS THAT HIS BELOVED UMBRELLAS CAN BE TROUBLESOME...
WHAT? UMBRELLAS--- SCATTERED EVERYWHERE

HEAVENS--- I NEVER DREAMED THEY COULD BE SUCH NUISANCES!

I CAN'T MOVE! I'M CAUGHT--- TRAPPED BY MY OWN UMBRELLAS!

TAKE THEM OFF! I NEVER WANT TO SEE THEM AGAIN!
HE SEEMS TO BE HAVING A LITTLE TROUBLE, ROBIN!
I KNOW A PLACE WHERE THEY'LL TAKE THEM OFF!

AND SO---FOR THE PRESENT, AT LEAST---THE PENGUIN BECOMES A JAILBIRD--- AND ALL BECAUSE OF TWO PEOPLE'S BOREDOM...
THE PENGUIN'S PLUMAGE SEEMS A BIT RUFFLED!
WITH ALL THOSE UMBRELLAS HE'S WEARING, YOU'D THINK HE COULD MANAGE TO KEEP DRY!
OH, DRY UP YOURSELF!
POLICE STATION
THE END

No. 88
JUNE...TEN CENTS
A SUPERMAN DC PUBLICATION
BATMAN
Detective
REG U S PAT OFF
COMICS

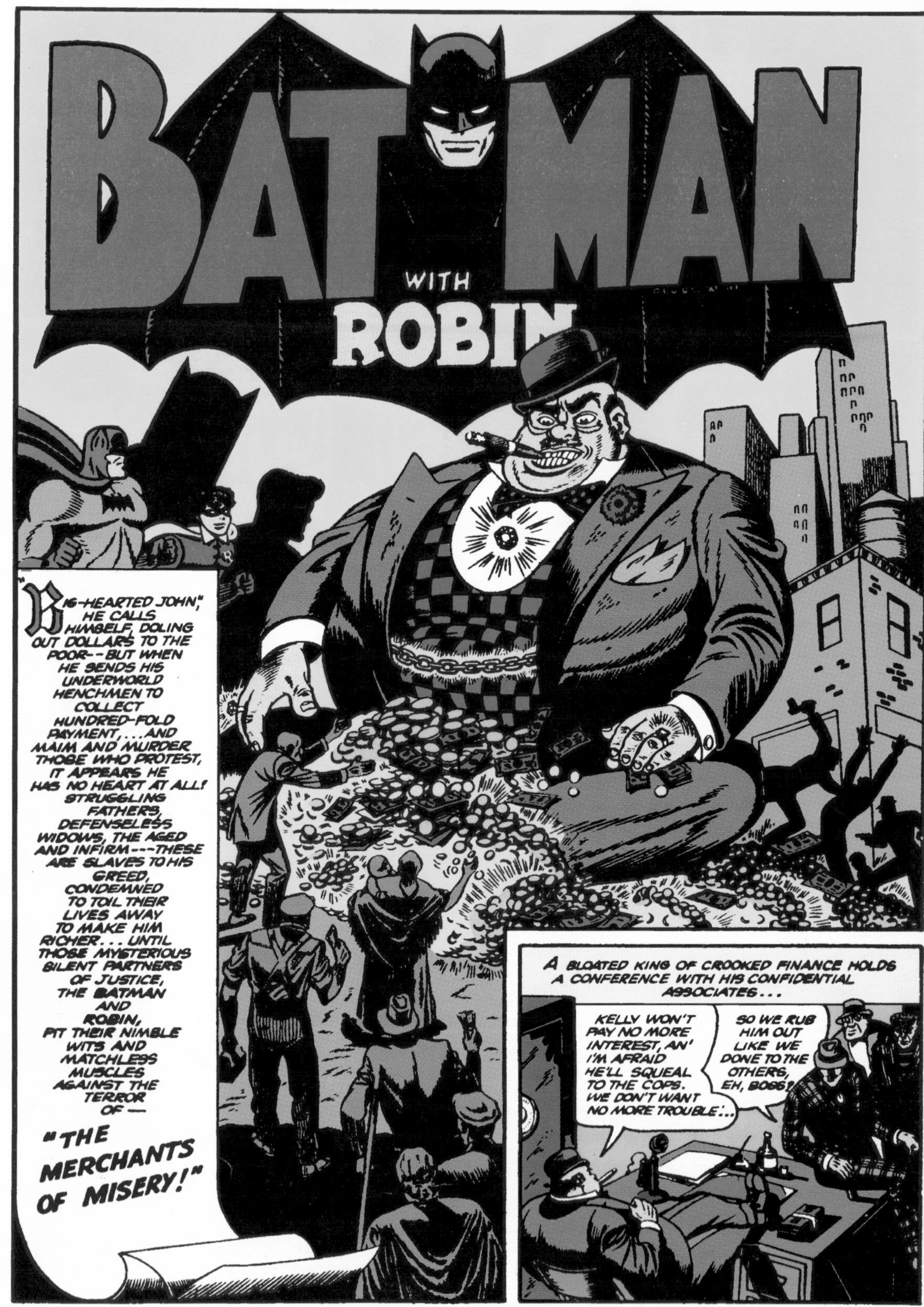
BATMAN
WITH
ROBIN
"BIG-HEARTED JOHN," HE CALLS HIMSELF, DOLING OUT DOLLARS TO THE POOR--BUT WHEN HE SENDS HIS UNDERWORLD HENCHMEN TO COLLECT HUNDRED-FOLD PAYMENT,...AND MAIM AND MURDER THOSE WHO PROTEST, IT APPEARS HE HAS NO HEART AT ALL! STRUGGLING FATHERS, DEFENSELESS WIDOWS, THE AGED AND INFIRM---THESE ARE SLAVES TO HIS GREED, CONDEMNED TO TOIL THEIR LIVES AWAY TO MAKE HIM RICHER... UNTIL THOSE MYSTERIOUS SILENT PARTNERS OF JUSTICE, THE BATMAN AND ROBIN, PIT THEIR NIMBLE WITS AND MATCHLESS MUSCLES AGAINST THE TERROR OF —
"THE MERCHANTS OF MISERY!"
A BLOATED KING OF CROOKED FINANCE HOLDS A CONFERENCE WITH HIS CONFIDENTIAL ASSOCIATES...
KELLY WON'T PAY NO MORE INTEREST, AN' I'M AFRAID HE'LL SQUEAL TO THE COPS. WE DON'T WANT NO MORE TROUBLE!...
SO WE RUB HIM OUT LIKE WE DONE TO THE OTHERS, EH, BOSS?

THAT NIGHT, IN A CANDY STORE IN THE TENEMENT DISTRICT...
I ALREADY PAID TEN TIMES MORE'N I BORROWED, AND--- AAAHHH-H-H!...
WE AIN'T COLLECTIN', KELLY,...WE'RE PAYIN' OFF-- IN LEAD!
STAR-PRESS
GOTHAM CITY GAZETTE EXTRA
SHOPKEEPER'S MURDER FOURTH THIS WEEK!
POLICE SAY SAME KILLERS GUILTY OF ALL......
THEN
MEANWHILE, TRAGEDY OF A DIFFERENT SORT HOVERS OVER THE HUMBLE HOME OF GEORGE SIMPSON...
THE DOCTOR SAYS SHE MUST HAVE AN OPERATION, GEORGE --BUT WHERE WILL WE GET THE MONEY?
I'LL BORROW IT SOMEWHERE, MARY. DON'T YOU WORRY!
BUT I'VE GOT TO GET MONEY SOMEWHERE!
IF I COULD HELP YOU, GEORGE, I'D DO IT IN A MINUTE!
DID I HEAR YOU MENTION MONEY, STRANGER?
I GOT A FRIEND WHO CAN FIX YA UP. BIG-HEARTED JOHN! ONLY YA GOTTA BE WORKIN'...
I'M A NIGHT WATCHMAN! I DON'T MAKE MUCH, BUT IT'S STEADY!
BOSS, HERE'S ANOTHER CUSTOMER!
MY LITTLE GIRL IS SICK! I'LL DO ANYTHING IF YOU'LL HELP ME!
SICK? AIN'T THAT TOO BAD! ALL YA GOTTA DO IS SIGN A PAPER..
DON'T BOTHER READIN' IT, YA CAN TRUST BIG-HEARTED JOHN! OF COURSE, THERE'LL BE A SMALL INTEREST CHARGE...
I'LL PAY YOU BACK AS SOON AS I CAN!
FIFTY DOLLARS! IF I ADD ALL MY WAGES TO IT, IT'LL BE ENOUGH! THIS IS MY LUCKY DAY!
YOUR LUCKY DAY? IT'S ONE OF THE UNLUCKIEST DAYS OF YOUR LIFE, GEORGE SIMPSON--AND OF YOUR WIFE'S LIFE, AND YOUR LITTLE GIRL'S! YOU'LL FIND OUT SOON ENOUGH...

SNEERING LAUGHTER ECHOES WHEN THE BORROWER IS OUT OF EAR-SHOT..
HAW, HAW! AINT IT A SCREAM, THE WAY THE CHUMPS SIGN AWAY EVERYTHIN' FOR A FEW BUCKS!
THIS IS THE SLICKEST RACKET I WAS EVER IN --- AN' ALMOST LEGAL, TOO!

WE GET OUR DOUGH BACK A HUNDRED TIMES IN INTEREST! THEY SIGN OVER THEIR FURNITURE, SO IF THEY DON'T PAY, WE SMASH IT-- AN' IF THEY SQUAWK, WE BEAT 'EM UP!
AN' IF THEY SQUEAL TO THE LAW, WE PUT 'EM AWAY FOR GOOD...ONLY MOST OF 'EM DON'T DARE TRY IT!

PAYDAY AT THE CONSTRUCTION JOB WHERE GEORGE IS EMPLOYED AS A WATCHMAN...
WON'T BE MUCH LEFT FOR GROCERIES WHEN I FINISH PAYING THE HOSPITAL BILL!
J. & J. CONSTRU
KEEP OUT

WE'LL TAKE THIS AS THE FIRST PAYMENT ON THAT LOAN!
BUT--BUT I DIDN'T EXPECT TO PAY IT BACK SO SOON! I'VE GOT TO HAVE THAT MONEY FOR MY FAMILY!

THAT PAPER YOU SIGNED GAVE US THE RIGHT TO COLLECT YOUR PAY... WANT US TO GO TO YOUR BOSS ABOUT IT?
PLEASE DON'T DO THAT-- I'D LOSE MY JOB!
JUST TO SHOW YA WE'RE RIGHT GUYS, HERE'S A DOLLAR FOR YOURSELF!

AND A FEW DAYS LATER...
BUT ALL I HAVE IS TWO DOLLARS WE BORROWED FROM A NEIGHBOR FOR FOOD!
HAND IT OVER, UNLESS YOU WANT A MILLION DOLLARS' WORTH O' TROUBLE!

WEEKS LATER..THE CLIMAX...COMES....
I TELL YOU, I CAN'T PAY A CENT MORE!
OH YEAH?... YOUR FURNITURE AIN'T WORTH TAKIN', BUT WE CAN BUST IT UP!
3

DID YA THINK MAYBE WE WERE FOOLIN'?

STOP IT! I'LL CALL THE POLICE!

THIS IS JUST A SAMPLE OF WHAT YA'LL GET IF YA EVER MENTION COPS AGAIN!

OH, GEORGE, I CAN'T STAND IT! WE MIGHT AS WELL BE DEAD AS GO ON LIKE THIS!

I'LL SEE BIG-HEARTED JOHN... WHEN HE UNDERSTANDS HOW THINGS ARE, HE'LL TELL THOSE THUGS TO LEAVE US ALONE!

BUT BIG-HEARTED JOHN'S KINDLY SMILE HAS TURNED TO A SCOWL...

I'VE PAID YOU TWICE WHAT I BORROWED ALREADY...MY WIFE AND BABY WILL STARVE IF THIS KEEPS UP!

I CAN'T WORRY ABOUT YOUR WIFE AN' KID! YOU AIN'T PAID NOTHIN' BUT INTEREST SO FAR.. IF YOU AIN'T MAKIN' ENOUGH, YOU BETTER START BEGGIN' OR STEALIN'!

HE WAS GONNA CALL THE COPS TODAY-- MAYBE ME AND THE BOYS SHOULD TEACH HIM A LESSON!

GOOD IDEA! — BUT DON'T HURT HIM SO BAD HE CAN'T WORK. HE'S ONE O' THEM MEEK GUYS WE CAN KEEP ON SQUEEZIN' FOREVER!

NEARBY, TWO MANTLED FIGURES PATROL THE NIGHT IN THE NAME OF JUSTICE... THE BATMAN AND ROBIN...
ALL THOSE MURDERS WERE COMMITTED IN THIS DISTRICT!
SOONER OR LATER WE'LL GET A LINE ON THE KILLERS!

AS THEY APPROACH THE SKELETON BUILDING...
LOOK, BATMAN-- THREE AGAINST ONE!
YOU AND I WILL MAKE THE ODDS EVEN... LET'S GO!

DON'T BREAK ANY BONES, AN' DON'T KNOCK HIM OUT TILL HE'S HAD A CHANCE TO FEEL WHAT ITS LIKE!
SOMEONE'S BUTTIN' IN!

BREAK IT UP, BOYS, AND LET'S START OVER!
IT'S THE BATMAN!

HERE'S WHERE THE BATMAN GETS THE WINGS OF AN ANGEL!
THIS CALLS FOR ALTITUDE!

LOW BRIDGE!
THANKS, ROBIN!

YOU LITTLE BRAT, I'LL...

OOOFF!
SPEAKING OF BRIDGE-- DON'T YOU KNOW SPADES BEAT CLUBS?
5

I SEE DIAMONDS!

ROBIN, YOU'RE A CARD!

WE'LL MAKE THIS ONE A GRAND SLAM!

HAVE A HEART!

THOSE BRICKS WILL SOFTEN THEM UP FOR THE POLICE!

PLEASE DON'T CALL THE POLICE... I'D LOSE MY JOB HERE!

YOUR JOB? WELL-- ALL RIGHT... WHEEL YOUR PALS OUT OF HERE, YOU TWO-BIT GUNMAN, BEFORE I CHANGE MY MIND!

YESSIR, MR. BATMAN!

NEXT MORNING...HAVING CHANGED THEIR MANTLED UNIFORMS FOR THEIR OLDEST CLOTHES, BRUCE WAYNE AND HIS YOUNG WARD, DICK GRAYSON, AGAIN INVADE THE TENEMENT DISTRICT....
WE'VE RENTED A TENEMENT FLAT, AND YOU'VE GOT A JOB...NOW WHAT?
NOW WE PAY A VISIT TO BIG-HEARTED JOHN!

YOU SAY YOU'RE A STEVEDORE ON THE DOCKS, MAKING THIRTY BUCKS A WEEK? SURE, I CAN MAKE A LOAN!
WHAT DO I HAVE TO SIGN?

THESE INTEREST RATES ARE PRETTY STEEP!
JUST A FORMALITY... DON'T WORRY ABOUT 'EM!

WE'LL TAKE HIM AT HIS WORD, EH, DICK? WE WON'T WORRY ABOUT THE INTEREST!
BUT I'LL BET HE WORRIES BEFORE WE'RE FINISHED!

AND WHEN A WEEK HAS PASSED...
I'M PAYING YOU BACK IN FULL, AT WHAT I CONSIDER A FAIR INTEREST RATE!
MISTER, YA JUST THINK YA ARE! WE SET OUR OWN INTEREST RATE! WE'LL BE SEEIN' YA PAYDAY!

LATER....AT THE DOCK WHERE BRUCE IS DISGUISED AS A STEVEDORE FOR A SHIPPING FIRM HE OWNS...
THIS IS PAY DAY... DO YOU COME ACROSS OR DO WE GO TO YOUR BOSS AN' GET YA' FIRED?
BUT BIG-HEARTED JOHN SAID I NEEDN'T WORRY ABOUT THAT PAPER I SIGNED!
PIER

YA DUMB CLUCK, YA BETTER START WORRYIN'!
WE'VE SENT GUYS TO HOSPITALS FOR NOT PAYIN' OFF!

THERE YOU GO, MAKING ME NERVOUS!
OOOH-H-H I SHOULDA STAYED IN BED!

WHEN I GET NERVOUS, I GET CLUMSY!
PIER
HALP! I'LL DROWN!
OOPS! DID I BUMP YOU, DUKE?
YA DONE IT ON PURPOSE, YA DOPE!
DON'T STAND THERE LIKE A NINNY! JUMP IN AND HELP YOUR FRIENDS!
IT SHOULDN'T HAPPEN TO A JAP!
GRIN ALL YA WANT... WE AIN'T THROUGH WITH YA!
WANT TO TRY IT AGAIN?
THAT EVENING, IN BRUCE'S TENEMENT FLAT...
CUTTING OUT PAPER DOLLS? THAT'S A BAD SIGN!
OUR FRIENDS ARE GOING TO CALL ON US TONIGHT... I MADE SURE OF THAT THIS AFTERNOON! THE BATMAN AND ROBIN WILL BE OUTSIDE WATCHING!
BUT UNLESS SOMEONE'S HERE, THEY WON'T START ANYTHING!
I GET IT!
GARBED ONCE AGAIN IN THE WEIRD GARMENTS THAT HAVE STRUCK DREAD TO THE HEARTS OF COUNTLESS WRONG-DOERS, THE DYNAMIC DUO SEEKS THE ROOF....
YOU WANT TO DO MORE THAN SPOIL THEIR LOAN SHARK RACKET, EH?
I'M SURE THEY'RE GUILTY OF MURDER, BUT THERE'S NO PROOF. BUT IF WE CATCH THEM AT ATTEMPTED MURDER, THEY'LL SPEND A LONG TIME IN PRISON!
SLOW MINUTES CRAWL PAST ... AND STEALTHILY, FIGURES SLINK THROUGH THE NIGHT, BENT ON THE DARKEST OF CRIMES...
HERE THEY ARE! NOW WHAT?
FOR THE TIME BEING, WE SIT TIGHT!
8

NO SLIPS! THE GUYS ARE TROUBLE-MAKERS, AN' THE BOSS SAYS THEY GOTTA BE RUBBED OUT!
WELL, YA GOT THE ERASER--AN' THEY'RE SITTIN' WHERE YA CAN'T MISS!
A MURDEROUS HAIL OF LEAD SMASHES THROUGH GLASS, CURTAIN--AND CARDBOARD...
THAT'LL TEACH 'EM TO THROW ME IN THE RIVER!
BUT THEY DON'T DROP-- THEY AIN'T EVEN MOVIN'! WE'RE BEIN' TRICKED!
A FEARSOME SHADOW SWOOPS LIKE A GIANT BAT UPON THE WOULD-BE MURDERERS...
IT'S HIM AGAIN!
I FEEL SICK!
SO YOU'D MURDER A MAN FOR A FEW CROOKED DOLLARS!
O-O-O-H-H! YOU'RE BREAKIN' MY BACK!
BUT I'LL FEEL BETTER WHEN I'VE PLUGGED HIM!
YOU JUST THINK YOU WILL!
IT'LL TAKE A TON OF ASPIRIN TO CURE YOUR HEADACHE!
THE BUILDIN'S FALLIN' ON ME!
BY AN IRONIC TWIST OF FATE, THE BOY WONDER'S TIMELY ATTACK SAVES BOTH THE BATMAN'S LIFE...AND BRINGS NEW PERIL!
HEY, LEGGO! I GOT TROUBLE ENOUGH... WITHOUT YOU!
I'M FALLIN'!
9

TOO LATE, THE YOUTHFUL CRIME-FIGHTER TRIES TO RESCUE HIS FRIEND...
GRAB MY HAND, BATMAN! I DIDN'T MEAN--
IT'S OKAY, ROBIN!

BUT OF ALL THE TRIO, THE BATMAN IS THE ONLY ONE WHO IS NOT "OKAY" AT THE FINAL RECKONING!
WHAT A SPOT FOR ME!
OUCH! MY FEET!
RUBBISH

HE'S OUT COLD! WE GOT HIM AT LAST!
WILL THE BOSS BE GLAD TO SEE HIM!

AND AS ROBIN LEANS OVER THE RAILING, FORGETTING ALL ELSE IN HIS DESPERATE ANXIETY...
BATMAN! WAKE UP!
GOT YA, YA LITTLE PEST!

THE THROBBING RETURN TO CONSCIOUSNESS BRINGS NO HOPE...
IT'S ALL MY FAULT!
QUIT TALKING LIKE THAT! WE'RE NOT LICKED YET!
IF YA THINK YOU'RE NOT, YOU'RE DUMBERN YA LOOK!
LOFT

SO THEY THOUGHT THEY'D SPOIL OUR MILLION-DOLLAR RACKET!
THE BATMAN AIN'T SO TOUGH, BOSS. I KNOCKED HIM OUT WITH ONE HAND!
10

YOU WON'T SPOIL NOTHIN' FOR NOBODY NO MORE, BATMAN! WHEN I GET THROUGH WITH YA, THE BOYS'LL SINK YA IN THE RIVER SO DEEP THE FISH WON'T EVEN FIND YA!
BOSS, I BET IT WAS THAT GUY GEORGE SIMPSON GOT THE BATMAN AFTER US!
WE'LL KILL HIM, TOO-- RIGHT NOW!
YOU VULTURES LEAVE HIM ALONE! HE HAD NOTHING TO DO WITH THIS!
WE'LL PUT 'EM HERE FOR SAFE-KEEPING WHILE WE TEND TO SIMPSON... WHEN WE GET BACK THEY'LL BE DEAD!
SAFE-KEEPING IS GOOD!
DO YA GO IN NICE AN' GENTLE-- OR DO I SLUG YA?
THEY'LL SMOTHER IN NO TIME!
YOU FIENDS! THE LAW WILL CATCH UP WITH YOU SOME DAY!
THE MASSIVE DOOR THUDS SHUT.. THE MULTIPLE BOLTS SNICK INTO THEIR SOCKETS...
BRUCE, I---I DON'T KNOW WHAT TO SAY! IF I HADN'T KNOCKED YOU OFF THE FIRE-ESCAPE!
QUIT BLAMING YOURSELF! WE KNEW THE CHANCES WERE AGAINST US... TWIST AROUND AND SEE IF YOU CAN UNTIE THESE KNOTS!
THEY'RE UNTIED... BUT WHAT GOOD ARE YOUR HANDS AGAINST FOUR-INCH STEEL WALLS?
THERE'S ONE SLIM CHANCE! IF IT DOESN'T WORK WE'RE NO WORSE OFF.. IF IT DOES, WE MAY SAVE GEORGE SIMPSON FROM THE KILLERS!
MIXING THE CHEMICAL CONTENTS OF TWO VIALS FROM A POCKET OF HIS UTILITY BELT, THE BATMAN PREPARES A MINIATURE BOMB..
I--CAN'T BREATHE! BUT I'M NOT SCARED-- NOT VERY..:
HOLD ON A LITTLE LONGER!
WONDER IF ANYONE EVER TRIED BLOWING A SAFE FROM INSIDE? IT MAY KILL US..BUT WE'RE DYING ANYWAY!
THESE LEDGERS WILL THROW THE FORCE OF THE BLAST AGAINST THE DOOR, INSTEAD OF US!
WELL, ROBIN, IF IT'S THE WINDUP, WE'LL MEET IT TOGETHER!

A RIPPING EXPLOSION PACKS THE NARROW VAULT WITH FLAME, THUNDER AND TERRIFIC CONCUSSION...

BOOM

THE BULGING DOOR OF THE ANCIENT SAFE SAGS OPEN ON BENT HINGES... BUT WHAT IS THIS?

LEDGER

HAS THE ARCH-FOE OF EVIL SUCCEEDED IN BURSTING HIS PRISON, ONLY TO LOSE HIS LIFE ON THE THRESHOLD OF FREEDOM?

ILENT MOMENTS TICK AWAY... AND FINALLY...

WHA--? NOW I REMEMBER! BIG-HEARTED JOHN...SIMPSON... ROBIN!

WHERE AM I? MY EARS ARE RINGING!

SNAP OUT OF IT ROBIN! YOU'RE ALIVE, BY A MIRACLE AND NOW WE'VE GOT TO PERFORM A MIRACLE TO SAVE SOMEONE ELSE'S LIFE!

ALL WE GOTTA DO IS TAKE THE ELEVATOR DOWN AN' LEAVE HIM HANGIN' HERE!

WILL THEY BE IN TIME? THE NIGHT WIND PLUCKS AT THEIR TREAMING CLOAKS WITH GHOSTLY FINGERS AS THEY STREAK THROUGH THE STREETS...

VE CAN MAKE IT FASTER ON FOOT HAN BY LOOKING FOR CAR...THERE N'T A SECOND TO LOSE!

IT'S JUST AROUND THE CORNER!

AND AS THEY REACH THE SKELETON BUILDING WHERE SIMPSON'S EMPLOYED....

LOOK! THEY'RE HANGING HIM!

12

THEY'VE GOT THE ELEVATOR, SO WE'LL HAVE TO TRAVEL THE HARD WAY!

I'D CLIMB TO THE MOON TO TAKE A POKE AT PIG-HEARTED JOHN!

HIGH AGAINST THE BLACK SKY, THE GREEDY MURDERERS FACE THEIR FEARSOME ENEMY...
IT'S THEM! IT AIN'T HUMAN!
LEMME GET BACK TO EARTH... IT'S MY ONLY CHANCE!

A HAIL OF BULLETS FLIES UPWARD AS THE ELEVATOR DESCENDS, LEAVING THE BATMAN ALONE ON HIS PERILOUS PERCH...
YOU KNOCKED OUT THE BATMAN WITH ONE HAND, DID YOU?

THAT ONE GOT ME!

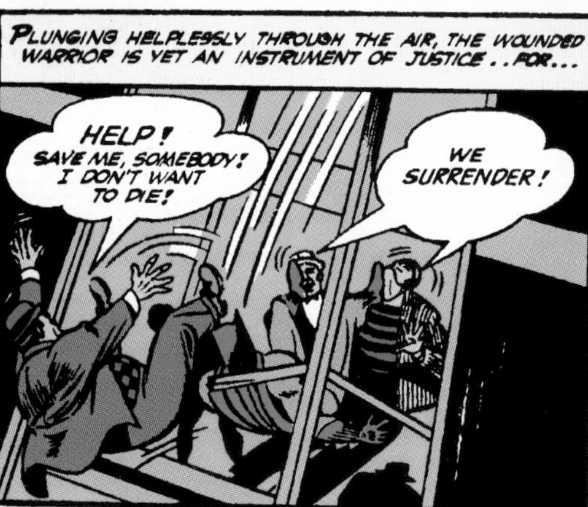
PLUNGING HELPLESSLY THROUGH THE AIR, THE WOUNDED WARRIOR IS YET AN INSTRUMENT OF JUSTICE...FOR...
HELP! SAVE ME, SOMEBODY! I DON'T WANT TO DIE!
WE SURRENDER!

SO DEATH COMES TO ONE WHO EARNED IT RICHLY... PROVING A MORAL THAT ALL OF US KNOW TOO WELL...
IF HE HADN'T SHOT THE BATMAN HE WOULDN'T BE DOWN THERE NOW!
THE BIGGEST COLLECTION AGENCY THERE IS HAS CAUGHT UP WITH HIM!

AND TO GEORGE SIMPSON AND HIS LITTLE FAMILY COMES HAPPINESS, OUT OF WHAT THREATENED TO BE DEEPEST TRAGEDY..
HERE'S ALL THAT BIG-HEARTED JOHN TOOK FROM YOU EXCEPT THE AMOUNT OF THE ORIGINAL LOAN..HIS OTHER VICTIMS WILL GET THEIR MONEY BACK, TOO-EXCEPT THE ONES HE MURDERED!
WE'LL NEVER FORGET WHAT YOU'VE DONE FOR US!
YOU-YOU'RE WONDERFUL, BATMAN!
HOME SWEET HOME

GOTHAM CITY GAZETTE
EXTRA
BATMAN ENDS CRIMINAL LOAN SHARK RACKET!
POLICE WAGE WAR ON GANGS WHO VICTIMIZED POOR
WAR BILL
DEAD

LATER, AT BRUCE WAYNE'S HOME....
BIG-HEARTED JOHN'S PALS WILL GET OUT OF PRISON IN TWENTY YEARS...DO YOU THINK THEY'LL HAVE LEARNED THEIR LESSON BY THEN?
IT'S HARD TO SAY... IF THEY HAVEN'T, THEY'LL GO RIGHT BACK. THEY ALWAYS DO!
The END

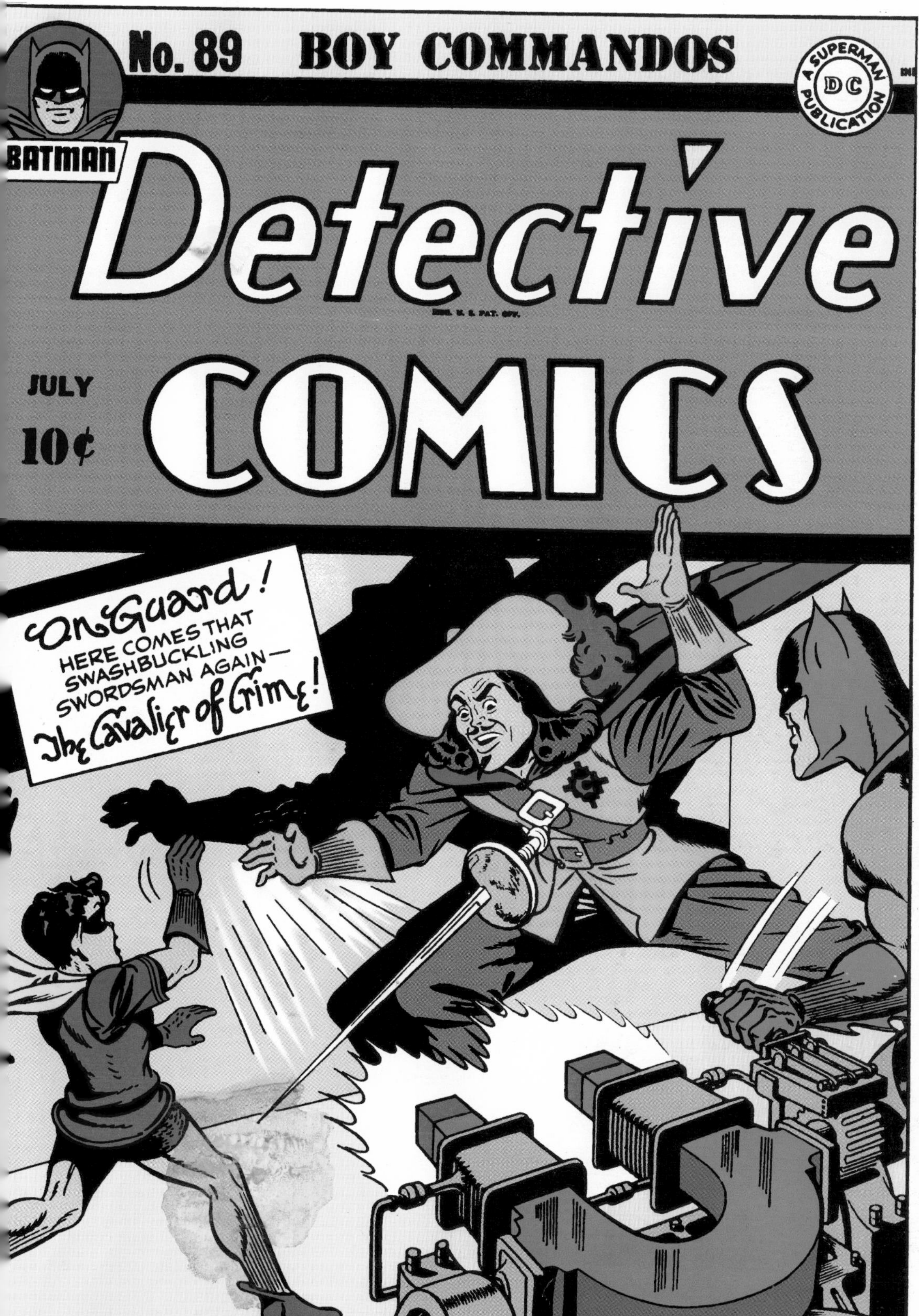
No. 89
BOY COMMANDOS
A SUPERMAN DC PUBLICATION
BATMAN
Detective
REG. U. S. PAT. OFF.
JULY
10¢
COMICS
On Guard!
HERE COMES THAT SWASHBUCKLING SWORDSMAN AGAIN—
The Cavalier of Crime!

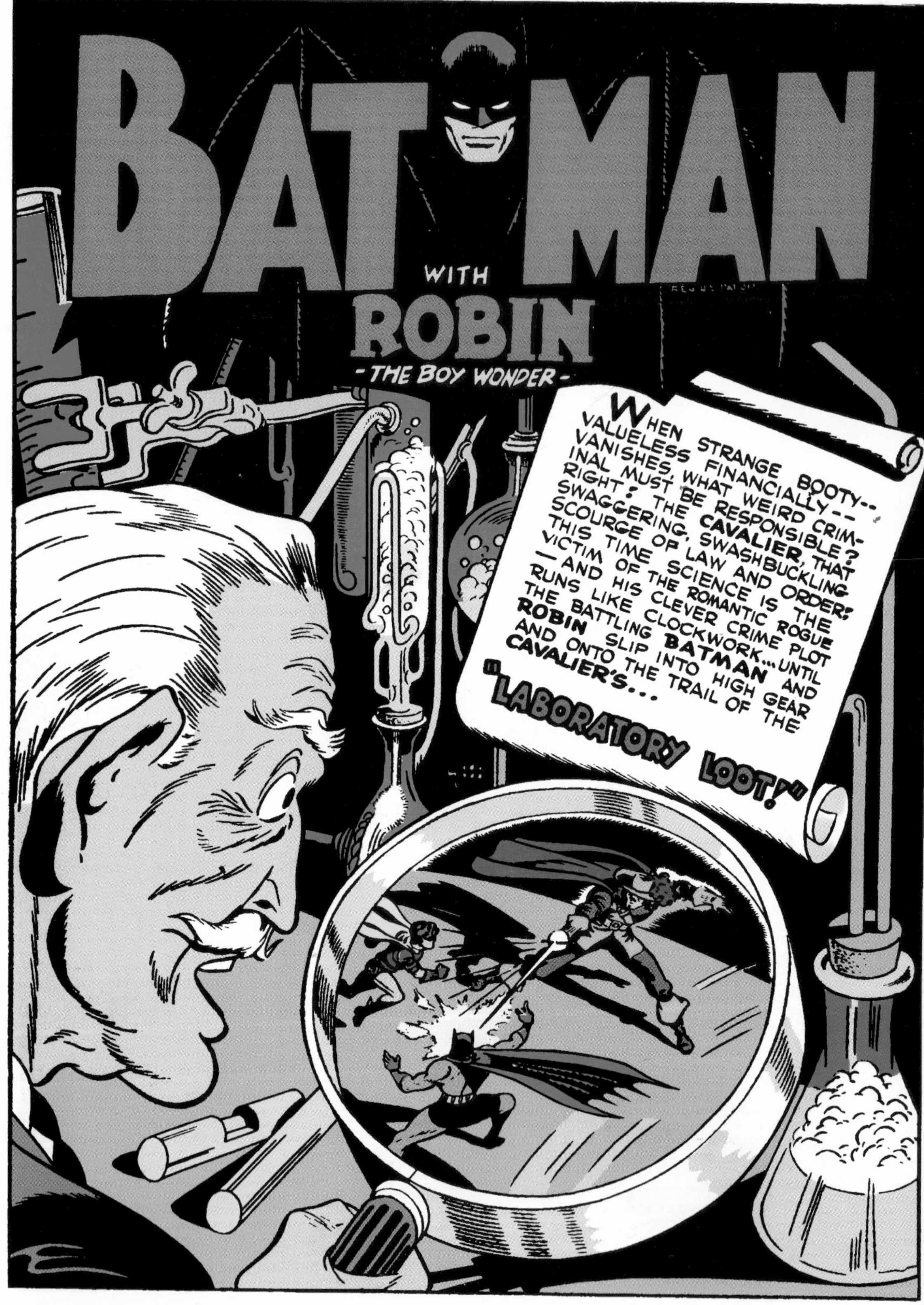
BATMAN
WITH
ROBIN
-THE BOY WONDER-
WHEN STRANGE BOOTY--VALUELESS FINANCIALLY--VANISHES, WHAT WEIRD CRIMINAL MUST BE RESPONSIBLE? RIGHT! THE CAVALIER, THAT SWAGGERING, SWASHBUCKLING SCOURGE OF LAW AND ORDER! THIS TIME SCIENCE IS THE VICTIM OF THE ROMANTIC ROGUE —AND HIS CLEVER CRIME PLOT RUNS LIKE CLOCKWORK...UNTIL THE BATTLING BATMAN AND ROBIN SLIP INTO HIGH GEAR AND ONTO THE TRAIL OF THE CAVALIER'S...
"LABORATORY LOOT!"

FATE PLAYS MANY PRANKS, BUT NONE AS GRIMLY HUMOROUS AS THIS — TO SEAT TWO SWORN ENEMIES SIDE BY SIDE — BRUCE WAYNE, IN REALITY THE **BATMAN**, AND MORTIMER DRAKE, IN REALITY, THE ***CAVALIER!***

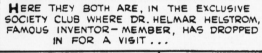

HERE THEY BOTH ARE, IN THE EXCLUSIVE SOCIETY CLUB WHERE DR. HELMAR HELSTROM, FAMOUS INVENTOR—MEMBER, HAS DROPPED IN FOR A VISIT...

IT'D BE WONDERFUL TO FEEL YOU'VE DONE AS MUCH AS DR. HELSTROM— BUT RATHER TIRING TO DO IT, EH, DRAKE?
YES, VERY! LIKE YOU, I PREFER TO HAVE FUN, WAYNE!

YOU PLAYBOYS IRRITATE ME! I WOULDN'T TRADE A SINGLE HOUR IN MY LABORATORY, WORKING ON MY INVENTIONS, FOR THE WHOLE OF YOUR LIVES!

NOW, DR. HELSTROM, THAT'S GOING A BIT TOO FAR!
NOT AT ALL, DRAKE! IT WAS FUN FOR ME TO INVENT ONE OF THE EARLIEST SEWING MACHINES AND TYPEWRITERS... WHICH REMINDS ME, THERE'S A LITTLE SECRET I CAN LET YOU IN ON THAT WON'T BE RELEASED UNTIL TOMORROW!
OH-OH!

I HOPE HE DOESN'T BLURT OUT ANYTHING ABOUT THE SECRET WORK HE'S DOING FOR THE GOVERNMENT!
I HAVE FINALLY SUCCEEDED IN BUYING THE WORKING MODEL OF THE TYPEWRITER I INVENTED YEARS AGO! IT SLIPPED OUT OF MY POSSESSION SOMEHOW, AND ALL I HAD WAS ONE OF THE PRODUCTION MODELS!

WHEW! THAT WAS CLOSE! I ASKED THE COMMISSIONER TO LET ME HELP PROTECT HELSTROM'S SECRET INVENTION, AND I THOUGHT THE OLD MAN WOULD TALK TOO MUCH!
GOOD NIGHT, GENTLEMEN! TAKE MY ADVICE AND TRY TO BE USEFUL TO HUMANITY!
SOME OTHER TIME, PERHAPS! I'M ENJOYING MYSELF TOO MUCH NOW!

YOU LEAVING EARLY TOO, DRAKE?
YES, WAYNE— BE RIGHT WITH YOU!
WELL, WELL! THIS HAS INDEED BEEN A PROFITABLE EVENING FOR THE CAVALIER!

AMUSING CODGER, THAT DR. HELSTROM! BUT RATHER A BORE WITH HIS ETERNAL PRATTLING ABOUT SCIENCE!
YES, I'M AFRAID HE MADE ME VERY DROWSY! SO I'LL BE HEADING FOR BED! GOOD NIGHT, DRAKE!

AND SO TWO MORTAL ENEMIES PART... LITTLE SUSPECTING THAT SOON EACH WILL BE LOCKED IN VIOLENT COMBAT WITH THE OTHER— AS THE MIGHTY **BATMAN** AND THE WILY ***CAVALIER!***

2

PRESENTLY, AT THE DRAKE HOME...
THIS IS ONE PRIZE THE BATMAN WILL NOT CHEAT ME OF!..
WORKING MODEL OF HELMAR HELSTROM TYPEWRITER

FOR THE CAVALIER STRIKES TONIGHT!

SOON, A SHADOWY SHAPE STALKS STEALTHILY INTO THE DARK LABORATORY OF THE NOTED SCIENTIST...
BY MY FAITH, I CAN SCARCELY WAIT UNTIL I HAVE IT IN MY POSSESSION!

BUT UNKNOWN TO HIM, A PHOTO-ELECTRIC BEAM FORMS AN INVISIBLE GUARD AT THE WINDOW...
...AND HIS ENTRY HAS BROKEN THE CIRCUIT!

A LIGHT FLASHES ON A BOARD AT POLICE HEADQUARTERS!
SOMEONE'S BROKEN INTO THE HELSTROM LABORATORY! CALL THE BATMAN IMMEDIATELY!
YES SIR!

AND THE NEXT INSTANT ... ACROSS THE SKY BLAZES THE SUMMONS THAT STRIKES FEAR DEEP INTO THE HEART OF CRIMEDOM—CALLING THE BATMAN!

AND MILES AWAY, LIKE A RUNAWAY COMET, THE BATMOBILE STREAKS INTO ACTION!
3

SOON...
LOOK, BATMAN! IN THE LABORATORY!
A FLASHLIGHT! LET'S GO, ROBIN!

ZOUNDS, MY NEMESIS! IS THERE NO WAY OF ELUDING YOU?
YES... IN PRISON! AND THAT'S WHERE YOU'RE GOING!
CLICK

FIRST, A LITTLE SOFTENING-UP PROCESS!
SOFTENING-UP? HE'LL BE MUSH WHEN WE GET THROUGH WITH HIM!

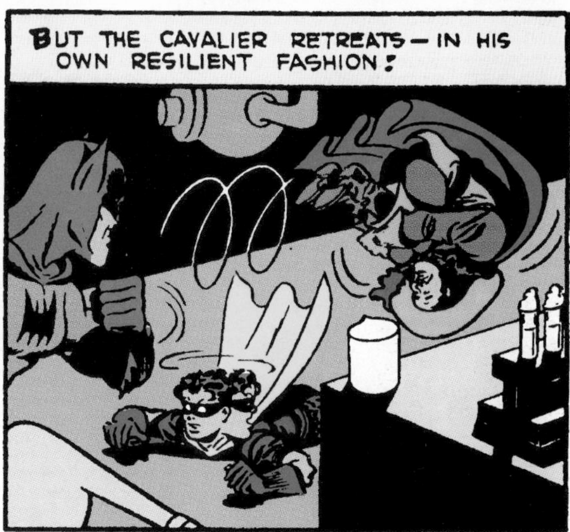
BUT THE CAVALIER RETREATS—IN HIS OWN RESILIENT FASHION!

THEN... AN UPWARD LEAP... AND HIS ELECTRIC-CHARGED SWORD LEAPS FROM ITS SCABBARD!
SPEAK NOT SO SURELY! OR DO MY ACTIONS SHOCK YOU?
OUCH!

HERE'S SOMETHING NEW FOR YOU, CAVALIER—AN ELECTRO-MAGNET TO SNATCH AN ELECTRIC SWORD!
CLANK!
PESTE! DISARMED!
4

BUT ONLY MOMENTARILY! THIS WINDOW POLE CAN BE AN EXCELLENT MAKESHIFT JAVELIN! OBSERVE...
UH-UH! I DON'T THINK I'M GOING TO LIKE THIS DEMONSTRATION!

THERE WON'T BE ANY!

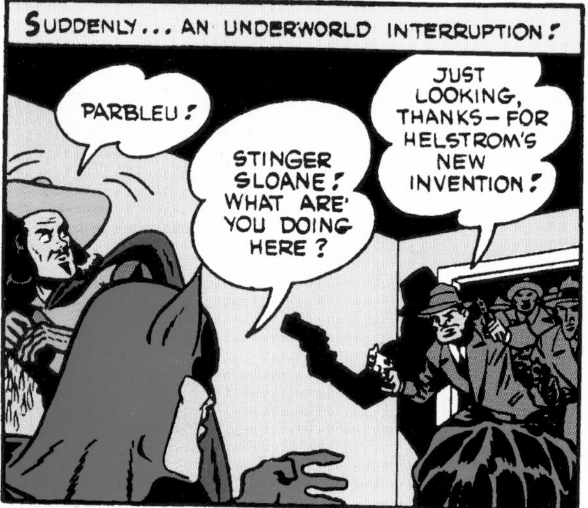
SUDDENLY... AN UNDERWORLD INTERRUPTION!
PARBLEU!
STINGER SLOANE! WHAT ARE YOU DOING HERE?
JUST LOOKING, THANKS— FOR HELSTROM'S NEW INVENTION!

YOU'VE GOT A SWEET CHANCE OF GETTING IT, SLOANE!...

WHAT'S THIS, CAVALIER? FIGHTING ON OUR SIDE?
TEMPORARILY, MON AMI, TO DEFEAT THESE FOUL THIEVES!

TEMPORARY IS RIGHT... BUT WE'LL DO THE DEFEATIN'!
5

OWWW
A BUNSEN BURNER TO KNOCK YOU COLD!

AND THEN...
ENJOY YOUR TRIP, BATMAN!

CRUDE OF ME TO SPILL THIS OIL UNDER YOU, HUH, BRAT?
CAN THE GAGS AND LET'S GET THAT INVENTION AND SCRAM!

TURN ON THE VACUUM PUMP! THEY'LL NEVER GET OUT OF THIS BELL JAR ALIVE! WHAT DO YOU SAY, MUGGS?.. GOT HOLD OF THAT INVENTION YET?
DON'T WORRY, STINGER! WE'LL FIND IT!

(PANT) THEY'RE PUMPING THE AIR OUT! (PANT) WE'LL SUFFOCATE IF WE DON'T GET OUT SOON! (PANT)
MUST DO SOMETHING! (PANT) CAN'T BUDGE THE JAR... VACUUM HOLDS IT--- WAIT A SECOND! VACUUM...

FROM HIS UTILITY BELT, BATMAN EXTRACTS A DIAMOND-TIPPED TOOL...
Y-YOU DON'T HAVE STRENGTH ENOUGH (PANT) TO CUT THROUGH THAT GLASS!
I DON'T— DON'T NEED TO! (PANT) IF I CAN JUST WEAKEN IT (PANT) AIR PRESSURE ON THE VACUUM WILL DO THE REST! COVER YOUR FACE!
6

CRASH!
WHOOSH!

A MOMENT LATER...
HUH? HOW'D YOU GET OUT?
WATCH FOR MY AUTOBIOGRAPHY IN ABOUT TWENTY YEARS! IT'LL EXPLAIN EVERYTHING!

MEANWHILE, UNNOTICED IN THE CONFLICT, THE CAVALIER IS WASTING NO OPPORTUNITIES!
ODSBODKINS, THIS IS NO PLACE FOR ME! I WOULD BUT BE CAUGHT BETWEEN TWO FIRES!

FORSOOTH, GLYCERINE IS A SPLENDID LUBRICANT! WITH IT, I CAN HANDILY SLIP THE ROPES FROM MY WRISTS!
GLYCERINE

NO TIME TO WASTE THESE GORILLAS ROBIN!
WHO'S WASTING TIME!

NOW? TO TAKE CARE OF OUR GAUDY FRIEND!.. WHERE IS HE?
GONE!
7

A SWIFT SUMMONS BRINGS THE POLICE AND DR. HELSTROM!
HEAVENS! THE ONLY THING THAT'S MISSING IS THE WORKING MODEL OF MY EARLY TYPEWRITER! BUT WHY! IT ISN'T WORTH ANYTHING TO ANYBODY BUT ME!
HMM! THIS IS BEGINNING TO TIE UP! SLOANE AND HIS GANG WERE AFTER THE SECRET INVENTION, AND THE CAVALIER MUST HAVE BEEN AFTER THE TYPEWRITER!
HELSTROM MENTIONED GETTING THE WORKING MODEL OF THE TYPEWRITER IN THE CLUB THIS EVENING, AND TOLD US IT WAS A SECRET! AND THE CAVALIER IMMEDIATELY TRIED TO STEAL IT! WHICH MEANS... THAT THE CAVALIER IS SOMEONE WHO BELONGS TO MY OWN CLUB SOMEONE I KNOW!

I HEARD THAT YOU MENTIONED IN YOUR CLUB TONIGHT THAT YOU HAD JUST RECEIVED THE WORKING MODEL! THAT WAS VERY FOOLISH... BUT YOU CAN STILL GET IT BACK, IF YOU DO WHAT I SUGGEST...
ANYTHING, BATMAN! ANYTHING!

AND SO, THE FOLLOWING NIGHT, PLAYBOY BRUCE WAYNE STOPS IN AT HIS CLUB...
IT DOESN'T SEEM POSSIBLE... THE CAVALIER IS SOMEBODY I KNOW!.. WHAT'S "WHO'S WHO" DOING OFF ITS SHELF?...

A CLIP HOLDING A PIECE OF PAPER INSIDE... LET'S SEE...
S BORN IN
SCHOOL
N 1915
E WAR
TED
NG
S
WHO'S WHO
43
BATMAN, THE... ONE OF THE MOST FAMOUS FIGHTERS IN THE ENTIRE HISTORY OF CRIME! HIS TRUE IDENTITY IS A CAREFULLY GUARDED SECRET, NEVER REVEALED TO ANYONE, SO FAR AS IS KNOWN!

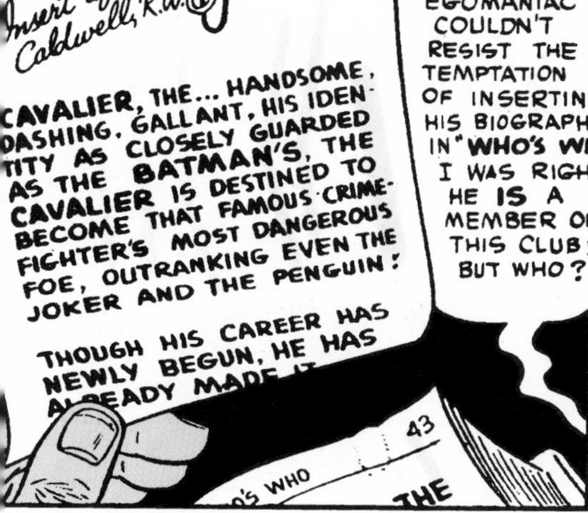
Insert after Caldwell, R.W.
CAVALIER, THE... HANDSOME, DASHING, GALLANT, HIS IDENTITY AS CLOSELY GUARDED AS THE BATMAN'S, THE CAVALIER IS DESTINED TO BECOME THAT FAMOUS CRIME-FIGHTER'S MOST DANGEROUS FOE, OUTRANKING EVEN THE JOKER AND THE PENGUIN!
THOUGH HIS CAREER HAS NEWLY BEGUN, HE HAS ALREADY MADE IT
43
WHO
THE
THE EGOMANIAC COULDN'T RESIST THE TEMPTATION OF INSERTING HIS BIOGRAPHY IN "WHO'S WHO"! I WAS RIGHT! HE IS A MEMBER OF THIS CLUB! BUT WHO?

SALUTATIONS, FELLOW LOAFERS! GOOD EVENING, DR. HELSTROM!
HI, BRUCE!
GOOD EVENING, WAYNE!
TO THINK, THE CAVALIER IS ONE OF THEM!
8

CAREFULLY FOLLOWING THE BATMAN'S INSTRUCTIONS, DR. HELSTROM CASUALLY BEGINS TALKING...
QUEER THING HAPPENED LAST NIGHT! REMEMBER MY TELLING YOU ALL ABOUT THE WORKING MODEL OF MY EARLY TYPEWRITER I RECENTLY RECEIVED? WELL, SOMEONE TRIED TO STEAL IT A LITTLE LATER!
MUST WATCH THEIR FACES! ONE MIGHT BETRAY HIMSELF!

SOMETHING ELSE HAPPENED THAT I'M NOT AT LIBERTY TO REVEAL! BUT ABOUT THE TYPE-WRITER... THE ONE THAT WAS STOLEN WAS AMONG THE FIRST OFF THE ASSEMBLY LINE! I HADN'T UNPACKED THE REAL MODEL YET AT MY HOME!
THAT WAS LUCKY!
YES, IT CERTAINLY WAS!
NO GO! THE CAVALIER'S TOO CLEVER TO— WHAT'S THAT?

STRANGE, THAT BLUE STAIN ON THE BACK OF THAT HAND! IT COULDN'T HAVE COME FROM WORK-- HELSTROM IS THE ONLY ONE HERE WHO USES HIS HANDS AT ALL!

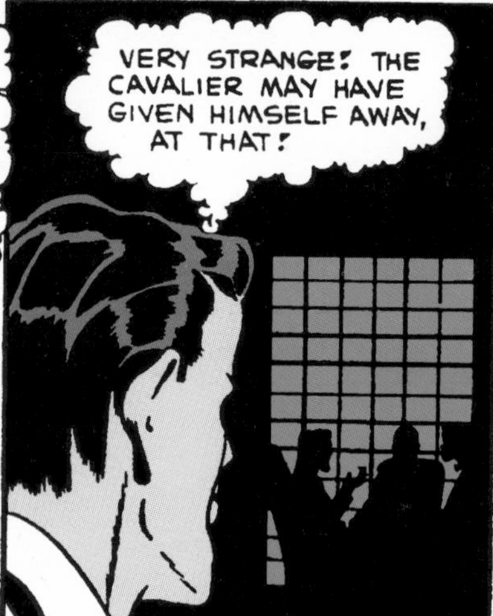
VERY STRANGE! THE CAVALIER MAY HAVE GIVEN HIMSELF AWAY, AT THAT!

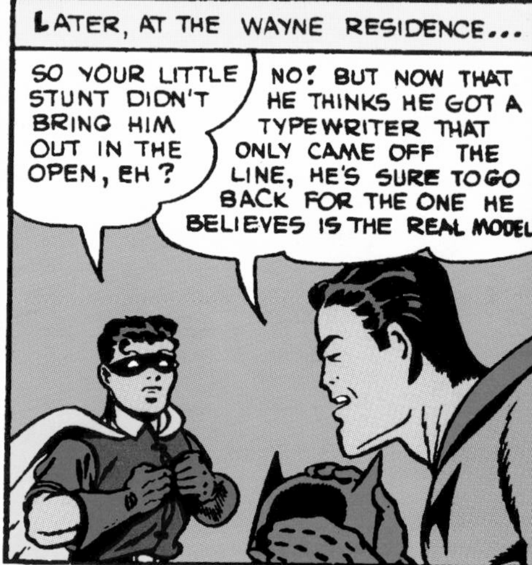
LATER, AT THE WAYNE RESIDENCE...
SO YOUR LITTLE STUNT DIDN'T BRING HIM OUT IN THE OPEN, EH?
NO! BUT NOW THAT HE THINKS HE GOT A TYPEWRITER THAT ONLY CAME OFF THE LINE, HE'S SURE TO GO BACK FOR THE ONE HE BELIEVES IS THE REAL MODEL!

AND THAT BLUE STAIN ON THE BACK OF THAT HAND— MAYBE WE'RE CLOSER TO KNOWING WHO THE CAVALIER IS THAN WE THINK!

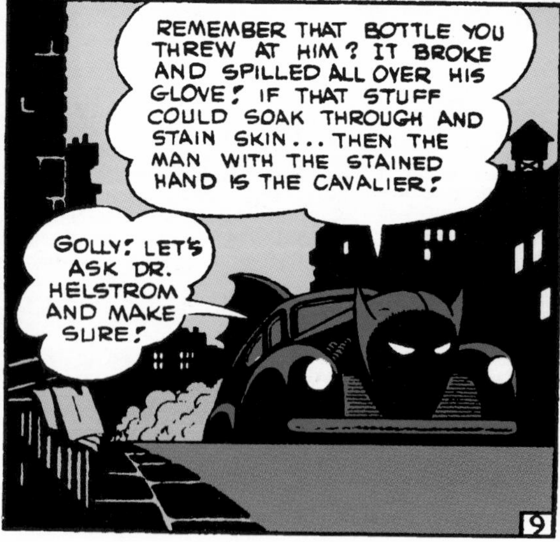
REMEMBER THAT BOTTLE YOU THREW AT HIM? IT BROKE AND SPILLED ALL OVER HIS GLOVE! IF THAT STUFF COULD SOAK THROUGH AND STAIN SKIN... THEN THE MAN WITH THE STAINED HAND IS THE CAVALIER!
GOLLY! LET'S ASK DR. HELSTROM AND MAKE SURE!
9

SOON, IN THE AGED SCIENTIST'S HOME...
DR. HELSTROM, ROBIN SMASHED A CHEMICAL BOTTLE IN YOUR LABORATORY LAST NIGHT! DO YOU REMEMBER WHAT IT CONTAINED?
WHY, YES! POTASSIUM FERROCYANIDE IN AN IRON CHLORIDE SOLUTION! I HAD A TERRIBLE TIME CLEANING IT UP! IT'S A VERY POWERFUL BLUE DYE, YOU KNOW!

THEN I WAS RIGHT! THAT STAIN WAS THE COLOR PRODUCED BY THE SOLUTION IN THAT BOTTLE!
WHO IS HE? QUICK!

YOU'LL SEE IN A LITTLE WHILE! HE'LL BE HERE SOON TO GRAB WHAT HE THINKS IS THE GENUINE WORKING MODEL!.. AND YOU'D BETTER STAY IN SOME SAFE PLACE, DR. HELSTROM! THERE'S GOING TO BE FIREWORKS IN THIS ROOM!
I CAN'T WAIT!

THE MINUTES MOVE SLOWLY PAST AS THE CAPED FIGURES WAIT IN DARKNESS! AND THEN, FURTIVELY...
TONNERRE! A BITTER PILL INDEED... TWO ROBBERIES TO ATTAIN A SINGLE ITEM!

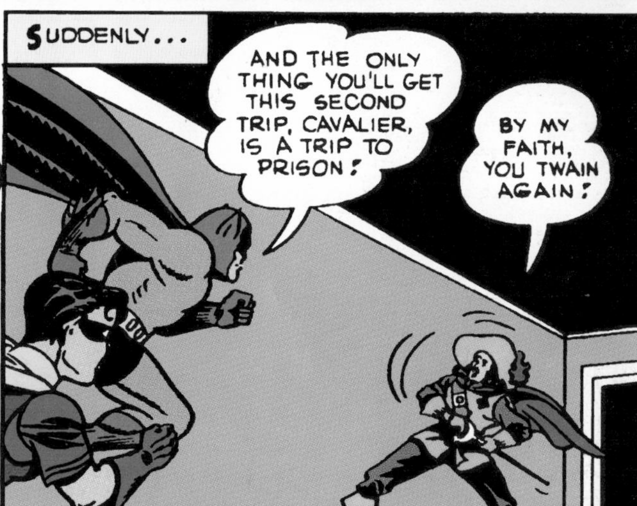
SUDDENLY...
AND THE ONLY THING YOU'LL GET THIS SECOND TRIP, CAVALIER, IS A TRIP TO PRISON!
BY MY FAITH, YOU TWAIN AGAIN!

RIGHT! AND THIS TWAIN ALWAYS MEETS.. ALL COMERS, FIST-FIRST!

I DEFEAT NOT THIS EASILY!
10

JUST A MINUTE, CAVALIER! BEFORE YOU TRY TO KNOCK ME OUT WITH THAT CHAIR, I THINK I OUGHT TO TELL YOU I KNOW WHO YOU ARE— MORTIMER DRAKE!

WHAT? HOW? WHO?...
IF WE NEED ANY MORE PROOF—

—HERE IT IS!

AND NOW, IF YOU DO OR DON'T MIND, I'LL FLATTEN YOU AND HAUL YOU OFF TO PRISON!
OH, NO! YOU'VE TRACKED DOWN MY IDENTITY, BUT YOU WON'T CAPTURE ME!

UNFORTUNATELY FOR YOU, YOU DON'T COME EQUIPPED WITH GAS-MASKS!
(COUGH) I'M STRANGLING!
AN AMMONIA BULLET! (COUGH!)

AFTER SEVERAL MINUTES OF TEARFUL AGONY...
HE'S SKIPPED OUT ON US AGAIN!
BUT THIS TIME WE KNOW WHERE TO CATCH HIM! C'MON!
11

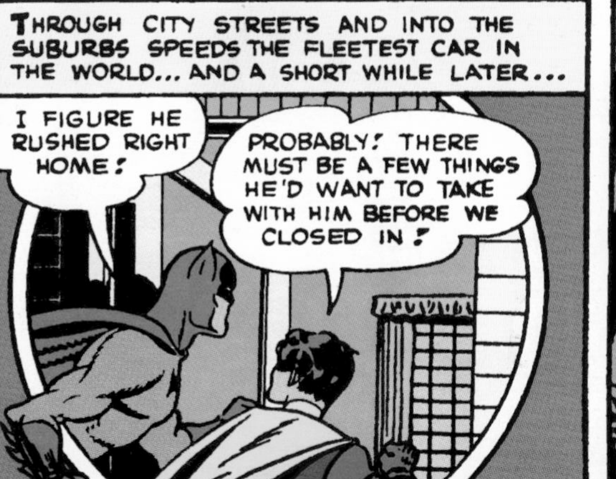
THROUGH CITY STREETS AND INTO THE SUBURBS SPEEDS THE FLEETEST CAR IN THE WORLD... AND A SHORT WHILE LATER...
I FIGURE HE RUSHED RIGHT HOME!
PROBABLY! THERE MUST BE A FEW THINGS HE'D WANT TO TAKE WITH HIM BEFORE WE CLOSED IN!

BUT A SWIFT SEARCH OF THE DRAKE HOME REVEALS...
NO SIGN OF HIM! WHAT'S THAT ROOM?
WOW! COME OVER HERE AND TAKE A LOOK!

SO THIS IS WHY HE KEPT TRYING TO STEAL QUEER THINGS LIKE SPORTS MINIATURES, JEWELER'S MODELS OF DIAMONDS...
RIGHT! HE'S A COLLECTOR— A CRIME COLLECTOR AND THIS WAS TO HAVE BEEN HIS PRIVATE, SECRET MUSEUM!
WORKING MODEL OF HELMAR HELSTROM TYPEWRITER

JUST THEN...
R-R-RING!
THERE'S THE DOORBELL!
CAREFUL! IT MAY BE A TRAP!

BUT WHEN THEY WARILY OPEN THE DOOR...
TELEGRAM FOR BATMAN AND ROB—G-GOLLY! I THOUGHT IT WAS A GAG!
HUH?
WHAT?!?

HOW'D ANYBODY KNOW WE WERE HERE? WHO'S IT FROM?
JUST A SECOND...
2

10:30 PM
BATMAN AND ROBIN
1605 GROVE AVENUE
YOU ARE WELCOME TO MY HOME AND FORTUNE... SINCE THE IDENTITY OF MORTIMER DRAKE IS NO LONGER SAFE FOR ME! THIS IS YOUR ROUND—BUT I SHALL BE SOMEONE ELSE WHEN NEXT WE MEET—AND MEET WE SHALL!
THE CAVALIER
THE END

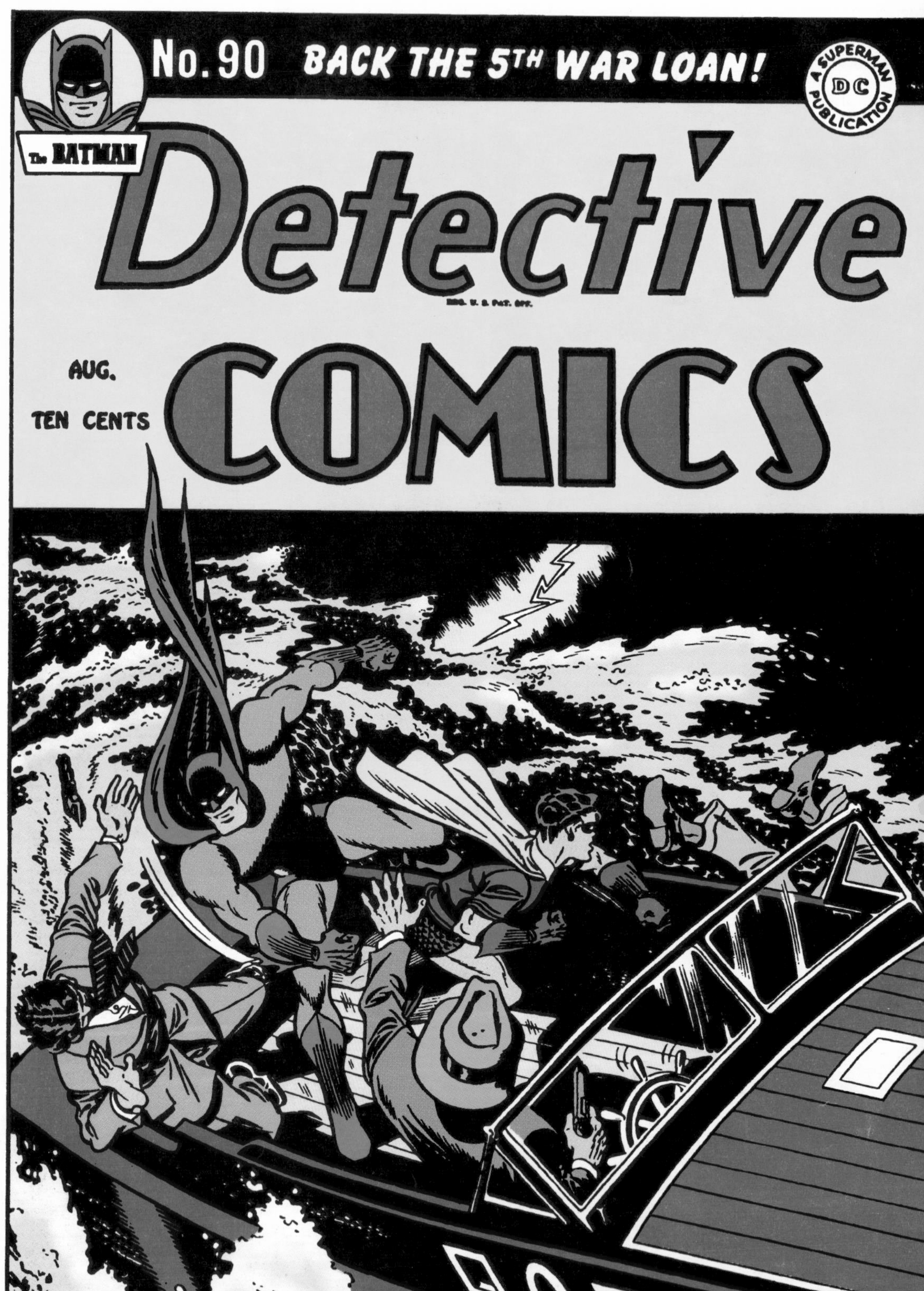
No. 90
BACK THE 5TH WAR LOAN!
A SUPERMAN DC PUBLICATION
The BATMAN
Detective
REG. U. S. PAT. OFF.
AUG.
TEN CENTS
COMICS

BATMAN
WITH
ROBIN
HERE COMES THE SHOWBOAT! FOR GENERATIONS THAT GLAD CRY HAS HERALDED THE APPROACH OF THE GAY, CAREFREE FLOATING THEATRE DEAR TO THE HEARTS OF RIVER FOLK. PROCLAIMING A NIGHT OF REVELRY--- AND THEN DAYS OF CHUCKLING MEMORIES! SUCH A CRAFT WAS THE MISSISSIPPI MERMAID--- BUT IN HER FOAMY WAKE SWIRLED A MURKY TRAIL OF CUNNING CRIME, OF BRAZEN BANDITRY, THAT LEFT THE OUTWITTED POLICE BAFFLED AND HELPLESS! HERE IS HOW BATMAN AND ROBIN, THE BOY WONDER, RISE TO MEET THE MENACING CHALLENGE OF---
"CRIME BETWEEN THE ACTS!"
STEAMBOAT 'ROUND THE BEND! AND JUBILANT CROWDS WELCOME CAPTAIN BEN'S RIVERCADE...
THE SHOW-BOAT'S COME TO TOWN!

THAT NIGHT TOWNSFOLK FLOCK TO THE CELEBRATED WATER CARNIVAL!
TAKE IT EASY, FOLKS! PLENTY OF ROOM INSIDE!
DIVING AND SWIMMING STARS---ALL IN ONE GREAT SHOW!
25

BUT WHILE THE PERFORMANCE IS AT ITS HEIGHT-- TERROR STALKS THE TOWN...
GOOD EV--- O-O-OH!
HERE'S MY CALLING CARD!

BURGLARY...
I'M CARRYING SO MUCH ICE I FEEL LIKE A TRUCK!
JEWELRY
JEWELRY

BANK ROBBERY...
WHAT A TINCAN! A FIRECRACKER WOULD POP IT OPEN!
BOOM

AND RUTHLESS GUNPLAY...
OKAY, COPPER--- STOP SOME LEAD!
STOP! STOP-

SUSPICION LEADS STRAIGHT TO THE MISSISSIPPI MERMAID...
I RECOGNIZED ONE OF THE GANG WHEN HIS MASK SLIPPED! HE'S A PERFORMER ON THE SHOWBOAT!
CAPTAIN BEN WILL HAVE SOME EXPLAINING TO DO!

QUIET, GENTLEMEN! YOU WILL DISTURB THE PERFORMANCE! I CAN VOUCH FOR EVERY MEMBER OF MY TROUPE--- AND SO CAN THE AUDIENCE WHO HAS BEEN WATCHING THEM FOR THE PAST HOUR!
HMM! IT'S THE PERFECT ALIBI!
2

HE NEXT DAY, AT THE HOME OF SOCIALITE **BRUCE WAYNE** AND HIS YOUNG WARD, **DICK GRAYSON**...

GOSH, HERE'S ANOTHER STORY ON THE MISSISSIPPI MERMAID! CARVER TOWN WAS CLEANED OUT WHILE THE SHOW-BOAT WAS AT THE DOCK!
H-M-M-M--- JEFFERSON, TALBERT, JOHNSVILLE, NOW CARVER TOWN! LET'S HAVE A LOOK AT THE ATLAS!

LOOK--- EVERY LITTLE TOWN VISITED BY THAT SHOWBOAT HAS BEEN A VICTIM OF THE RIVER GANG! WE HAVE A JOB ON OUR HANDS, DICKEY!

MISSISSIPPI, HERE WE COME!

MEANWHILE, THE BEGUILING MERMAID SAILS ON TO FRESH TRIUMPHS!

WELCOME, LADIES AND GENTLEMEN! WELCOME TO THE FINEST AQUATIC SHOW ON EARTH!

UT--- WHILE DALESTOWN APPLAUDS THE SHOWBOAT PERFORMANCE, THE RIVER GANG STRIKES AGAIN!

UP WITH YOUR HANDS---AND KEEP YOUR TRAP SHUT!

COME ON, GRAMPA--- GET IT OPEN BEFORE I OPEN YOU!

PEN! BUT THE CLICKING TUMBLERS RING--- THE BATMAN AND ROBIN!

YOU HIT THE JACKPOT THIS TIME!
DID YOU RING SIR?

ONE
THE BATMAN!
UHHH
TWO
3

-THREE!
CHECK YOUR GUN, SIR!
YOWW
TIME TO UNMASK, BROTHER--- PARTY'S OVER!
LOOK OUT!

LIGHTNING-FAST. THE BOY WONDER LASHES OUT WITH AN AGILE TOE!

SORRY--- BUT YOU'VE GOT TO CALL YOUR SHOTS IF YOU WANT TO PLAY IN OUR LEAGUE!
BANG
THAT'S TELLING HIM, ROBIN!

BUT PERVERSE FATE INTERVENES.. AND THE STRAY BULLET SEVERS A SUPPORTING WIRE!

THAT'S ALL FOR THE BATMAN!
NOW FOR THAT BRAT!

A SPLIT-SECOND OF CONSTERNATION--- BUT IT SPELLS DISASTER FOR ROBIN!

LITTLE BOYS SHOULD BE SEEN AND NOT HEARD!
LET'S SCRAM, GUYS!

LATER...A FRANTIC ROBIN CRIES IMPLORINGLY AT A STILL BATMAN...

THE BANK'S BEEN ROBBED!
THEY'RE LOOTING THE WHOLE TOWN!
BATMAN-- BATMAN!

AND WHEN THE CURTAIN OF FOG LIFTS FROM THE CRIME-FIGHTER'S MIND...

ALL RIGHT, MEN, LET'S GET THEM! I HAD A GOOD LOOK AT ONE OF THEM---AND I KNOW WHERE WE'LL FIND HIM!
ON THE SHOWBOAT!

UT SUAVE CAPTAIN BEN IS READY AT THE GANGPLANK!
I ASSURE YOU YOU ARE MISTAKEN, GENTLEMEN! I CAN VOUCH FOR EVERY MEMBER!
WE'RE HAVING A LOOK- FOR OURSELVES, CAPTAIN!
GET THE CROOKS!

ABOARD THE MERMAID THE RIVERCADE IS IN FULL SWING...
THAT FELLOW ON THE BOARD--- I UNMASKED HIM IN THE HOTEL!
IMPOSSIBLE! THAT'S GUS HENKEL, OUR STAR SWIMMER!

T TEN
INUTES
O NINE
E WAS
STAR
OLD-UP
MAN!

BUT HE HASN'T LEFT THE BOAT ALL EVENING!

HE'S RIGHT, BATMAN! HENKEL WAS GIVING A DIVING EXHIBITION AT TEN TO NINE!

HENKEL'S OKAY!

I'M SORRY, CAPTAIN! I GUESS THE BATMAN WAS MISTAKEN!

FORGET IT, BATMAN! PERHAPS THIEVES ARE FOLLOWING THE MERMAID AND MASQUERADING AS MEMBERS OF OUR COMPANY!

POSSIBLY SO!

PERHAPS... BUT THE BATMAN KNOWS BETTER...
WHY DID YOU SAY YOU MIGHT HAVE BEEN MISTAKEN? YOU KNOW THAT WAS HENKEL IN THE HOTEL!
OF COURSE, BUT THERE WAS NO USE BUCKING THAT SET-UP! THIS SCHEME IS MIGHTY SLICK, DICK--- BUT WE'RE GOING TO CRACK IT WIDE OPEN!

HE FOLLOWING WEEK... WHEN THE RIVERCADE OPENS IN ANDRE'S BEND, BRUCE WAYNE IS READY FOR THE NEXT ROUND...
ENKEL HASN'T EEN OUT OF IGHT FOR THE AST HOUR!
AND WITH ONLY FIVE MINUTES INTERMISSION THERE WON'T BE TIME FOR HIM TO GET UP TO TOWN AND BACK! HE MUST BE INNOCENT!

AND NOW, LADIES AND GENTLEMEN, THERE WILL BE AN INTERMISSION OF FIVE MINUTES! AT 9:05 OUR COMPANY WILL RETURN! UNTIL THEN--- THE WATER IS YOURS!
H RAY

SUDDENLY INSPIRATION FLASHES
I'VE GOT IT, DICK! THAT CLOCK IS THE ANSWER! AND I KNOW HOW TO PROVE IT!
5

MOMENTARILY BRUCE AND HIS YOUNG WARD VANISH---
YOU GET THE IDEA?
YOU'RE MILES AHEAD OF ME---BUT I KNOW WHAT TO DO!
---TO MAKE WAY FOR THE BATMAN AND ROBIN...
THE BATMAN!
AND ROBIN!
WHAT'S WRONG? WHY ARE THEY HERE?
THERE IS NOTHING WRONG, FOLKS! DURING THE INTER-MISSION THERE IS TO BE AN EXHIBITION OF SPEED SWIMMING BY THE BATMAN, WHO WILL TRY TO SET A NEW RECORD! OKAY, BATMAN!

LIKE A DARK FLASH, THAT LITHE FIGURE CUTS THROUGH THE WATER...
SIX TIMES AROUND THE TANK IS A QUARTER-MILE!
THAT'S HIS EIGHTH LAP! HE'S SMASHED THE WORLD'S RECORD!
A QUARTER MILE IN TWO MINUTES! WOW!

THIS MAKES LESS THAN FOUR MINUTES FOR A HALF-MILE! AND THE WORLD'S RECORD IS 10:07.6! THAT'S ALL I NEED TO KNOW, CAPTAIN BEN!

THUNDEROUS APPLAUSE HAILS THAT INCREDIBLE PERFORMANCE!
JUST AS I THOUGHT---THIS FIVE-MINUTES INTERMISSION HAS BEEN AT LEAST TEN MINUTES!
YEA... BATMAN!!!

BUT BACKSTAGE AWAITS ANOTHER RECEPTION...
DOWN, ROBIN!
6

TOO BAD, BUT THIS BAT CAN SEE IN THE LIGHT---AND THE ONE YOU'RE SWINGING CAN'T!

THE CHIN YOU LOVE TO TOUCH!
NICE WORK, ROBIN! THESE GENTLEMEN PROVE THAT WE'VE SOLVED THE RIVER GANG'S SCHEME!

THAT BIG CLOCK WAS MANIPULATED SO THAT AT NINE O'CLOCK THE TIME WAS ACTUALLY 8:45! THEN, WITH THE INTERMISSION, IT WAS SLOWED DOWN TO GIVE THE PERFORMERS TIME FOR THEIR DEVILTRY ASHORE!
A NEAT STUNT!

HOW THE GANG TRICKED TIME!
CLOCK TIME
ACTUAL TIME

AND, WITHOUT WATCHES, THE BATHING SPECTATORS HAD ONLY THE ALTERED CLOCK TO TELL THE TIME!

MEANWHILE, DOWN THE RIVER, AN UNLIGHTED CRAFT DARTS AWAY FROM THE SHORE....
THIS IS THE RICHEST HAUL YET!
NOW WATCH THE SAPS COME SQUEALING TO THE BOAT!

NOISELESSLY THE FRONT OF THE MERMAID OPENS TO RECEIVE ITS FURTIVE FLEDGELING.
HEADS DOWN!

BUT AT THAT INSTANT THE DARK NIGHT TURNS INTO GLARING MID-DAY....
THIS'LL THROW SOME LIGHT ON THE SUBJECT!

YOU BLASTED FOOL! DOUSE THAT LIGHT!
I'LL DOUSE IT--- WITH LEAD!
7

AND OUT OF NOWHERE FLASHES THE NEMESIS OF CRIME...
TOO MUCH LIGHT FOR YOU RATS? I'LL PUT IT OUT!
THE BATMAN!
LIKE THIS!
GET HIM! STOP HIM!
LOW BRIDGE, BOYS!
FOUR TO ONE---BUT THAT ONE IS BATMAN!
GIVE HIM THE HOOK!... YOU'RE FINISHED, BATMAN!
SUCH MANNERS!
NOT QUITE FINISHED---- BUT ALMOST!
AND NOW FOR THE RIVER GANG!
SORRY I CAN'T STAY ANY LONGER, BOYS, BUT I MUSTN'T KEEP THE CAPTAIN WAITING!
THAT'S RIGHT--- YOU TWO GET TOGETHER AND TALK IT OVER!
CRACK
WHAT HIT ME?
I KNEW WE'D BE BOMBED SOME DAY!
8

NAWARE OF THE DISASTER BELOW-DECK, CAPTAIN BEN GUARDS HIS GANGPLANK...
WE CHASED THEM TO THE RIVER AND SAW THEM HEADING FOR YOUR BOAT, CAP-TAIN! THEY'RE ON THE MERMAID!
IMPOSSIBLE! I CAN VOUCH FOR MY TROUPE AND NOT ANOTHER SOUL HAS COME ABOARD SINCE!
UNTIL---
I WOULDN'T BE TOO SURE OF THAT, CAPTAIN!
BUT WILY CAPTAIN BEN THINKS FAST...
THE BATMAN... THERE'S YOUR ANSWER, CONSTABLE! HE WAS IN THE TOWN WHEN IT WAS LOOTED! HE'S HERE! HE'S USING MY BOAT AS A HIDEOUT! LOOK---HE'S STILL WET FROM SWIMMING ABOARD!
HE SLY RUSE WORKS...
MY TOWN'S BEEN ROBBED CLEAN, AND I AIN'T TAKIN' CHANCES WITH NOBODY! HOW DO WE KNOW YOU ARE THE BATMAN?
AND IF YOU ARE THE BATMAN, WHAT ARE YOU DOING HERE?
I'M DOING WHAT YOU OUGHT TO BE DOING--- HUNTING THE RIVER GANG! WE HAD THE BRAINS HERE A MINUTE AGO, BUT NOW--- THANKS TO YOU--- HE'S SLIPPED AWAY! GET MOVING AND WE MAY STILL NAB HIM!
TOO LATE! YOU HELD ME JUST LONG ENOUGH TO LET HIM MAKE HIS GET-A-WAY!
I--- I DIDN'T KNOW! I COULDN'T TELL!
THERE HE GOES, CONSTABLE! THAT'S THE LAST YOU'LL SEE OF CAPTAIN BEN---AND THE LOOT HIS GANG TOOK OUT OF YOUR TOWN!
WHY, THE DOUBLE-CROSSING LIAR! AND HE SOUNDED SO HONEST!
9

MINUTES LATER, OUT OVER THE RIVER STREAKS AN EERIE, BAT-SHAPED CRAFT--- THE BATPLANE!
OKAY, CAPTAIN BEN--- HERE I COME WHEREVER YOU ARE!
BUT WHERE IS ROBIN? THAT'S WHAT PUZZLES ME!
WHILE FAR BELOW, SKIMMING OVER THE DARK SURFACE OF THE MISSISSIPPI---
LISTEN, CAPTAIN--- A PLANE!
SO THE BATMAN STILL IS WITH US... WELL, HERE IS WHERE WE PART COMPANY!
BAYOU LAMONT! EVEN IN DAY-LIGHT THIS ENTRANCE IS COMPLETELY HIDDEN FROM ABOVE!
BYE-BYE, BATMAN!
MILES UP THE SWAMPY BAYOU LIES A REMOTE RENDEZVOUS...
TOO BAD WE LOST YOUR PLAY-MATE, HENKEL! ALMOST WISH HE'D CALL ON US HERE!
NO FEAR OF THAT! I'VE SEEN THE LAST OF THE BATMAN AND HIS PESKY BRAT!
BUT EVEN BEFORE THE ECHO OF HIS COCK-SURE WORDS FADES...
PESKY BRAT, EH? WE'LL TAKE THAT UP LATER, HENKEL!
HALF AN HOUR LATER... CAPTAIN BEN TALLIES HIS LOOT...
CARVER TOWN---$175,000. ANDRE'S BEND---$240,000. BETTER AND BETTER!
WHAT'S THAT? I HEAR A NOISE!
A NOISE? YES, I HEAR IT TOO! IT SEEMS MY WISH IS ABOUT TO BE GRANTED!
10

THE SHATTER OF GLASS...AND THE MANTLED BATMAN HURTLES IN!
SO YOU GOT HERE, BATMAN! TOO BAD YOU MISSED THE BOAT!
YOUR BOAT'S FINISHED, CAPTAIN BEN! THE RIVER GANG IS ALL WASHED UP!

BUT CAPTAIN BEN'S HAND IS BENEATH THE TABLE, HIS FINGERS REACHING...

AND PRESSING...
HO-HO! WHAT A GRACE-FUL EXIT!
MUST YOU GO SO SOON? NICE TO HAVE YOU DROP IN!

THE PIT OF DEATH...
YOU'RE SO AT HOME IN THE WATER, NO DOUBT YOU'LL GET ALONG EXCELLENTLY WITH ANNIE!
LET'S SEE YOU MAKE A RECORD WITH HER, BATMAN!

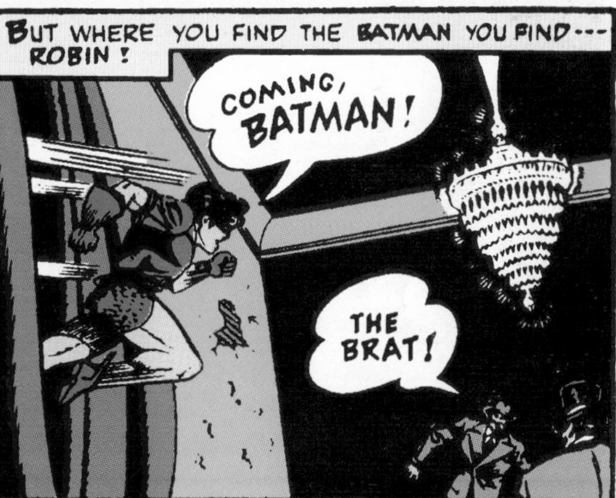
BUT WHERE YOU FIND THE BATMAN YOU FIND---ROBIN!
COMING, BATMAN!
THE BRAT!

I'VE BEEN SAVING THAT FOR YOU, HENKEL!

AND SEE WHAT I BROUGHT FOR YOU, CAPTAIN!
YOU LITTLE SNIPE--
11

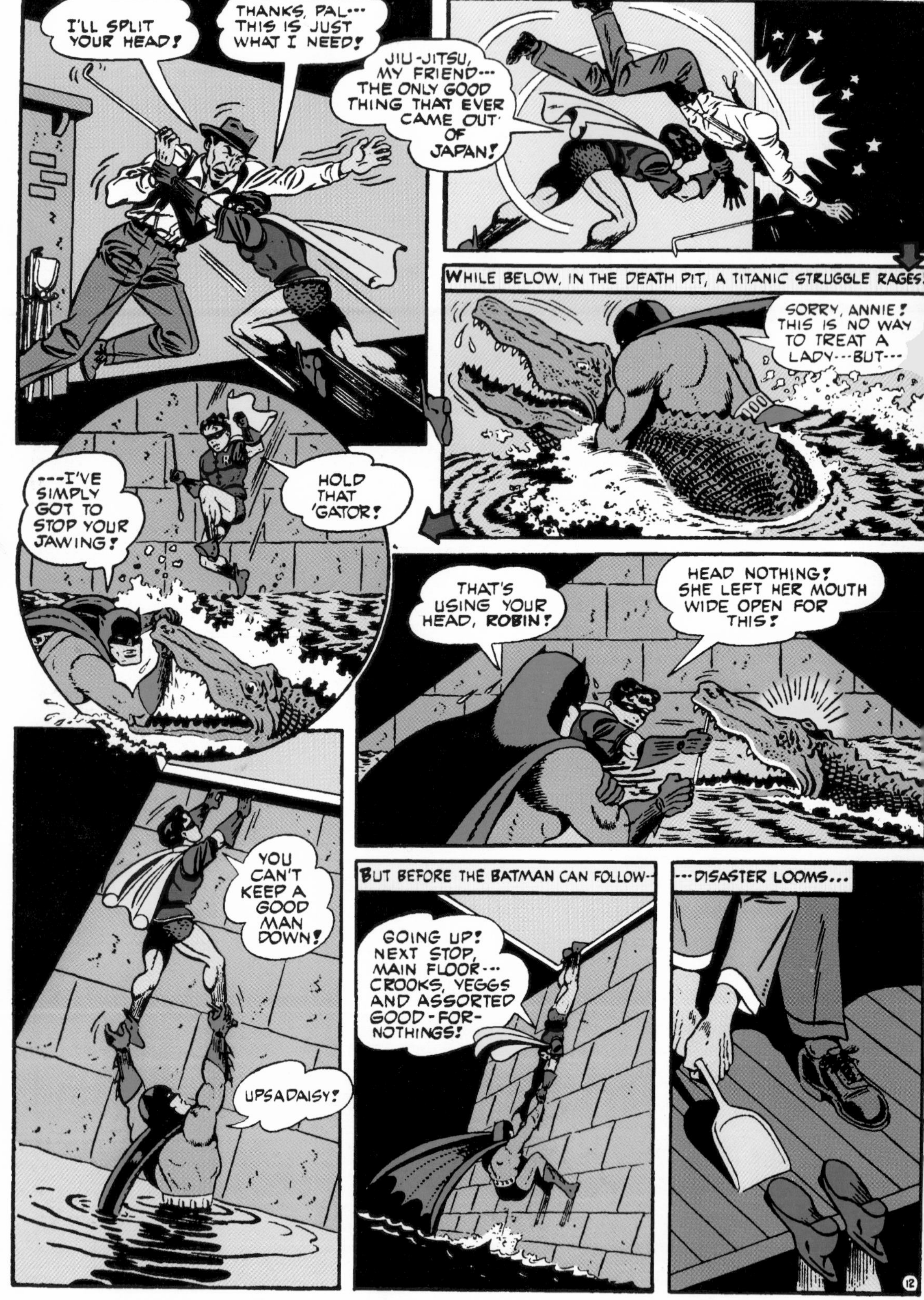
I'LL SPLIT YOUR HEAD!
THANKS, PAL--- THIS IS JUST WHAT I NEED!
JIU-JITSU, MY FRIEND--- THE ONLY GOOD THING THAT EVER CAME OUT OF JAPAN!
WHILE BELOW, IN THE DEATH PIT, A TITANIC STRUGGLE RAGES!
SORRY, ANNIE! THIS IS NO WAY TO TREAT A LADY---BUT---
---I'VE SIMPLY GOT TO STOP YOUR JAWING!
HOLD THAT 'GATOR!
THAT'S USING YOUR HEAD, ROBIN!
HEAD NOTHING! SHE LEFT HER MOUTH WIDE OPEN FOR THIS!
YOU CAN'T KEEP A GOOD MAN DOWN!
UPSADAISY!
BUT BEFORE THE BATMAN CAN FOLLOW--
GOING UP! NEXT STOP, MAIN FLOOR--- CROOKS, YEGGS AND ASSORTED GOOD-FOR-NOTHINGS!
---DISASTER LOOMS...
12

ONLY THE ACROBATMAN'S PERFECT COORDINATION OF MIND AND MUSCLE CAN MEET THAT PERIL..

ALLEY-OOP!

GLAD TO GIVE YOU A LIFT, HENKEL!

BUT WHERE IS CAPTAIN BEN? IN A FLASH THE PEERLESS PARTNERS ARE AFTER THE FLEEING RIVER RENEGADE...

HE'LL NEVER GET THE BOAT STARTED--- I FIXED THAT!

NICE GOING, ROBIN!

YOU'RE NOT TAKING ME!

HE'S GOING OVERBOARD! HE'S AFTER THE BATPLANE!

THE POOR FOOL! HE'LL NEVER MAKE IT!

BARRACUDA

THERE'S ONLY ONE CHANCE---IF I CAN LOOP THE BATPLANE!

THE ALLIGATORS ARE CLOSING IN ON HIM!

THE HEMPEN NOOSE FLASHES THRU SPACE IN AN UNERRING THROW...

CAPTAIN BEN'S ONE CHANCE- AND THE BATMAN TAKES IT!

HOLD THEM OFF FOR A MOMENT!

HELP!

AND THE VILLAINOUS CAPTAIN BEN'S OUTLAW CAREER IS ENDED!

CAN'T LET THE 'GATORS HAVE YOU, BEN! YOU'RE GOING TO DO TIME--- PLENTY OF IT--- AND BY A CLOCK YOU WON'T BE ABLE TO FIX!

YOU WIN, BATMAN--- AND IT'S THE FIRST TIME I'M GLAD YOU DID!

SNAP SNAP

SNAP

The END

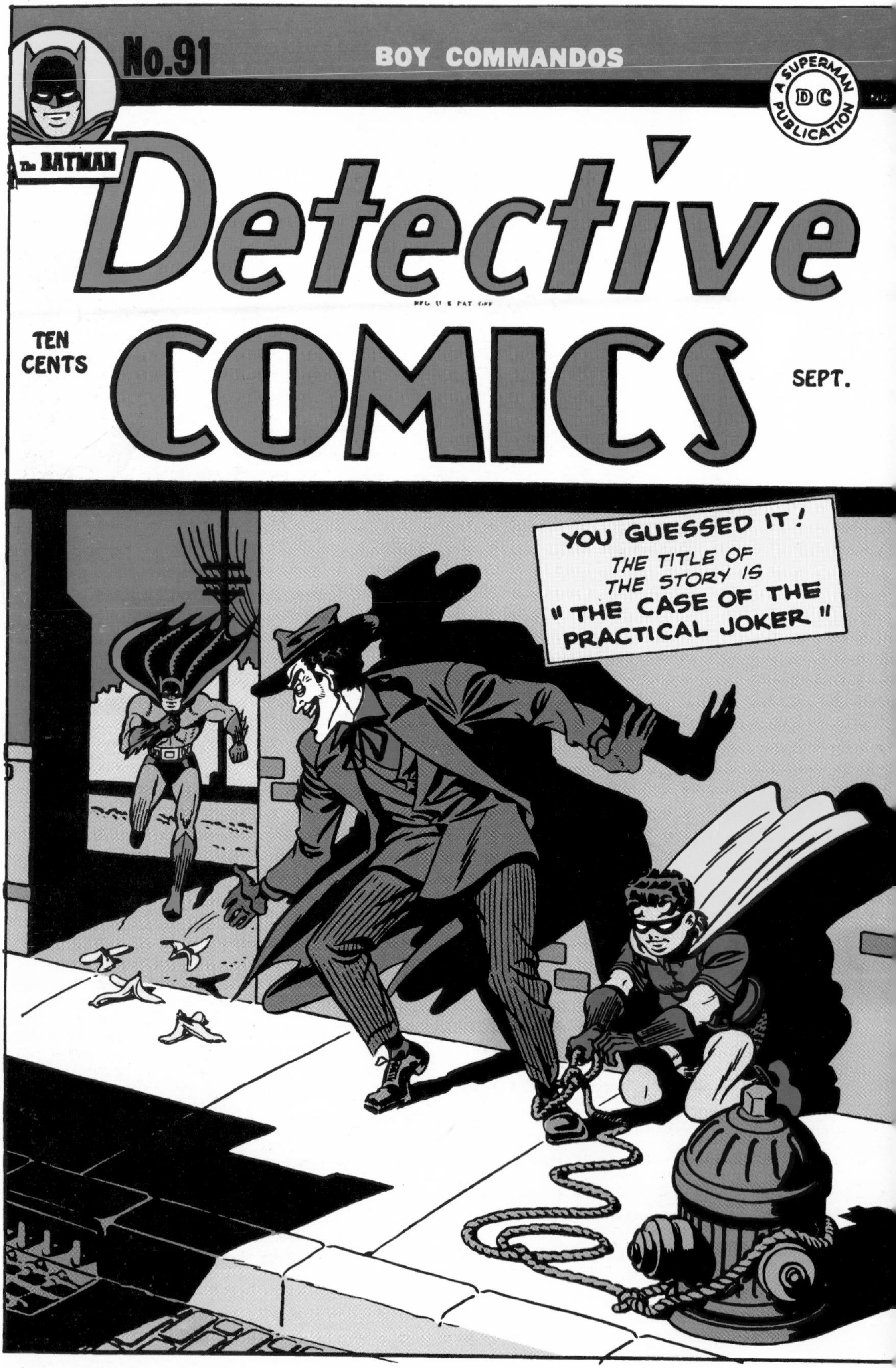

No.91
BOY COMMANDOS
A SUPERMAN DC PUBLICATION
The BATMAN
Detective
TEN CENTS
COMICS
SEPT.
YOU GUESSED IT!
THE TITLE OF THE STORY IS
"THE CASE OF THE PRACTICAL JOKER"

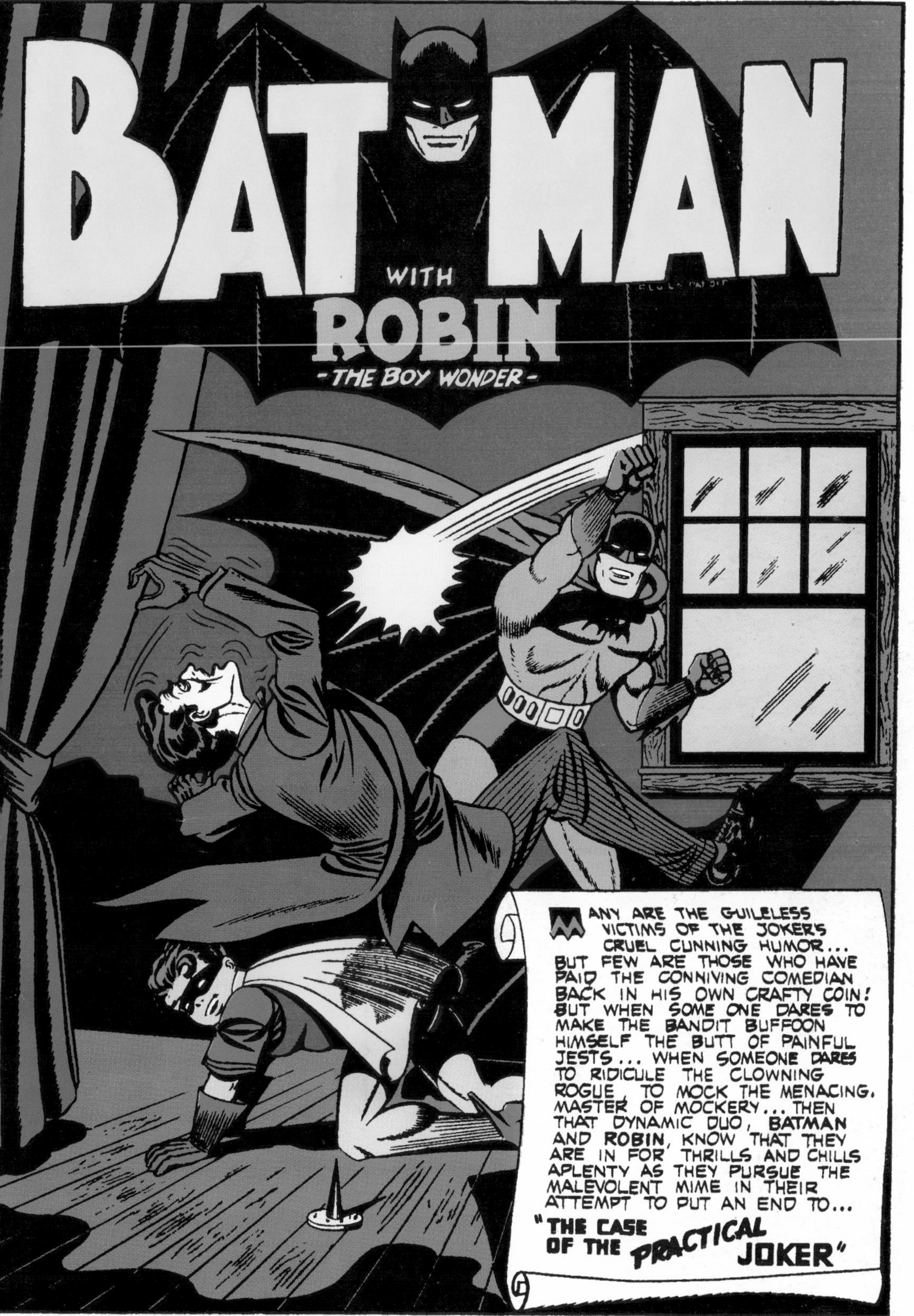
BATMAN
WITH
ROBIN
-THE BOY WONDER-
MANY ARE THE GUILELESS VICTIMS OF THE JOKER'S CRUEL CUNNING HUMOR... BUT FEW ARE THOSE WHO HAVE PAID THE CONNIVING COMEDIAN BACK IN HIS OWN CRAFTY COIN! BUT WHEN SOME ONE DARES TO MAKE THE BANDIT BUFFOON HIMSELF THE BUTT OF PAINFUL JESTS... WHEN SOMEONE DARES TO RIDICULE THE CLOWNING ROGUE, TO MOCK THE MENACING. MASTER OF MOCKERY... THEN THAT DYNAMIC DUO, BATMAN AND ROBIN, KNOW THAT THEY ARE IN FOR THRILLS AND CHILLS APLENTY AS THEY PURSUE THE MALEVOLENT MIME IN THEIR ATTEMPT TO PUT AN END TO...
"THE CASE OF THE PRACTICAL JOKER"

FROM BEHIND STEEL BARS COMES MOCKING, SPINE-CHILLING LAUGHTER...

THE WAY THE JOKER LAUGHS GIVES ME THE CREEPS! WONDER WHAT HE'S GOT UP HIS SLEEVE NEXT!

HA HA HA HA HA HA HA HA

THE SOUND OF MIRTHLESS GAIETY ECHOES DOWN THE GRIM CORRIDORS...

YOU'VE GOT NOTHING TO LAUGH AT, JOKER! YOU'RE GOING TO SPEND THE REST OF YOUR LIFE IN JAIL!

HA, HA! TIME WILL TELL! HA! HA!

BUT TIME BRINGS THE HARLEQUI OF HATE NO CAUSE FOR AMUSEMENT!.. THAT NIGHT...

YEEEEOW

QUIET, THERE! WHAT'S GOING ON, JOKER?

SOMEBODY PUT THAT IN MY BED!

LOOKS LIKE THE KIND OF PRACTICAL JOKES YOU PLAY YOURSELF, JOKER! BUT THIS TIME THE JOKE'S ON YOU! HA, HA!

AND AT BREAKFAST...

SOMEBODY PUT VINEGAR IN MY COFFEE!

IT'S SURE TURNED YOU INTO A SOURPUSS, JOKER! HA, HA!

DURING THE REST PERIOD...

SOMEBODY PULLED THAT CHAIR AWAY FROM UNDER ME! WHEN I FIND OUT WHO IT IS, I'LL KILL HIM! I'LL KILL HIM!

JOKER, YOU'RE A RIOT! FUNNIER THAN EVER!

HA, HA!

DON'T BE SO SURE OF THAT, DICK! I CAN'T SEE AN ORDINARY CONVICT OR GUARD PUTTING ANYTHING OVER ON HIM!
IT DOES SEEM STRANGE!
WHEN SOMEBODY SEEMS TO BE GETTING THE BETTER OF THAT CUNNING SCOUNDREL, IT'S TIME TO BE SUSPICIOUS! I'D BETTER DO A LITTLE INVESTIGATING!
HAT EVENING...
HA, HA, I CAN'T HELP LAUGHING EVERY TIME I THINK OF THE JOKER! HE'S SO BURNED UP HE'S FUNNY!
HEY, WHAT... UGH...
SORRY, FELLOW, THIS CAN'T BE HELPED!
HE DOESN'T KNOW IT, BATMAN, BUT HE'S LUCKY! ALL HE'LL HAVE TO DO IS TAKE THINGS EASY...
... WHILE I DO HIS WORK FOR HIM! I HOPE HE'S GRATEFUL WHEN HE FINDS OUT!
ATER, A MASTER OF DISGUISE TRANSFORMS HIS FEATURES WITH STOUNDING SKILL...
GEE, BRUCE, YOU LOOK SO MUCH LIKE HIM, YOU'D EVEN FOOL ME!
I HAVE TO DO A GOOD JOB, ROBIN! THE JOKER WON'T BE EASY TO DECEIVE!
AND SOON BRUCE WAYNE, PRETENDED PLAYBOY, ENTERS A NEW PHASE OF HIS EXCITING CAREER...
HE DOESN'T SUSPECT I'M NOT REALLY HIS GUARD!
WHAT ARE YOU DOING NOW, JOKER, PLANNING HOW TO ROB A BANK?
I'M THROUGH WITH ROBBING BANKS! MY NEXT CRIME WILL BE... THE THEFT OF AN ENTIRE CITY!

THE THEFT OF A CITY! I WONDER IF THE JOKER IS LOSING HIS GRIP!
HA, HA! YES, I AM DOING NOTHING! BUT REMEMBER, NERO FIDDLED WHILE ROME BURNED! HA, HA!
YOU TALK BIG, JOKER... BUT YOU'RE DOING NOTHING WHILE SOMEBODY IS PLAYING PRACTICAL JOKES ON YOU!
THE JOKER IS TALKING IN RIDDLES TODAY! BUT THERE MUST BE SOMETHING BEHIND HIS WORDS! NERO FIDDLED... HMM...
LATER...
HELP
FIRE
NOW'S MY CHANCE TO SEE THE JOKER AS A VICTIM!
SOMEBODY SET FIRE TO MY MATTRESS!
AND YOU'RE ALL BURNED UP! HA, HA!
I'VE BEEN WATCHING THAT CELL ALL THE TIME... HMM... I'M BEGINNING TO UNDERSTAND!
I'LL GET THE MAN WHO'S PLAYING THESE TRICKS ON ME, AND MAKE HIM LAUGH ON THE OTHER SIDE OF HIS FACE!
I THINK I KNOW WHO HE IS
HAS THE BATMAN SOLVED THE MYSTERY SO SOON? CAN YOU GUESS WHO THE MYSTERIOUS PRANKSTER IS
NEXT DAY...
THIS IS A PERFECT CHANCE FOR A PRACTICAL JOKE! HERE'S WHERE THE JOKER GETS SOAKED!
WATER
IT'S JUST AS I THOUGHT! THAT BUCKET WAS WAITING FOR HIM!
STILL ANOTHER TRICK ON THE JOKER! HA, HA!
WHAT...

SUDDENLY, WHILE EVERYONE LAUGHS AT THE PLIGHT OF THE KILLER-CLOWN ... MENACING MISSILES COME HURTLING FROM OUTSIDE THE PRISON WALL!
LAUGH, FOOLS, LAUGH! SOON IT WILL BE MY TURN!
THE JOKER DELIBERATELY WALKED UNDER THAT BUCKET! I'LL HAVE TO BE ON THE ALERT!
HA HA HA
BITING, CHOKING TEAR-GAS FILLS THE PRISON YARD! LAUGHTER GIVES WAY TO UNWILLING WEEPING!
HA, HA! THE LIQUID IN THAT BUCKET CONTAINED A CHEMICAL THAT NEUTRALIZES TEAR-GAS! I'M THE ONLY ONE HERE NOW WHO ISN'T CRYING!
THIS HANDKERCHIEF ISN'T AS EFFECTIVE AS THE JOKER'S, BUT IT WILL PROTECT MY EYES UNTIL I CAN GET OUT OF THE YARD!
WE'VE TAKEN CARE OF THE GUARDS ALONG THE WALL, BOSS, BUT YOU'D BETTER HURRY BEFORE THEY STOP CRYIN'!
GOOD-BYE, FOOLS! I'M LEAVING! GIVE MY REGARDS TO THE WARDEN!
JUST A SECOND TO SHUCK OFF THESE CLOTHES, AND THEN...
JUST A MINUTE, JOKER, YOU FORGOT TO SAY GOOD-BYE TO ME!
BATMAN! WHERE DID YOU COME FROM?
MAYBE THAT GAS COULDN'T DO IT, BUT THIS PUNCH WILL BRING TEARS TO YOUR EYES!
UGH!...
YOU MEDDLING FOOL...
SPRINGING FROM BEHIND THE MANTLED NEMESIS OF CRIME, TWO NEWCOMERS SUDDENLY JOIN THE FRAY!
TOO BAD YOU DIDN'T REALIZE, BATMAN, THAT I HAD A COUPLE OF MEN IN RESERVE!
THAT GAS IS FINALLY GETTING ME! MY EYES ARE BEGINNING TO SMART!
AS THE BATMAN STUMBLES BLINDLY...
GOOD-BYE, MEDDLER! IF I HAD THE TIME, I'D STAY TO FINISH YOU OFF!
I CAN'T SEE WHERE I'M GOING!

A SUDDEN GUST OF WIND DISPELS THE LINGERING CLOUD OF GAS... BUT THE BATMAN, EYES STILL SMARTING...
MUST BE A TRICK! THE JOKER WOULDN'T DO ME ANY FAVORS!
BUT IF YOU INSIST ON FOLLOWING US, BATMAN... WE'LL HOLD THE NET FOR YOU! HA, HA!
GUIDED BY THE SOUND OF THE BANDIT BUFFOON'S VOICE, THE BATMAN TWISTS TO ONE SIDE AS HE PLUNGES DOWN...
THANKS FOR BREAKING MY FALL AND SAVING MY LIFE, JOKER!
YOU'LL PAY FOR THIS YET, BATMAN! GET HIM, MEN!
BUT NOW A YOUTHFUL, DYNAMIC FIGURE CATAPULTS INTO THE FRAY ...ROBIN, THE BOY WONDER...
I'M TIRED OF BEING A ROBIN PERCHED ON A TELEGRAPH POLE! BATMAN PHONED ME TO WAIT THERE... BUT NOW IT'S TIME FOR ACTION!
HERE'S ANOTHER PRACTICAL JOKE... A HOT FOOT, IN YOUR FACE!
THAT ISN'T FUNNY, YOU BIRD-BRAINED BRAT!
I MAY BE ONLY A ROBIN... BUT I KNOW HOW TO HANDLE A JAILBIRD!
OKAY, KID, YOU ASKED FOR IT!
THIS WILL HOLD YOU TILL WE DISPOSE OF YOUR INTERFERING FRIEND!
HEY!
AND NOW TO FINISH OFF THE BATMAN!
IT'S TIME I DID A LITTLE FINISHING MYSELF, FUNNYMAN!
6

BUT UNEXPECTEDLY, FROM THE PRISON WALLS COMES THE RATTLE OF MACHINE-GUN FIRE!

THE GUARDS MUST HAVE GOT OVER THE EFFECTS OF THE TEAR-GAS, BOSS!

BUT THEY CAN'T SEE WELL YET, AND THEY DON'T REALIZE THEY'RE SHOOTIN' AT THE **BATMAN**, TOO! HA, HA!

AHHH

RATATAT

RATATAT

ZINNG-G

PING-G-G

AS THE GUARDS FIRE WILDLY, THE CRIME CLOWN AND HIS MOB MAKE THEIR ESCAPE! BUT THE **BATMAN**...

MY LEG! UGH... JUST AS I WAS GOING TO LAND THE JOKER!

HEY, STOP SHOOTIN'! DON'T YOU SEE IT'S THE **BATMAN**!

ECONDS LATER, AS **ROBIN** FINALLY ELEASES HIMSELF FROM THE NTANGLING MESHES OF THE NET...

BATMAN! YOU'RE NOT HURT BADLY...

JUST A FLESH WOUND, **ROBIN**! I'LL BE ALL RIGHT!

WE'RE SORRY WE SHOT AT YOU, **BATMAN**! BUT OUR EYES WERE STILL SMARTING FROM THAT TEAR GAS!

AS THE GUARDS DEPART...

WELL, **BATMAN**, THE JOKER TOOK THE WINNING TRICKS THAT TIME! EVEN THOUGH YOU GUESSED HE WAS PLAYING THOSE PRACTICAL JOKES ON HIMSELF!

YES, ROBIN, HE WAS JUST SETTING THE STAGE FOR THAT ESCAPE! ONCE OR TWICE HE USED A CONFEDERATE, BUT MOST OF THE TIME HE WAS BOTH JESTER AND VICTIM!

BUT I THINK WE'LL RUN INTO HIM AGAIN SOON! HE BOASTED HE WAS GOING TO STEAL A WHOLE CITY... HM... FIRST I'LL RELEASE THAT GUARD WHOSE PLACE I TOOK...

EVERAL DAYS LATER...

HE JOKER MUST BE RAZY! HE'S RACTICALLY URRENDERING O THE POLICE!

GOTHAM SQUARE IS A BIG PLACE, **ROBIN**! HE'S COUNTING ON THAT!

DONT MISS THE FUNNIEST STUNT OF ALL TIME! AT 8 P.M. TUESDAY, THE JOKER WILL SLIP ON A BANANA PEEL IN GOTHAM SQUARE! SEE THE MASTER MUMMER VICTIMIZED AS HE HAS VICTIMIZED OTHERS!

DONT MISS

AT THE APPOINTED TIME, A MILLING, EXCITED CROWD PACKS GOTHAM SQUARE.

WE WANT TO SEE THE JOKER! IT'S TIME HE SHOWED UP!

KEEP MOVIN', THERE! KEEP MOVIN'!

7

AS DEEP BELLS CHIME THE HOUR OF EIGHT...
HERE I AM, BOYS! I ALWAYS KEEP MY PROMISES!
WE'VE GOT HIM SURROUNDED! HE CAN'T ESCAPE THIS TIME!
JEWELRY
OOPS! THE JOKE'S ON ME! I SLIPPED!
HERE'S WHERE YOU SLIP BACK TO JAIL!
JEWELER
SUDDENLY, FROM THE WINDOWS OF A NEARBY BUILDING, COMES A SHOWER OF BANANA PEELS, CAST BY THE JOKER'S THUGS!
HA-HA! HAPPY LANDINGS, COPPERS! I DIDN'T SAY I'D BE THE ONLY ONE TO SLIP!
JEWELR
CRASH
HERE'S THE TREASURE I CAME FOR! A MODEL OF GOTHAM CITY... MADE WITH PRECIOUS STONES, AND DONE WITH SKILL THAT CAN'T BE MATCHED! IT'S WORTH A MILLION!
AHH
AS THE EVIL HARLEQUIN'S HENCHMEN DESCEND FROM THE UPPER STORIES OF THE BUILDING...
CARRY IT INTO THE ELEVATOR, AND WE'LL TAKE IT UP TO THE ROOF! QUICK, BEFORE THOSE COPS RECOVER!
SURE, BOSS! AND IF THOSE COPS TRY TO BOTHER US, WE'LL LET 'EM HAVE A FEW MORE BANANA PEELS!
SUDDENLY... FROM THE DOOR TO THE CELLAR...
I FIGURED THIS MIGHT BE WHAT THE JOKER MEANT WHEN HE SAID HE'D STEAL A CITY!
THAT PAIR BUTTING IN AGAIN

HOW ABOUT LETTING ME HAVE THE KEY TO THE CITY, JOKER?
SURE, IN JUST A MOMENT...

YOU CAN EVEN HAVE THIS SKYSCRAPER!
SO YOU'RE A TWENTY-SECOND STORY MAN NOW!

THIS WILL BRING YOU DOWN TO MY LEVEL!
OOOOOFFF

THIS WILL SHAKE YOU LOOSE FROM YOUR BRIDGEWORK, KID!
LOW BRIDGES FOR ME!

AND FOR YOU A LESSON ON HOW TO RIGHT-CROSS YOUR BRIDGES WHEN YOU COME TO THEM!
OWWW

BUT THE CUNNING CRIME CLOWN STILL HAS A TRICK UP HIS SINISTER SLEEVE...

I HOPE YOU AND YOUR BRAT DON'T MISS THE TRAIN, BATMAN! WHA--- THE COPS!
UGH!

BEFORE THE DYNAMIC DUO CAN RECOVER, THE EVIL KING OF COMEDIANS IS ON HIS WAY TO SAFETY...
CURSE YOU, BATMAN! YOU SPOILED MY PLANS! I'LL PAY YOU BACK FOR THAT!
COME ON, ROBIN! WE'VE GOT A LONG CLIMB AHEAD OF US!
ELEVATOR
BATMAN AND ROBIN WILL TAKE CARE OF HIM! WE'D BETTER RETURN TO THE STREET! THOSE BANANA PEELS CAUSED A RIOT!

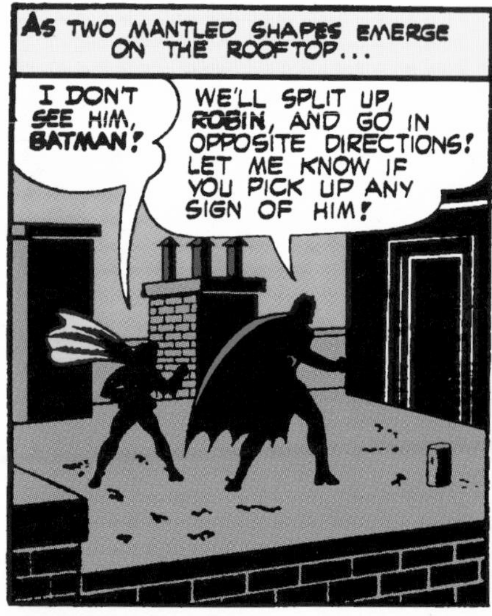
AS TWO MANTLED SHAPES EMERGE ON THE ROOFTOP...
I DON'T SEE HIM, BATMAN!
WE'LL SPLIT UP, ROBIN, AND GO IN OPPOSITE DIRECTIONS! LET ME KNOW IF YOU PICK UP ANY SIGN OF HIM!

ON A NEARBY ROOFTOP, AN OPEN DOORWAY BECKONS! AS BATMAN MOVES FORWARD CAUTIOUSLY...
BETTER WATCH MY STEP! THE JOKER MAY BE LYING IN WAIT FOR ME!

SUDDENLY, THE MASTER CRIME FIGHTER SEES THE LEERING FACE OF THE HARLEQUIN HAT
WAITING FOR ME, JOKER WELL, I DON'T WANT YOU TO WASTE YOU TIME ... HERE I COME!

YOU'RE SLIPPERY, JOKER ... BUT YOU'RE NOT SLIDING OUT OF THIS!
THIS IS GOING TO HURT YOU MORE THAN IT DOES ME, BATMAN!

HA, HA! HIT ME AGAIN, BATMAN!
WHAT... HUH...?
CRASH

I SEE... MIRRORS!
NOT ALL THE FIGURES ARE REFLECTIONS, BATMAN! ONE OF THEM IS REAL!

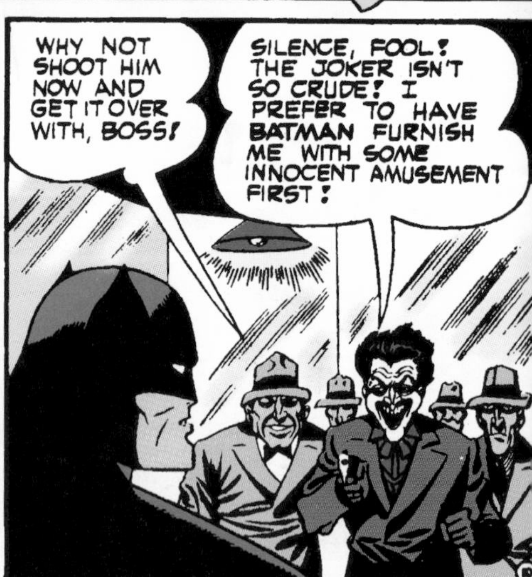
WHY NOT SHOOT HIM NOW AND GET IT OVER WITH, BOSS!
SILENCE, FOOL! THE JOKER ISN'T SO CRUDE! I PREFER TO HAVE BATMAN FURNISH ME WITH SOME INNOCENT AMUSEMENT FIRST!

THE BOUND FIGURE OF THE EVIL JESTER'S ARCH-FOE IS CARRIED TO THE ROOF ONCE MORE...

SO YOU'RE GOING IN FOR PEA-SHOOTING NOW, JOKER!

YES, BATMAN! MIXED IN WITH THESE PEAS IS A POISONED DART-- YOU DON'T KNOW WHEN IT'S COMING, BUT WHEN IT DOES... JUST A TOUCH, AND IT'S CURTAINS FOR YOU!

MEANWHILE, UNSUCCESSFUL IN PICKING UP THE JOKER'S TRAIL, THE BOY WONDER RETRACES HIS STEPS... AND HEARS A TAUNTING LAUGH...

BULL'S-EYE AGAIN! SOON I'LL BE SHOOTING THAT POISON DART, BATMAN! HA, HA!

GOLLY! BATMAN CAPTURED -- IN DANGER! GOT TO DO SOMETHING, BUT THERE ARE TOO MANY OF THEM!.. AH, HERE'S SOMETHING THAT OUGHT TO BE USEFUL!

THE WIND MUST HAVE BLOWN IT HERE... NOW, WITH THIS HEAVY RUBBER BAND I PICKED UP TO TURN IN FOR SALVAGE, AND SOME STONES FROM THE ROOF...

HA, HA! MAYBE THIS ONE IS THE POISONED DART!
THE JOKER IS IN A LAUGHING MOOD! I HOPE HE APPRECIATES THE HUMOR OF THIS!

IT MUST BE A COP! HE'S SHOOTIN' AT US WITH A SILENCED GUN!

WHAT...

THIS PROVES THAT THE SLINGSHOT IS MIGHTIER THAN THE PEASHOOTER!

NOW TO DISGUISE MY VOICE...

BETTER SURRENDER, JOKER! I'VE GOT YOU COVERED!

OWW... I'M WOUNDED... I'M KILLED...
BETTER GET OUT OF HERE, BOSS, BEFORE THAT SHARP-SHOOTER PICKS US ALL OFF!
YOU'RE LUCKY THIS TIME BATMAN, BUT YOU WON'T ESCAPE SO EASILY AGAIN!

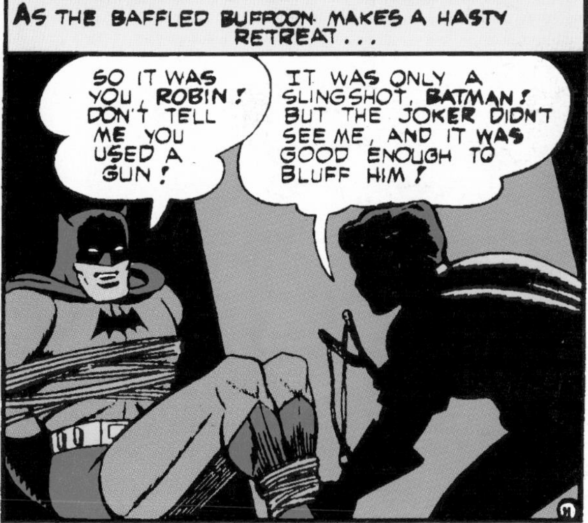

AS THE BAFFLED BUFFOON MAKES A HASTY RETREAT...
SO IT WAS YOU, ROBIN! DON'T TELL ME YOU USED A GUN!
IT WAS ONLY A SLINGSHOT, BATMAN! BUT THE JOKER DIDN'T SEE ME, AND IT WAS GOOD ENOUGH TO BLUFF HIM!

A FEW DAYS LATER... THE MIRTHFUL MENACE SHOWS HIS SINISTER HAND ONCE MORE...
Dear Commissioner Gordon: Tonight you will see the Joker become the victim of a whole series of practical jokes in Gotham Square! I will not play any jokes on the police this time! I'll be counting on you to be there! The Joker
A FURIOUS POLICE COMMISSIONER SCANS THE JOKER'S IMPUDENT LETTER...
THIS TIME THE JOKER HAS GONE TOO FAR! THE MOMENT HE SETS FOOT IN GOTHAM SQUARE, WE'LL NAB HIM!
EVERY POLICEMAN WE CAN SPARE WILL BE COVERING THE PLACE!
THAT NIGHT AS THE POLICE WAIT IMPATIENTLY..
IT'S THE JOKER, ALL RIGHT!
BUT NOT IN PERSON IT'S ONLY A MOVIE!
OOF
SOMEBODY'S MAKING A FOOL OF THE JOKER... BUT ONLY IN THE MOVIE!
HEY
THE JOKER KEPT HIS WORD... BUT HE TRICKED US, ANYWAY!
THE JOKE'S ON US!
MEANWHILE, LEARNING OF THE JOKER'S MISSIVE, THE BATMAN HAS MADE PLANS OF HIS OWN...
GOTHAM MUSIC CO.
RARE MUSICAL INSTRUMENTS
I THINK WE'RE GOING TO FIND AN OLD FRIEND, ROBIN! HE USED A TRICK TO GET THE POLICE AWAY FROM HERE, BUT I KNOW HE'LL BE HAPPY TO SEE US!
WHAT'S THE IDEA OF COMING HERE, BATMAN?
HOW'D YOU KNOW WE'D FIND THE JOKER HERE?
A REMARK OF HIS IN JAIL ABOUT NERO FIDDLING WHILE ROME BURNED! IT REVEALED WHAT WAS ON HIS MIND!
THIS RARE OLD STRADIVARIUS IS WORTH $50,000! IT... WHAT...!?!
12

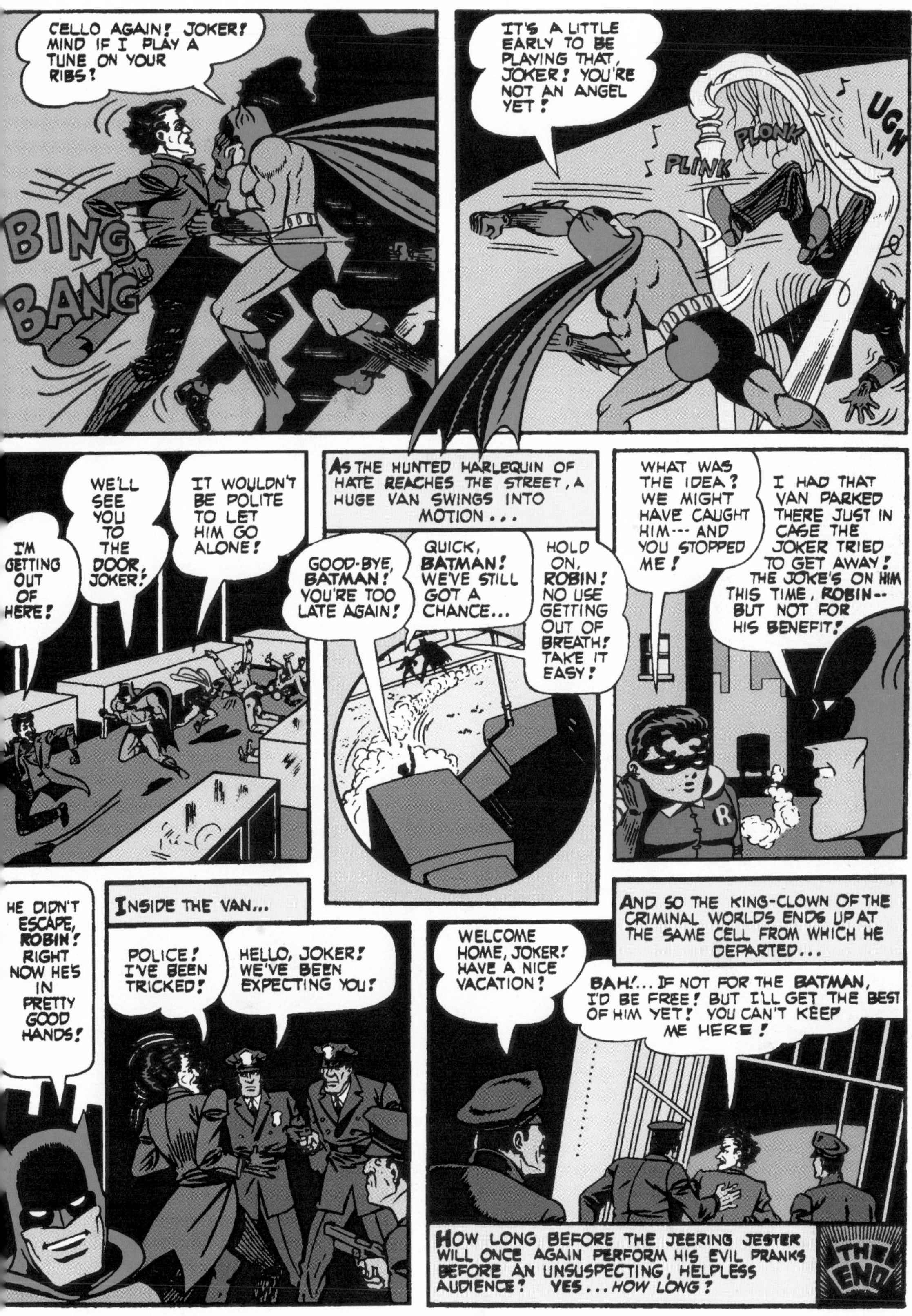
CELLO AGAIN! JOKER! MIND IF I PLAY A TUNE ON YOUR RIBS?
BING
BANG
IT'S A LITTLE EARLY TO BE PLAYING THAT, JOKER! YOU'RE NOT AN ANGEL YET!
PLINK
PLONK
UGH
I'M GETTING OUT OF HERE!
WE'LL SEE YOU TO THE DOOR, JOKER!
IT WOULDN'T BE POLITE TO LET HIM GO ALONE!
AS THE HUNTED HARLEQUIN OF HATE REACHES THE STREET, A HUGE VAN SWINGS INTO MOTION...
GOOD-BYE, BATMAN! YOU'RE TOO LATE AGAIN!
QUICK, BATMAN! WE'VE STILL GOT A CHANCE...
HOLD ON, ROBIN! NO USE GETTING OUT OF BREATH! TAKE IT EASY!
WHAT WAS THE IDEA? WE MIGHT HAVE CAUGHT HIM--- AND YOU STOPPED ME!
I HAD THAT VAN PARKED THERE JUST IN CASE THE JOKER TRIED TO GET AWAY! THE JOKE'S ON HIM THIS TIME, ROBIN-- BUT NOT FOR HIS BENEFIT!
HE DIDN'T ESCAPE, ROBIN! RIGHT NOW HE'S IN PRETTY GOOD HANDS!
INSIDE THE VAN...
POLICE! I'VE BEEN TRICKED!
HELLO, JOKER! WE'VE BEEN EXPECTING YOU!
AND SO THE KING-CLOWN OF THE CRIMINAL WORLDS ENDS UP AT THE SAME CELL FROM WHICH HE DEPARTED...
WELCOME HOME, JOKER! HAVE A NICE VACATION?
BAH!... IF NOT FOR THE BATMAN, I'D BE FREE! BUT I'LL GET THE BEST OF HIM YET! YOU CAN'T KEEP ME HERE!
HOW LONG BEFORE THE JEERING JESTER WILL ONCE AGAIN PERFORM HIS EVIL PRANKS BEFORE AN UNSUSPECTING, HELPLESS AUDIENCE? YES... HOW LONG?
THE END

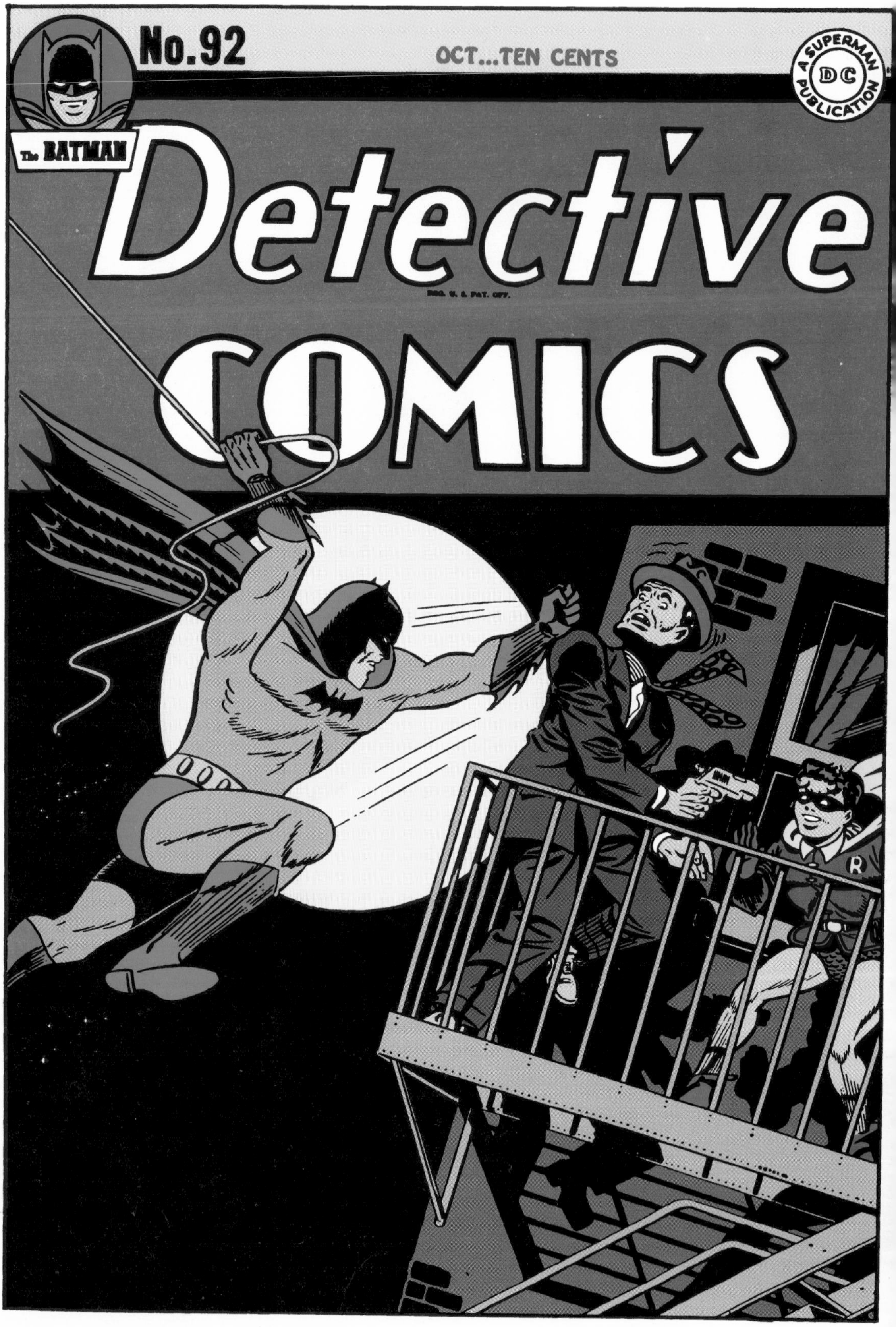

No.92

OCT...TEN CENTS

A SUPERMAN DC PUBLICATION

The BATMAN

Detective COMICS

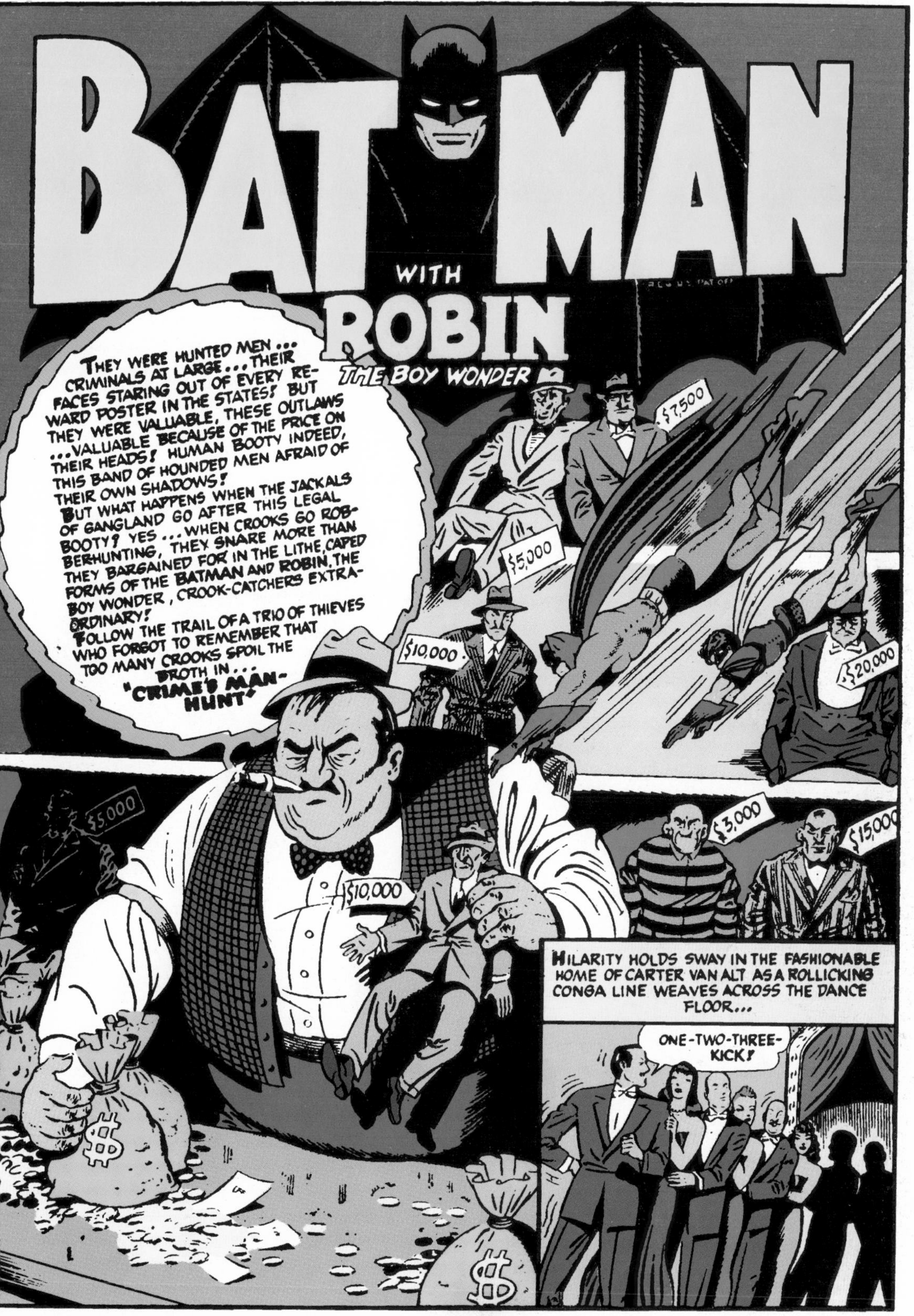
BATMAN
WITH
ROBIN
THE BOY WONDER
THEY WERE HUNTED MEN ... CRIMINALS AT LARGE ... THEIR FACES STARING OUT OF EVERY REWARD POSTER IN THE STATES! BUT THEY WERE VALUABLE, THESE OUTLAWS ... VALUABLE BECAUSE OF THE PRICE ON THEIR HEADS! HUMAN BOOTY INDEED, THIS BAND OF HOUNDED MEN AFRAID OF THEIR OWN SHADOWS! BUT WHAT HAPPENS WHEN THE JACKALS OF GANGLAND GO AFTER THIS LEGAL BOOTY? YES ... WHEN CROOKS GO ROBBERHUNTING, THEY SNARE MORE THAN THEY BARGAINED FOR IN THE LITHE, CAPED FORMS OF THE BATMAN AND ROBIN, THE BOY WONDER, CROOK-CATCHERS EXTRAORDINARY! FOLLOW THE TRAIL OF A TRIO OF THIEVES WHO FORGOT TO REMEMBER THAT TOO MANY CROOKS SPOIL THE BROTH IN ... "CRIME'S MAN-HUNT"
$7,500
$5,000
$10,000
$20,000
$5,000
$3,000
$15,000
$10,000
HILARITY HOLDS SWAY IN THE FASHIONABLE HOME OF CARTER VAN ALT AS A ROLLICKING CONGA LINE WEAVES ACROSS THE DANCE FLOOR...
ONE-TWO-THREE-KICK!

SUDDENLY THREE GRIM FIGURES MENACE THE MERRYMAKERS...

KEEP SWINGING, FOLKS! RIGHT THIS WAY--- AND KEEP YOUR HANDS HIGH!

THE WAITERS!

OH! OH! ...IT'S A HOLD-UP! ... MY JEWELS!

AH-AH! NO HOLDING OUT! IS THAT NICE!

CAN'T SOMEBODY STOP THEM?

THEN, MIRACULOUSLY, THAT DESPERATE PLEA IS ANSWERED--FROM THE BALLROOM'S CRYSTAL-DOMED ROO

THE BATMAN AND ROBIN!

COMING!

BETTER LATE THAN NEVER

STRAIGHT FOR THEIR MARK THE DYNAMIC DUO PLUNGE!

THAT'S MY CONTRIBUTION!

SORRY MINE MISSED THE BAG!

THESE AREN'T YOUR WAITERS, VAN ALT! THEY KNOCKED OUT THE REGULAR MEN AND TOOK THEIR PLACES!

NEXT MOMENT, THE FLASH OF THE BATARANG THRU SPACE, AND THE TRIO ARE SNARLED IN BOLO FASHION...

THREE BIRDS WITH ONE STONE!

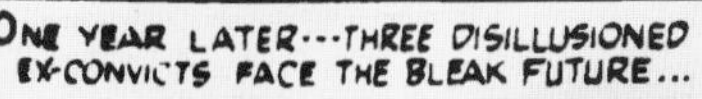
ONE YEAR LATER---THREE DISILLUSIONED EX-CONVICTS FACE THE BLEAK FUTURE...

WE MIGHT AS WELL BE ACK IN THE BIG HOUSE! THE RACKETS IS ALL WASHED UP!
YEAH ... WITH THE BATMAN AROUND, A FELLOW CAN'T MAKE AN HONEST DOLLAR!

AN HONEST DOLLAR--- YOU GOT SOMETHIN' THERE, SLUG! THE RACKETS ARE WASHED UP! BUT I GOT AN IDEA---A RACKET THAT'S SAFE AND LEGITIMATE! LOOKA HERE---

$5000 REWARD
BOBO NELSON
WANTED FOR HIGHWAY ROBBERY AND FELONIOUS ASSAULT. HE

USE YOUR BRAINS THE WAY I DO, SLUG! WE BRING IN BOBO---AND THAT FIVE GRAND IS OURS! THEN WE CAN GO AFTER DOZENS OF THE OTHER REWARDS! LISTEN...
YEAH, BUT WHAT'S THAT O US?
GEE, BRAINY---IT'S A PERFECT RACKET--- AN' HONEST, TOO!

LOOK--- BOBO WAS SHOT DURING THAT HOLD-UP! HE'S HIDIN' OUT WITH HEINY DIPP, AND THE DOC SEES HIM EVERYDAY! NOW, SLUG, WE RIG YOU UP LIKE THE DOC, AND THEN---

THE NEXT MORNING... HEINY OPENS HIS DOOR TO THE DOCTOR AS USUAL---BUT---
TODAY YOU COME EARLY, DOCTOR, NO? YOU---
THIS IS WHAT THE DOCTOR ORDERED, HEINY!

OBO NELSON'S USUAL QUICK SUSPICION IS DULLED BY FEAR...
WHAT'S THE MATTER, OC? AIN'T T COMIN' ALONG OKAY?
NOT SO GOOD, BOBO! I'LL HAVE TO GIVE YOU A SLEEPING POWDER!

MINUTES LATER...
HE'LL BE FAST ASLEEP FOR HOURS!
GREAT, BOYS! WHAT'D I TELL YOU? EASY AS ROLLIN' OFF A LOG!
3

A WEEK LATER...
PRETTY SOFT, BRAINY---FIVE GRAND AND "THE THANKS OF THE COMMUNITY"!
BETTER THAN DUCKIN' THE COPS, EH, SLUG? NOW LET'S GET DOWN TO BUSINESS! "TWISTY" HERMAN'S GONNA BE OUR NEXT MEAL TICKET!
YEAH, BUT TWISTY IS HIDING OUT OVER IN JERSEY! HE NEVER COMES OVER THE STATE LINE!
SEVEN AND A HALF GRAND!
THAT'S WHERE I COME IN, BOYS! NOW LISTEN!..
$7,500 REWARD
NEXT DAY, AT TWISTY HERMAN'S RAMAPO MOUNTAIN HIDEOUT...
NIFTY HIDEOUT YOU HAVE UP HERE, TWISTY! SAFE FROM NEW YORK COPS TOO!
YEAH, BRAINY! THAT'S WHY I BROUGHT YOU TO THIS HILL! I LIK TO COME HERE AND LAUGH AT THEM! THAT'S NEW YORK, DOWN THER BUT THIS IS JERSEY---
SUDDENLY...
SURPRISE! HAPPY LANDING!
HEY---WHAT'S THE IDEA? I'M OFF-BALANCE-A-A-R-K!
PROPELLED BY BRAINY'S TREACHEROUS SHOVE, TWIST MAKES A DISASTROUS DESCENT...
Y-I-I-I-I-I
---BUT "AID" COMES SWIFTLY!
WELCOME BACK TO NEW YORK TWISTY!
YOU CROSSED THE STATE LINE IN NOTHING FLAT!
SUCCESS! AND AS THE LOOT PILES UP, THE RACKETEERS MOVE TO MORE PALATIAL QUARTERS...
PRETTY SOFT! AND ALL GOOD, HONEST DOUGH!
THAT'S CHICKEN FEED! NOW WE'RE GOIN' AFTER REAL DOUGH! THERE'S TEN GRAND ON SAM AZARRA, AND HE'S HIDIN' RIGHT HERE IN TOWN! NOW HERE'S HOW WE'LL GRAB HIM...
4

EXT DAY, WARY SAM AZARRA CAUTIOUSLY OPENS THE DOOR OF HIS APARTMENT...
WINDOW WASHER!
YOU'RE A NEW MAN, EH? AWRIGHT, COME IN--- AND GET DONE WITH IT IN A HURRY!

THREE LITTLE PELLETS TUMBLE NOISELESSLY INTO THE WINDOW WASHER'S SCRUB-PAIL...

OUTSIDE THE CLOSED WINDOW, THE WASHER TOILS INDUSTRIOUSLY...
GO TO SLEEP, MY BABY, MY BA-A-A-BY!
THOSE SLEEPING GAS TABLETS ARE BEGINNING TO WORK!

SO-O-O SLEEPY... CAN'T KEEP MY--- EYES--- OPEN---

THAT'S OKAY, BROTHER! NOW YOU'RE READY FOR DELIVERY--- C.O.D! YES, SIR--- THE D.A. WILL SHELL OUT TEN GRAND FOR YOU!

REWARDS! REWARDS! THE GOLDEN HARVEST ROLLS IN!
TEN GRAND! GEE, BRAINY, I HATE TO THINK ABOUT THE YEARS WE WASTED IN THE PEN!
YEAH, BUT WHAT DO WE DO NOW? WE'RE RUNNIN' OUT OF GUYS TO GRAB!

NO MORE GUYS TO GRAB? THE PEN IS FULL OF THEM! ALL WE GOTTA DO IS SPRING A GUY, WAIT FOR THE REWARD FOR HIS RECAPTURE, AND THEN HAND HIM BACK AGAIN! NOW LET'S SEE---THERE'S NICK ROSSI---

PRESENTLY, HALF A DOZEN GIFT RADIOS ARRIVE AT STATE PRISON--- BUT THE ONE DESTINED FOR NICK ROSSI'S CELL PRODUCES MORE THAN MUSIC!
THINK OF FINDING YOU HERE! HEH, HEH---YOU SURE LOOK MEAN, BABY! ...HERE'S WHERE I GO INTO ACTION!
5

"ACTION!"
GUARD! HELP! THAT SNAKE'LL KILL ME!
STAND STILL, ROSSI! I'LL KILL IT!

SHAME ON YOU, YOU BIG BULLY---HITTING A POOR LITTLE SNAK

THE GUN AND THE GUARD'S UNIFORM OPEN THE PRISON DOORS---TO WHERE BRAINY WAITS...
THANKS, BRAINY! YOU'RE A SWELL GUY!
HIYA, NICK!

AND NOW, THE NEXT ACT IN THIS DRAMA OF DUPLICITY...
SO TONIGHT HENCHELL WILL BROADCAST THE TIP I SENT HIM, AND ROSSI WILL BE SCARED STIFF! I COME TO SNEAK HIM OUT OF TOWN---AND YOU TWO SOCK HIM WHEN WE COME OUT!

BUT THAT NIGHT WALLY HENCHELL'S GOSSIP BROADCAST IS PICKED UP BY UNEXPECTED EARS...
...AND I HAVE IT ON GOOD AUTHORITY THAT PUBLIC ENEMY NICK ROSSI IS HIDING IN A CERTAIN WATER-FRONT BOWLING ALLEY...
"A WATERFRON BOWLING ALLE ---THAT MUST BE DUNN'S! SUPPOSE WE TAKE A LOOK, ROBIN!

LATER...
THIS ROOM OUGHT TO LEAD INTO THE ALLEYS---RIGHT UP BEHIND THE BOWLERS! ---HERE I GO!
RIGHT BEHIND YOU!

THE BATMAN!
HUH- WHO TOLD HIM I WAS HIDING OUT HERE?
6

GET IT NOW! RAINY--- YOU'RE A OUBLE-CROSSING AT! YOU SPRUNG E OUT OF STIR--- ND NOW YOU'RE ANDING ME OVER O THE BATMAN OR THE REWARD!
NO, NICK--- I DIDN'T! I DON'T KNOW ANYTHING---

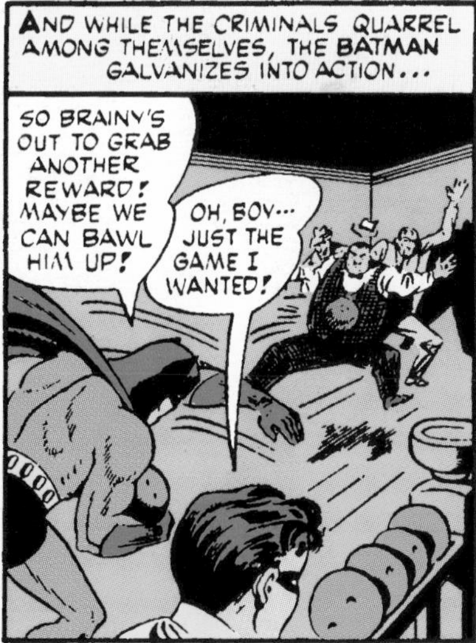
AND WHILE THE CRIMINALS QUARREL AMONG THEMSELVES, THE BATMAN GALVANIZES INTO ACTION...
SO BRAINY'S OUT TO GRAB ANOTHER REWARD! MAYBE WE CAN BAWL HIM UP!
OH, BOY--- JUST THE GAME I WANTED!

BUT NOT EVEN THE GREAT CRIME-FIGHTER CAN STEM THE TIDE OF THUGS...
I HAVE A SCORE TO SETTLE WITH YOU, BATMAN!

OKAY, NICK--- CHALK IT UP THERE!
SCORE

MEANWHILE, THE LAUGHING BOY WONDER HAS HIS LITTLE FLING...
COME ON AND GET YOUR EARS PINNED BACK!
GET THE LITTLE BRAT!
BUT A PIECE OF CHALK PROVES THE STALWART YOUNG DAREDEVIL'S UNDOING...
O-H-H-H... I'M SLIPPING!
RIGHT... AND I'M GONNA SLIP YOU A HAYMAKER!

NOT WHILE I CAN MAKE HAY FIRST--- THIS WAY!

STRIKE!
7

ROSSI REACHES THE HEAD OF THE STAIRS---TO FIND THE WAY TO FREEDOM BLOCKED BY A MERE BOY!
OUT OF THE WAY, KID!
ANYTHING TO OBLIGE, BUT---
---YOU'D BETTER TAKE A CUE FROM ME!
AND AT THAT MOMENT BRAINY'S WILD SHOUTING BRINGS A RESPONS
A PERFECT CAROM SHOT, ROBIN! YOU'RE GETTING GOOD!
WANT TO KNOW MY SECRET? I STUDIED UNDER A MASTER!
YOU'LL GET HURT PLAYING ON THE STAIRS!
HEADS UP, PAL!
IN A FLASH THE PEERLESS PAIR HAVE THEIR MAN--- ON THEIR WAY TO THE WAITING BATMOBILE...
TEN THOUSAND DOLLARS ON THE HOOF WEIGHS PLENTY, EH, ROBIN ?
LUCKY FOR US WE DIDN'T PICK UP A MILLION!
NEXT DAY, BRAINY'S BEAUTIFUL GOLDEN BUBBLE HAS BURST...
THE BATMAN MUSCLES IN ON OUR RACKET AND SWIPES OUR REWARD---AND THEN WHAT DOES HE DO WITH IT? TURNS IT OVER TO THE U.S.O.!
THE DIRTY, CHISEL-ING CROOK!
THAT'S WHAT HAPPENS WHEN WE TRY TO GO STRAIGHT!
AND THEN COMES THE BOOMERANG!
EXTRA! $1000 REWARD FOR BRAINY BULOW! READ NICK ROSSI'S CONFESSION!
NICK SQUEALED! NOW EVERY RAT IN TOWN WILL BE READY TO TURN ME IN FOR THE REWARD!
H-M---IT'S ONLY ONE GRAND! WE WOULDN'T---
8

IN FAR MORE COMFORTABLE SURROUNDINGS THE SAME HEADLINES INTEREST BRUCE WAYNE AND DICK GRAYSON...

H-M-M---SO THERE'S A REWARD OUT FOR BRAINY FOR HELPING ROSSI BREAK JAIL! THAT'S ONE REWARD BRAINY WON'T GO AFTER!
BUT THE BATMAN WILL! TURNING IN CROOKS FOR THE REWARDS IS ONE THING---BUT ARRANGING JAIL-BREAKS IS QUITE ANOTHER MATTER!
the NEWS
HUGE REWARD FOR BR

BRAINY WILL BE IN HIDING, SO WE'LL NEED BAIT TO BRING HIM OUT---BAIT HE CAN'T RESIST! LET'S SEE NOW...
MAYBE SOME OF THESE ROGUES GALLERY VALENTINES WILL HELP YOU!
REWARD

SO, IN A FEW DAYS, A NEW REWARD NOTICE IS CIRCULATED THROUGHOUT GOTHAM CITY...

$25,000 REWARD FOR THE CAPTURE OF SOUPY McCUE

ON THE NIGHT OF MARCH 10 THIS VETERAN CRACKSMAN AND EX-CONVICT BROKE INTO THE SAFE OF THE GOTHAM JEWELERS AND MADE OFF WITH GEMS TO THE VALUE OF MORE THAN $250,000. THE MISSING GEMS ARE DESCRIBED AS FOLLOWS:

THE FERRET EYES OF THE UNDERWORLD SPY THE STARTLING POSTERS...

TWENTY-FIVE GRAND! AND NO QUESTIONS ASKED! OH, BOY!

GEE, I'D TURN MYSELF IN FOR THAT!

WHO IS THIS SOUPY McCUE?

$25,000 REWA... SOUPY

WHO IS SOUPY McCUE? THAT QUESTION IS ON HUNDREDS OF LIPS, BUT NOBODY SEEMS TO KNOW--- UNTIL---
YEAH, I KNOW WHERE SOUPY McCUE IS HIDING! I TAKE FOOD UP TO HIM EVERY NIGHT!---SLIP ME A HUNDRED SMACKERS AND I'LL TELL YOU WHERE HE IS...
SURE, PAL! HAVE ANOTHER COFFEE! HOW ABOUT SOME PIE?...

HALF AN HOUR LATER...

IT WENT OFF LIKE CLOCKWORK! FOR A COUNTERFEIT HUNDRED-DOLLAR BILL AND A HAMBURGER I GAVE SLIM ALL THE DOPE!

AND TONIGHT WE GO TO WORK!

AND AT THAT VERY MOMENT...
TWENTY-FIVE GRAND! I CAN'T COLLECT IT, BUT SLIM CAN! THEN WE CAN BLOW THIS TOWN AND START UP SOMEWHERE ELSE---WITH NO PESKY BATMAN TO MUSCLE IN ON US!
IT'S A CINCH, BRAINY!
9

MIDNIGHT...AND BRAINY LEADS THE WAY OUT ONTO THE TERRACE OF A PENTHOUSE FAR ABOVE THE SURROUNDING ROOFS...
FINE! THERE'S A LIGHT! SOUPY'S IN--- WAITING TO BE GRABBED!
I TOLD YOU MY TIP WAS ON THE LEVEL!

SOUPY McCUE--- THERE HE IS!
TWENTY-FIVE GRAND!
SWELL! NOW BE READY WHEN I TRY THE DOOR!

TENSELY BRAINY PRESSES THE BELL-AND---
IT'S MIKE, SOUPY! I'VE GOT YOUR FOOD!
OKAY, PAL! COME IN!

HOLD IT, SOUPY! WE GOT YOU COVERED!
STICK 'EM UP OR WE'LL DRILL YOU!
HE SURE FELL FOR OUR GAG!

BUT SOUPY MAKES NO ATTEMPT TO STICK 'EM UP...
HOLY MACK---

TOO LATE, SLIM'S EYES FLASH UPWARD!
THE BATMAN!

TAG--- YOU'RE OUT!
TATTLE TALE--- THAT'S WHAT YOU GET FOR SNITCHING!
UGH-H

BUT AT THAT MOMENT PERVERSE FATE INTER-VENES...
WHACK
BATMAN!
10

DAZED, THE BATMAN IS MOMENTARILY HELPLESS---AND THAT SPLIT SECOND IS ALL BRAINY NEEDS...
SO YOU TRIED TO GYP ME AGAIN, EH, BATMAN? BUT I'VE PUT A REWARD ON YOUR HEAD---AND THE NOTICE READS, "DEAD OR ALIVE!"
LISTEN, BATMAN--- LISTEN!

THE TRIGGER-FINGER TIGHTENS---BUT EVEN AS DEATH BLASTS FROM THE GUN THE BATMAN SPEEDS INTO ACTION...
ROLL, ROBIN--- ROLL! BACK OF THE SETTEE!

SAFE AT FIRST, ANYWAY!
BUT THAT'S A LONG WAY FROM HOME!
BANG
BANG
BANG

FEW SECONDS REPRIEVE---BUT THE BATMAN ASKS NO MORE---
WHERE DO WE GO FROM HERE?
THROUGH THAT BEDROOM DOOR! THIS GADGET OUGHT TO INTEREST OUR FRIEND BRAINY! HERE GOES!
ING-3-3
ING-3-3

HERE'S SOME SOLID THOUGHT FOR YOU, BRAINY!
CLUNK

AFE IN THE BEDROOM! BUT A THIN WOODEN DOOR IS LIGHT PROTECTION AGAINST LEAD SLUGS...
THIS GAME SURE IS TOUGH ON URNITURE!

ONE DOOR IS SAFE---BUT IN FROM THE OTHER...
DON'T BLAME ME FOR THAT, BATMAN--- IT'S THESE GENTS WHO BARGE IN WITHOUT KNOCKING!

HOW DO YOU LIKE MY MAGIC CARPET?
THAT'S TAKING OUT THE INTERFERENCE, ROBIN!
11

---AND WINS FAR MORE EFFECTIVELY THAN HE DARED HOPE!

ROBIN!

CRASH

AND NOW YOU'LL FOLLOW THE KID, BATMAN! HUH---

THAT'S ONE FOR ROBIN!

SWIFTLY THE BATMAN'S LIGHTNING BRAIN FORMULATES A DESPERATE PLAN...
HERE COMES THE LINE, ROBIN! CATCH!
RIGHTO!
ALL IN HAND BELOW, SIR!
GOOD BOY! NOW HANG ON!
A DEADLY HAIL RIDDLES THE BATMAN'S SABLE WINGS AS HE LEAPS INTO SPACE!
BANG
BANG
BANG
BUT DOOM HOVERS TENACIOUSLY ABOVE HIM...
ALL RIGHT, ROBIN--- ALL SET?
SWING AWAY BATMAN! I GOT LOTS OF BULLETS!
I GET IT!
YOU WON'T HOLD STILL, EH? WELL, SUPPOSE I PICK OFF THE KID INSTEAD!
GO ON---YOU COULDN'T HIT THE SIDE OF A BARN!
THE DEADLY MUZZLE TURNS TO ROBIN'S BARELY MOVING FIGURE... BUT BRAINY MISSES THE SIGNIFICANCE OF THAT DESPERATE PINWHEEL--- UNTIL---
SORRY BUT THIS IS WHERE I GET OFF!
UGH!
AND SO WE REACH THE END OF THE SORDID RACKET TRAIL...
HELLO, COMMISSIONER! WE HAVE THREE CUSTOMERS HERE WAITING FOR THE PATROL WAGON! AND THERE'S A LITTLE REWARD WE WANT TO DONATE TO---
TO THE RED CROSS! I HAVE IT ALL PRINTED!
TO THE AMERICAN RED CROSS WE HEREBY DONATE OUR REWARD RIGHTS IN BRAINY BULOW PASTMASTER IN THE DOUBLE-CROSS! THE BATMAN & ROBIN
The END

No.93
NOV...TEN CENTS
A SUPERMAN DC PUBLICATION
The BATMAN
Detective
REG. U. S. PAT. OFF.
COMICS

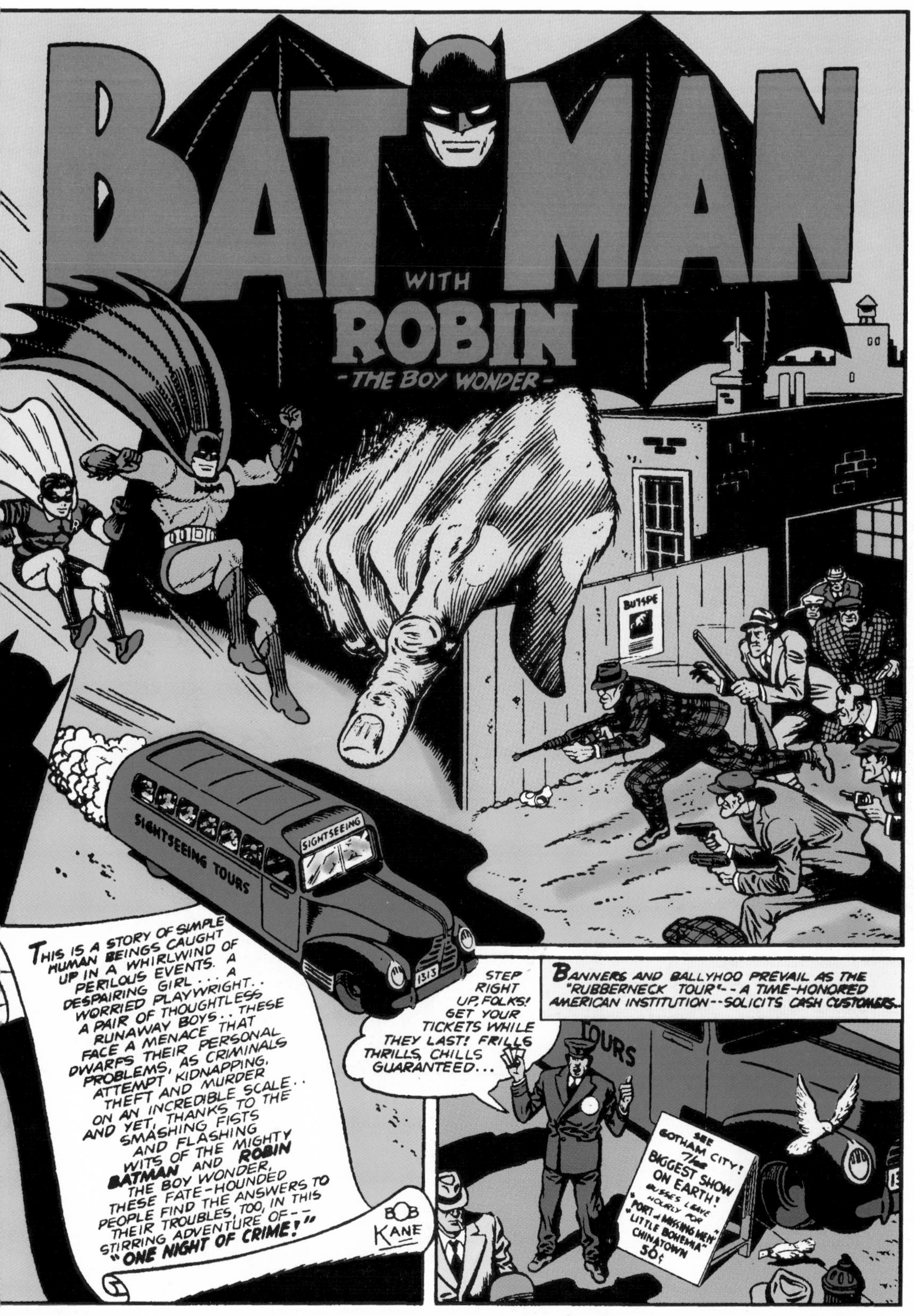
BATMAN
WITH
ROBIN
-THE BOY WONDER-
SIGHTSEEING
SIGHTSEEING TOURS
1313
THIS IS A STORY OF SIMPLE HUMAN BEINGS CAUGHT UP IN A WHIRLWIND OF PERILOUS EVENTS. A DESPAIRING GIRL... A WORRIED PLAYWRIGHT.. A PAIR OF THOUGHTLESS RUNAWAY BOYS.. THESE FACE A MENACE THAT DWARFS THEIR PERSONAL PROBLEMS, AS CRIMINALS ATTEMPT KIDNAPPING, THEFT AND MURDER ON AN INCREDIBLE SCALE.. AND YET, THANKS TO THE SMASHING FISTS AND FLASHING WITS OF THE MIGHTY BATMAN AND ROBIN THE BOY WONDER, THESE FATE-HOUNDED PEOPLE FIND THE ANSWERS TO THEIR TROUBLES, TOO, IN THIS STIRRING ADVENTURE OF-- "ONE NIGHT OF CRIME!"
BOB KANE
BANNERS AND BALLYHOO PREVAIL AS THE "RUBBERNECK TOUR"-- A TIME-HONORED AMERICAN INSTITUTION--SOLICITS CASH CUSTOMERS..
STEP RIGHT UP, FOLKS! GET YOUR TICKETS WHILE THEY LAST! FRILLS THRILLS, CHILLS GUARANTEED...
TOURS
SEE GOTHAM CITY! The BIGGEST SHOW ON EARTH! BUSSES LEAVE HOURLY FOR "PORT of MISSING MEN" "LITTLE BOHEMIA" CHINATOWN 50¢

WHAT SORT OF PEOPLE ARE THESE, WHO SEEK AMUSEMENT OR KNOWLEDGE, BY PEERING INTO THE LIVES OF OTHER HUMANS? LET US LOOK CLOSELY AT SOME OF THEM..

LOVELY MARY DALE DREAMED OF BECOMING A GREAT ACTRESS... BUT REPEATED REBUFFS HAVE LEFT HER DISHEARTENED AND ALL BUT DESTITUTE...
I REALLY CAN'T AFFORD IT-- BUT PERHAPS IT WILL TAKE MY MIND OFF MY TROUBLES..

FOOLISH JOHNNY REID AND EDDIE BARTON HAVE DREAMS ALSO.. THEY HAVE RUN AWAY FROM THEIR HOMES IN FALLS CORNERS TO BECOME "AMATEUR DETECTIVES!"
GOLLY, OUR MONEY IS GOING FAST HERE IN THE CITY!
WELL, WE HAVE TO KNOW OUR WAY AROUND IF WE'RE GOING TO BE AMATEUR DETECTIVES, DON'T WE!

WEALTHY VICTOR CLEMENT, SUCCESSFUL PLAYWRIGHT AND PRODUCER, IS SEARCHING DESPERATELY FOR A NEW DRAMATIC PLOT....
MAYBE A SIGHTSEEING TOUR WILL START MY BRAIN CLICKING AGAIN...

SPEAKING OF DRAMA... AT THIS MOMENT THE NIGHT REVERBERATES WITH IT, A SCANT TWO BLOCKS AWAY..
LOAN CO.

TWO CAPED FIGURES STREAK THROUGH THE DARKNESS TOWARD THE SOUND OF SHOOTING---THE BATMAN AND ROBIN..
BET IT'S THAT HOLDUP GANG THAT HAS BEEN OPERATING IN THIS PART OF TOWN!
WE'LL SOON KNOW!

WINDMILL FISTS LASH OUT AT THE FLEEING OUTLAWS..
WHAT'S YOUR HURRY?
IT'S THE BATMAN!
2

HAVEN'T YOU BOYS DONE ENOUGH SHOOTING?

ONE OF THE THIEVES HAS REMAINED IN THE BACKGROUND, ESCAPING NOTICE IN THE TURMOIL...

HERE'S MY CHANCE TO BEAT IT!

AS THE CROOK MELTS INTO THE GATHERING CROWD, A LOITERER SHADOWS HIM FURTIVELY...

POLICE ARRIVE TO FIND FOUR OF THE GUNMEN THOROUGHLY SUBDUED....
TAKE THEM AWAY, CAPTAIN!
FINE WORK, BATMAN! IS THIS ALL OF THEM?
P.D.

NOT ALL OF THEM! THE MOST IMPORTANT ONE GOT AWAY WITH THE $50,000. THEY TOOK FROM ME!
YOU'RE THE MANAGER, EH?

TOO BAD THE ONE WITH THE LOOT GOT AWAY!
IN A CITY THIS BIG, IT WOULD BE HOPELESS TO START LOOKING FOR HIM WITHOUT A CLUE!
POME

SO IT HAPPENS THAT "TIGER" RAGLAND, NOTORIOUS THIEF AND GUNMAN, JOINS OUR "RUBBERNECK" PARTY...
NO ONE'D EVER THINK TO LOOK FOR ME ON A SIGHTSEEING TOUR!
TO
3

AS THE GREAT BUS STARTS ON ITS FAMILIAR ROUTE...A TELEPHONE CALL OPENS A GRIM GAME IN WHICH FATE IS THE DEALER AND HUMAN LIVES ARE AT STAKE!
DUTCH? THIS IS FRENCHY... GET THIS--A RUBBERNECK BUS JUST LEAVING TRIBUNE SQUARE WILL BE IN CHINATOWN IN ABOUT HALF AN HOUR.. YEAH... NOW LOOK..
QUAINT SCENES ENGAGE THE SIGHTSEERS' ATTENTION...
WE ARE NOW PASSING THROUGH LITTLE BOHEMIA, THE HAUNT OF ARTISTS AND WRITERS...WHERE LIFE IS UNCONVENTIONAL AND EXCITING!
TOO MANY PLAYS HAVE BEEN WRITTEN ABOUT THIS SORT OF THING..
THE PURPLE PIG
ARTE SHOPPE
SIGHTSEEING
HERE IS THE STREET CALLED THE PORT OF MISSING MEN WHERE DOWN-AND-OUTERS WIND UP!
POOR FELLOWS! I SUPPOSE A LOT OF THEM WERE ALWAYS BUMS...BUT SOME MUST HAVE TRIED HARD AND FAILED, AS I HAVE!
ROOMS 15¢ HOTEL
ELECTRIC TATTOOING
HOTEL
HAIRCUT
POP-EYED WONDER FILLS JOHNNY AND EDDIE, THE THOUGHTLESS RUNAWAYS, IN A CHINATOWN JOSS HOUSE...
BUDDHA IS THE BEST LOVED OF ALL THE EASTERN DEITIES
GEE---WHILLIKERS--THIS IS BETTER'N A MOVIE!
WE'LL HAVE LOTS TO TELL THE FELLOWS BACK HOME--IF WE EVER GO BACK!
BUT UGLY EVENTS IN THE WAITING BUS MAKE IT SEEM DOUBTFUL WHETHER THE TWO LADS WILL EVER RETURN TO THEIR ANXIOUS PARENTS...
YOU AREN'T IN OUR PARTY! WHAT DO YOU WANT?
NOTHIN' BUT YOUR RUBBERNECK WAGON--AND YOUR CAP!
NICE GOIN', DUTCH!
AS THE SIGHTSEEING GROUP LEAVES THE JOSS HOUSE, WITH THE BARKER BRINGING UP THE REAR...
I'M TAKIN' OVER YOUR JOB, CHUM!

UNSUSPECTING, THE PASSENGERS RESUME THEIR SEATS...
ENJOYING IT?
AS MUCH AS I'VE ENJOYED ANYTHING LATELY...
"TIGER RAGLAND" IS THE FIRST TO NOTICE THAT ALL IS NOT WELL..
OVER HERE, LADIES AND GENTS, IS THE NEW CITY JAIL, WHERE I HAVE SPENT MANY HAPPY, HAPPY HOURS!
WHA--? IT'S FRENCHY LAVOIS!
TWO MEN REACH FOR HIDDEN GUNS WITH EYE-BLURRING SPEED... BUT ONE IS FASTER...
I WAS AFRAID I'D HAVE TO DO THIS!
OH, HOW PERFECTLY AWFUL!
EVERYBODY SIT STILL AND KEEP QUIET! THIS IS A STICKUP!--A SNATCH--CALL IT ANYTHING YOU WANT! THE FIRST ONE TO MAKE TROUBLE GETS SPRAYED WITH LEAD!
THAT'S TELLIN' 'EM, LEFTY!
GOSH-ALL--FISHHOOKS, EDDIE--THEY'RE REAL GANGSTERS!
I BROUGHT MY SLINGSHOT BUT IT'S NO GOOD AGAINST GUNS!
CAREENING THROUGH DESERTED STREETS, THE STOLEN BUS SWERVES INTO A DINGY GARAGE.
GARAG
GOOD OLD DUTCH! HE ALWAYS BRINGS HOME THE GRAVY!
MEANWHILE, THE SLUGGED BARKER HAS RECOVERED..
BUT I TELL YOU, IT REALLY HAPPENED!
SOMEBODY STOLE A SIGHTSEEING BUS WITH ALL ABOARD? ARE YOU SURE YOU HAVEN'T BEEN DRINKING?
A RADIO ALARM BLANKETS THE CITY...
ALL CARS BE ON LOOKOUT FOR MISSING SIGHTSEEING BUS FILLED WITH PEOPLE... STOLEN IN CHINATOWN!
FOR THE LOVE OF MIKE, WHAT WILL THEY THINK OF NEXT?
P.D.

BRUCE WAYNE AND HIS YOUNG WARD DICK GRAYSON-- WHO ARE IN REALITY THE BATMAN AND ROBIN, THE BOY WONDER -- HEAR THE MESSAGE . . .
. . . NO REPORT AS YET OF BUS BEING SEEN AFTER THEFT . . . MAY BE HEADED IN ANY DIRECTION . . .
BRUCE, DO YOU THINK THERE'S A CHANCE--?
WON'T DO ANY HARM TO FIND OUT!
THE FLEET ROADSTER SPEEDS THEM TOWARD CHINATOWN . . .
THE BUS WOULD HAVE BEEN SEEN IF THEY'D DRIVEN IT THROUGH THE CITY. THEY MUST HAVE HIDDEN IT NEAR WHERE IT WAS STOLEN!
WE'RE THINKING ON THE SAME WAVELENGTH, DICK!
AND IN THE CRIMINALS' HIDEOUT . . .
SIT TIGHT, FOLKS. TILL THE BOSS MAKES UP HIS MIND WHAT TO DO WITH YOU!
WE CAN'T LET 'EM GO; THEY SAW ME KILL TIGER! THEY'D IDENTIFY US, SEND US ALL TO THE CHAIR!
WE'LL TAKE 'EM TO THE CELLAR . . . SHUT THEIR MOUTHS FOR GOOD!
THEY'RE GOING TO KILL US ALL A-A-A-H-H-H . . .
YOU CAN BE THE FIRST TO GO, GRANDPA!
THE MURDEROUS DEVILS!
INSIDE THE BASEMENT, THE HUGE VEHICLE IS DRIVEN INTO A VAST, STONEWALLED CELLAR . . .
YOU BRING THE ROPES, FRENCHY?
THEY'RE INSIDE!
I DEMAND TO KNOW WHAT YOU'RE GOING TO DO WITH US!
FIRST OF ALL, WE'RE GONNA TIE YOU IN YOUR SEATS!
6

UDDENLY MARY DALE SLUMPS . . .
I'M GOING TO FAINT . . . OH-H-H-H . . .
LEAVE HER ALONE! SHE'S OKAY WHERE SHE IS!

TERROR HOLDS THE ERSTWHILE SIGHTSEERS MOTIONLESS AS THEY ARE BOUND TIGHTLY . . .
HOW ABOUT HER?
FORGET HER! I'VE SEEN DAMES FAINT BEFORE! WHEN SHE WAKES UP IT'LL BE TOO LATE!

WE'LL CLOSE THE WATERTIGHT DOORS AND LET THE PLACE FILL UP! EVEN IF THEY GET LOOSE, THEY CAN'T TURN OFF THE WATER!
CHIEF, YOU THINK OF EVERYTHING!

IN A DAY OR TWO, WHEN THE HEAT'S OFF, WE'LL DRAIN THE PLACE AND RUN THE BUS AND THE BODIES INTO THE RIVER!

AS THE DOORS BANG SHUT, MARY STIRS . . .
WHAT A GIRL!
HAVE THEY GONE? I ONLY PRETENDED TO FAINT, HOPING THEY WOULDN'T TIE ME! NOW I CAN UNTIE YOU PEOPLE!

OHNNY AND EDDIE SUFFER A ARDY ATTACK OF HOMESICKNESS . .
WHAT I OULDN'T E TO BE CK IN FALLS CORNERS!
ME, TOO--AND MAYBE I KNOW HOW WE CAN GET THERE! GOT A PENCIL AND PAPER?

FIND ME A BOLT OR A NUT OR SOMETHING, JOHNNY--AND A PIECE OF STRING OR A FIBER FROM SOME OF THAT ROPE!
OKAY, BUT I DON'T SEE WHAT FOR!

I'LL SHOW YOU WHAT FOR, IF YOU AREN'T DETECTIVE ENOUGH TO GUESS!

I GET IT! IF ONLY YOU DON'T MISS!
AND IF ONLY SOMEBODY FINDS IT BEFORE IT'S TOO LATE!
SIGHTSEEING TOURS
GAR
THIS IS ABOUT THE ONLY PART OF THE CITY WHERE THE CROOKS COULD HAVE HIDDEN THE BUS SO QUICKLY!
BUT HOW DO WE PICK OUT THE RIGHT BUILDING?
A TINKLE OF BROKEN GLASS... A FLASH OF WHITE AGAINST THE DARKNESS... AND THE BATMAN STREAKS FORWARD!
MAYBE WE'VE FOUND IT ALREADY!
Help! We are prisoners and gangsters are trying to drown us! We are in cellar and think they are upstairs! Please hurry!! Johnny Reid and Eddie Barton Amateur Detectives
IF THE OTHERS ARE TRAPPED THERE, WE PROBABLY WOULD BE, TOO!
WHY NOT TRY THE CELLAR?
DON'T SLIP!
COMING RIGHT AT YOU!
PAYOFF TIME FOR THE KILLERS...
FIFTY THOUSAND! THAT'S TEN GRAND APIECE!
I FEEL LIKE A MILLIONAIRE!
SEEMING TO PLUMMET DOWN FROM THE NIGHT SKY, TWO OMINOUS SHADOWS POUNCE UPON THE OUTLAWS..
IT'S THE BATMAN!!
YOU WERE HAVING SUCH A GOOD TIME, WE JUST HAD TO JOIN YOU!

YOU LOVE
MONEY--BUT
AN YOU TAKE IT
ON THE CHIN?
LEMME PLAY MY FIDDLE FOR HIM!
COMING DOWN!
OOOHHH!
GOING UP!
AAAHH...
THAT'S PICKING A SOFT SPOT TO LAND ON!
THINK YOU'RE A TOUGH KID, EH?
LOOK OUT, ROBIN!
E DARK-CLAD WARRIOR ROCKETS TOWARD THE SLUGGER...
LET'S SEE YOU TRY THAT ON SOMEONE YOUR OWN SIZE!
HELP, SOMEBODY!
WHAM
9

BLACK FURY MAKES THE BATMAN FORGET HIS OTHER FOES FOR A SPLIT SECOND...
GET UP AND FIGHT, RAT!

AND THAT MOMENT IS SUFFICIENT TO TURN THE TIDE OF THE BATTLE...
GOT HIM!

LATER..
IN WITH THEM! LET THEM DROWN WITH THE OTHERS!
IT'S A PLEASURE!

IT'S THE BATMAN!
AND THAT ROBIN KID!
THE SHOCK OF COLD WATER REVIVES THE DYNAMIC DUO...
I'M AFRAID WE DROPPED IN ON YOU RATHER ABRUPTLY!
ABRUPTLY ISN'T THE WORD!
I'M GLAD TO SEE YOU BOTH---BUT NOT IN THIS MESS!

THERE DOESN'T SEEM TO BE ANY ESCAPE! WE CAN'T SHUT OFF THE WATER.. WE CAN'T OPEN THE DOORS.. WE CAN'T REACH THE WINDOW!
I HAVE A PLAN THAT MAY WORK... BUSES OF THIS TYPE ARE USUALLY FLOORED WITH STRIPS OF STEEL RUNNING LENGTHWISE...

RACING THE MOUNTING TIDE, THEY LABOR FEVERISHLY...
ONE END OF THIS PIECE IS LOOSE!
LUCKY WE FOUND A KIT OF TOOLS!
I'M NOT SCARED ANYMORE, MR. BATMAN!
10

SO YOU'RE THE
AMATEUR DETECTIVES
WHO SHOT THAT
NOTE THROUGH
THE WINDOW!
THAT WAS
SMART!
YESSIR! WE RAN
AWAY FROM
FALLS CORNERS
TO PRACTICE
DETECTING!
BUT WE'RE
GOING HOMB
WHEN WE
GET OUT
OF HERE!
PROPPED AGAINST
THE WALL, THE
STEEL STRIPS
FORM A RUDE RAMP...
NOW IF THE WATER
HASN'T FLOODED
THE CARBURETOR
OR SHORT-CIRCUITED
THE IGNITION--
AH!
THERE SHE
GOES!
THE
ENGINE'S
RUNNING!
SLOWLY THE FRONT
WHEELS OF THE
GREAT VEHICLE
INCH UP THE
FLIMSY RUNWAY...
NO IT ISN'T!
OH, IT
MUSN'T!
THE STEEL'S
BUCKLING!
MASSIVE TIRES
REACH
THE END OF
STRIPS, REST
AGAINST THE
CONCRETE
WALL...
HE'S MAKING
IT!
AND KEEP
RIGHT ON
CLIMBING
AS THE
REAR WHEELS
THRUST
POWERFULLY
AGAINST
THE FLOOR!
HE MADE
IT!
GOLLY, I'D LIKE
TO BE YOU--HELPING
THE BATMAN IN
ALL HIS CASES!
IT ISN'T ALL
FUN! SOMETIMES
I WISH I WAS JUST
A PLAIN ORDINARY
KID IN--WELL, IN
FALLS CORNERS!
11

I DON'T KNOW HOW I CAN THANK YOU!
NEITHER DO I BUT I WANT TO!
FORGET IT! I SAVED ROBIN AND MYSELF AT THE SAME TIME, REMEMBER! WILL ONE OF YOU GO FOR THE POLICE?..
I'D GO FOR THEM MYSELF BUT I HAVE WORK TO DO!
THAT MEANS ME TOO!
SLIDING OPEN A WINDOW, THE BATMAN FLINGS A SILKEN NOOSE TOWARD THE CEILING...
THIS TIME WE'LL TRY A DIFFERENT APPROACH!
I HOPE OUR DEPARTURE WILL BE DIFFERENT TOO!
AS ONE MAN THE DYNAMIC DUO SWOOPS DOWN UPON THE UNWARY CRIMINALS...
WE SHOULD CELEBRATE TONIGHT! BESIDES GRABBIN' OFF ALL THIS DOUGH, WE GOT RID OF THE BATMAN FOR GOOD!
THE WHOLE UNDERWORLD OUGHTTA BLOW US TO A PARTY!
I WOULDN'T DO THIS, CHUM, IF YOU HADN'T HIT ME WHEN I WASN'T LOOKING!
HERE'S A HEEL FOR EACH OF YOU HEELS!
HE'S IN AGAIN!
YOU OUGHT TO TOUGHEN UP THOSE STOMACH MUSCLES!
DIDN'T YOU SLUG ME WITH A GUN A WHILE AGO?
I DIDN'T MEAN TO! IT SLIPPED!
OOPS! EXCUSE ME! MY HAND SLIPPED!

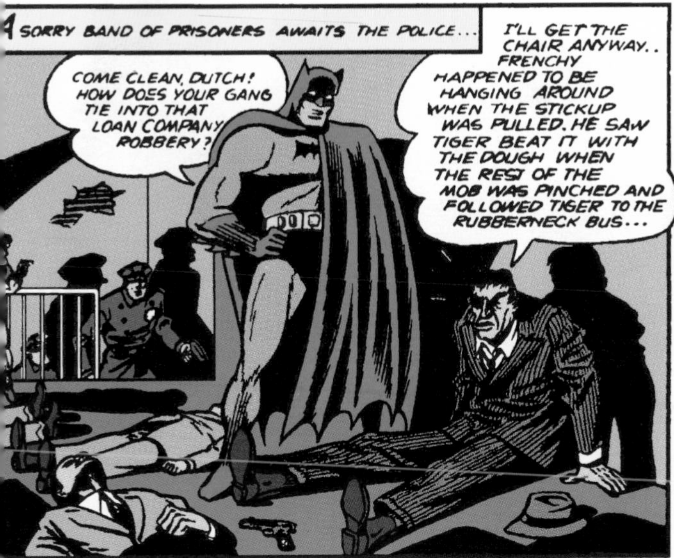
A SORRY BAND OF PRISONERS AWAITS THE POLICE...
COME CLEAN, DUTCH! HOW DOES YOUR GANG TIE INTO THAT LOAN COMPANY ROBBERY?
I'LL GET THE CHAIR ANYWAY.. FRENCHY HAPPENED TO BE HANGING AROUND WHEN THE STICKUP WAS PULLED. HE SAW TIGER BEAT IT WITH THE DOUGH WHEN THE REST OF THE MOB WAS PINCHED AND FOLLOWED TIGER TO THE RUBBERNECK BUS...
WE DECIDED TO HIJACK THE LOOT FROM TIGER. WE SNATCHED THE BUS AND KILLED TIGER WHEN HE PULLED A GUN . . . THEN WE FIGURED WE'D NEVER GET NAILED FOR THE MURDER IF WE'D DROWNED ALL THE WITNESSES!
LEST THIS SHOULD SEEM TO BE ONLY ANOTHER STORY OF A GANGSTER'S GREED AND THE WAGES OF SIN, LET US SEE WHAT BYPRODUCTS OF HAPPINESS IT BROUGHT FORTH...

REMEMBER CLEMENT'S WORRIES?...
I HAVE THE PLOT FOR MY NEW DRAMA NOW! IT WILL BE A CRIME STORY THAT WILL TAKE THE COUNTRY BY STORM! AND I KNOW JUST THE ACTRESS TO PLAY THE LEADING ROLE!
AND MARY'S DESPAIR?
ANY GIRL WHO COULD PULL THAT FAINTING STUNT WITH DEATH STARING HER IN THE FACE-- AND STILL REMAIN COOL AND COLLECTED--IS A GREAT ACTRESS! WILL YOU HONOR MY NEXT PRODUCTION WITH YOUR TALENT?
AND TO THINK I WAS ALMOST READY TO GIVE UP!
HENCEFORTH TWO "AMATEUR DETECTIVES" WILL CONFINE THEIR SLEUTHING TO LESS DANGEROUS FIELDS....
THE BATMAN AND ROBIN ARE TAKING US BACK TO FALLS CORNERS IN THE BATPLANE! WE'LL BE HEROES TO THE OTHER KIDS!
AND WE'LL BE JUST AS GLAD TO SEE OUR MOTHERS AND FATHERS AGAIN AS THEY'LL BE TO SEE US!

I FEEL PRETTY GOOD ABOUT THE WHOLE THING--DON'T YOU, ROBIN?
AND HOW!

No. 94
DEC...TEN CENTS
A SUPERMAN DC PUBLICATION
The BATMAN
Detective
COMICS

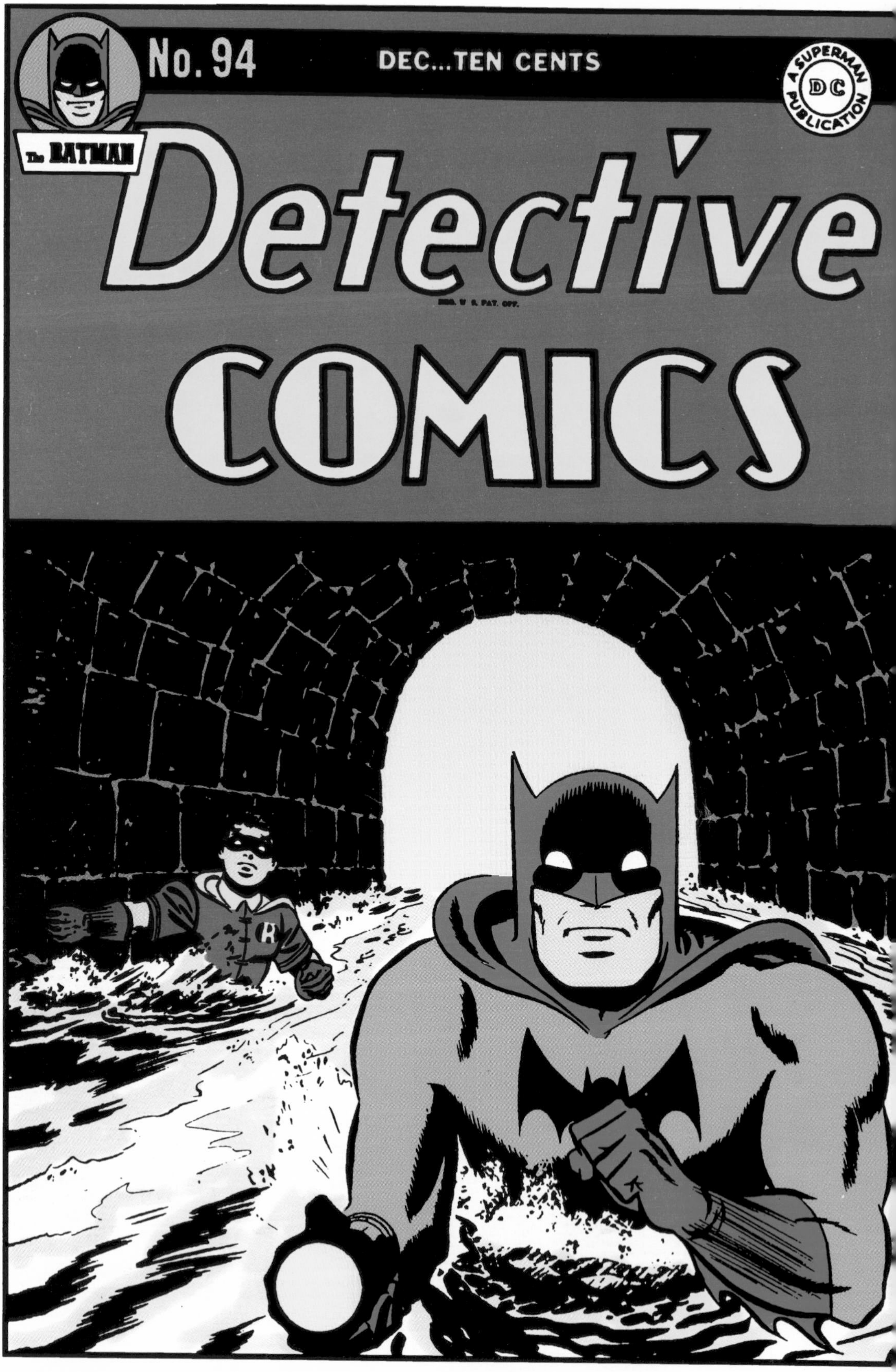

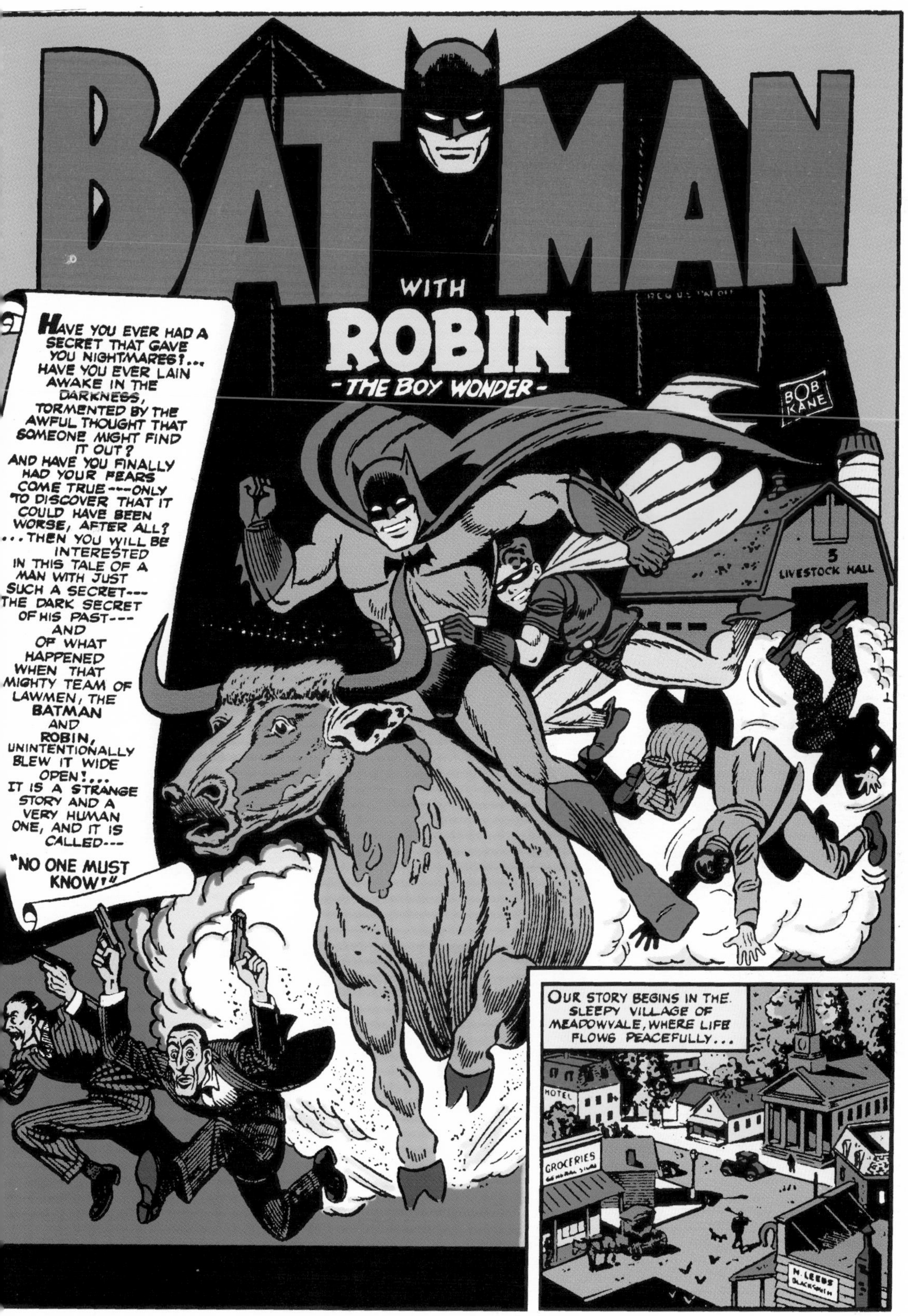
BATMAN
WITH
ROBIN
-THE BOY WONDER-
BOB KANE
HAVE YOU EVER HAD A SECRET THAT GAVE YOU NIGHTMARES?... HAVE YOU EVER LAIN AWAKE IN THE DARKNESS, TORMENTED BY THE AWFUL THOUGHT THAT SOMEONE MIGHT FIND IT OUT? AND HAVE YOU FINALLY HAD YOUR FEARS COME TRUE---ONLY TO DISCOVER THAT IT COULD HAVE BEEN WORSE, AFTER ALL? ...THEN YOU WILL BE INTERESTED IN THIS TALE OF A MAN WITH JUST SUCH A SECRET--- THE DARK SECRET OF HIS PAST--- AND OF WHAT HAPPENED WHEN THAT MIGHTY TEAM OF LAWMEN, THE BATMAN AND ROBIN, UNINTENTIONALLY BLEW IT WIDE OPEN!... IT IS A STRANGE STORY AND A VERY HUMAN ONE, AND IT IS CALLED---
"NO ONE MUST KNOW!"
5
LIVESTOCK HALL
OUR STORY BEGINS IN THE SLEEPY VILLAGE OF MEADOWVALE, WHERE LIFE FLOWS PEACEFULLY...
HOTEL
GROCERIES
N. LEEDS BLACKSMITH

WHERE THE BANK PRESIDENT HAS A DEEP INTEREST IN THE WELFARE OF HIS HUMBLEST CLIENT...
DON'T WORRY ABOUT YOUR MORTGAGE, SILAS---AT LEAST, NOT TILL YOU GET YOUR CROPS IN!
THANKS, MR. BURLING!

WHERE EVEN THE LAW IS FRIENDLY.
NOW, EDDIE, I KNOW YOU CAN'T AFFORD TO PAY A FINE---SO IF YOU'LL PROMISE NOT TO FIGHT ANY-MORE, WE'LL FORGET ABOUT IT!
THANKS, JUDGE WATTS!

AND EVERY CITIZEN TAKES PART IN THE AFFAIRS OF THE COMMUNITY...
I AGREE WITH THE MAYOR... WE SHOULDN'T SPEND ANY MORE MONEY ON IMPROVEMENTS TILL THE CASH IS IN THE TREASURY!
GEORGE BARROW IS RIGHT!

NATURALLY, ROMANCE FLOURISHES IN MEADOWVALE--- IN THIS CASE BETWEEN YOUNG JIMMY BARROW AND PRETTY MARY WATTS...
DAD, JUDGE WATTS HAS JUST GIVEN HIS CONSENT! MARY AND I ARE ENGAGED!
ENGAGED? WELL--ER-- THAT'S SPLENDID, CHILDREN!

SO MY SON IS GOING TO MARRY INTO THE JUDGE'S FAMILY... BUT WHAT IF THE JUDGE KNEW I WAS AN EX-CROOK, AN ESCAPED CONVICT?

IF IT WERE KNOWN, EVEN NOW, I'D HAVE TO GO BACK TO PRISON! I'D BRING SHAME AND DISGRACE ON JIMMY AS WELL AS ME!

IT ISN'T SO MUCH MYSELF I CARE FOR---BUT I CAN'T SEE THE HAPPINESS OF THOSE TWO YOUNG PEOPLE RUINED! NO ONE MUST EVER DISCOVER MY SECRET!

IT'S ALL VERY WELL TO MAKE RESOLUTIONS, GEORGE BARROW---BUT THE FACT REMAINS THAT A MAN'S MOST CAREFULLY HIDDEN SINS HAVE A WAY OF CATCHING UP WITH HIM--- SOMETIMES MANY YEARS LATER... SOMETIMES AT THE VERY MOMENT WHEN HE WOULD GIVE HIS LIFE TO KEEP THEM HIDDEN JUST A LITTLE LONGER!

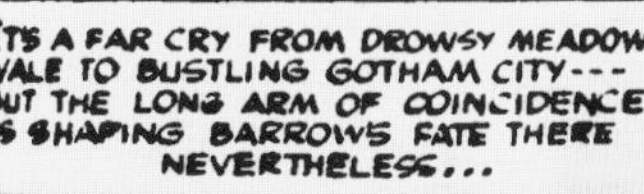
IT'S A FAR CRY FROM DROWSY MEADOW-VALE TO BUSTLING GOTHAM CITY--- BUT THE LONG ARM OF COINCIDENCE IS SHAPING BARROWS FATE THERE NEVERTHELESS...

LOOK! THOSE OIL STOCKS YOU SOLD ME ARE WORTHLESS! WHY, YOU---YOU SWINDLER! I'LL GO TO THE POLICE!
EASY ON THAT SORT OF TALK, BUDDY!

THIS'LL SHUT YOU UP!
OHHHH

WHAT RE WE GONNA DO WITH HIM, LEFTY?
WHAT D'YA THINK, SLATS? WE'RE GONNA DUMP HIM IN THE RIVER! WE CAN'T AFFORD TO HAVE COPS FINDIN' OUT WE'RE CONFIDENCE MEN!

BUT AT THAT MOMENT TWO MANTLED FIGURES APPROACH ALONG THE STREET OUTSIDE--- THE BATMAN AND ROBIN, ON THE PROWL FOR EVIL-DOERS!
LOOK, BATMAN--- TWO MEN CARRYING ANOTHER!
I'M LOOKING--- BUT I WANT A CLOSER VIEW!

JUST A MINUTE, STRANGERS!
IT'S THE BATMAN INSIDE, QUICK!
I'M RIGHT BEHIND YOU, LEFTY!

THAT GUY AND HIS BOY FRIEND ARE POISON! LOCK THE DOOR WHILE I CALL THE MOB TO TAKE CARE OF 'EM!

THE POOR FELLOW IS ONLY STUNNED--- BUT I RECOGNIZED THE OTHERS! THEY'RE LEFTY GORAN AND SLATS MACER, WANTED CON MEN!
OH, BOY! EXCITEMENT TODAY!
3

WITHIN THE CROOKED BROKERAGE OFFICE...
MIND IF I TAKE A LITTLE FLYER?
CRASH
HE'S IN!
LEAVE HIM TO ME!
YOU SEEM TO HAVE GONE UP A FEW POINTS!
HEY---THIS AIN'T THE SOCK EXCHANGE!
I SOLD WILDCAT STOCKS, BUT I NEVER RAN INTO A WILDCAT BEFORE!
WE OUGHT TO MAKE YOU A CHAIR-MAN OF THE BOARD--- IF IT ISN'T TOO BAD A PUN!
I'LL PICK UP A LITTLE EVIDENCE BEFORE I TURN YOU OVER TO THE LAW!
LOOK OUT, BATMAN!
WHAT, ROB---?
UGH!
YOU RAT--- IN A SECOND THE MARKET'S GOING TO CRASH ALL OVER YOU!
A DOME FOR A DOME!
AN' I GOT SOMETHIN' FOR YOUR DOME, KID!
4

SLOW MINUTES TICK BY BEFORE THE SKULL-SPLITTING AWAKENING COMES...
OH-H-H! PLEASE MAKE THE ROOM STOP SPINNING!
I'VE BEEN TRYING TO!
3

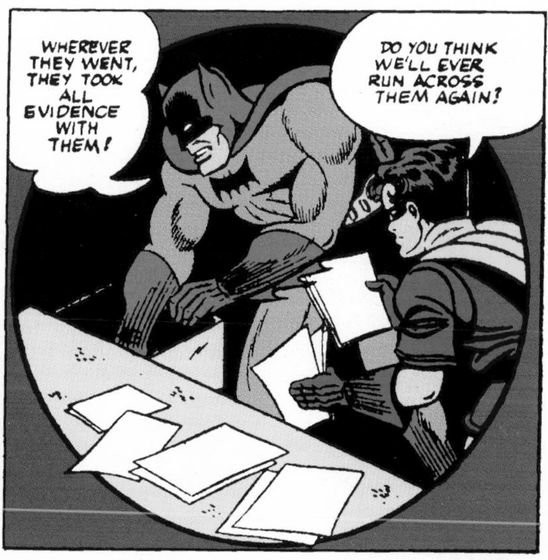
WHEREVER THEY WENT, THEY TOOK ALL EVIDENCE WITH THEM!
DO YOU THINK WE'LL EVER RUN ACROSS THEM AGAIN?

IT'S FUNNY, AND I
AN'T EXPLAIN IT---
BUT I'VE GOT A
ELING WE'LL SEE
HEM AGAIN REAL
SOON!
OH, BOY---AND WILL I HAVE A DIVIDEND TO PAY THEM ON THIS DEAL!

JUST TO SHOW HOW MYSTERIOUSLY FATE BRINGS ABOUT CRISES IN THE LIVES OF MEN AND WOMEN, LET'S SEE WHAT HAPPENED TO LEFTY AND SLATS WHEN THEY FLED FROM THE WRECKAGE OF THEIR PHONY BROKERAGE BUSINESS...

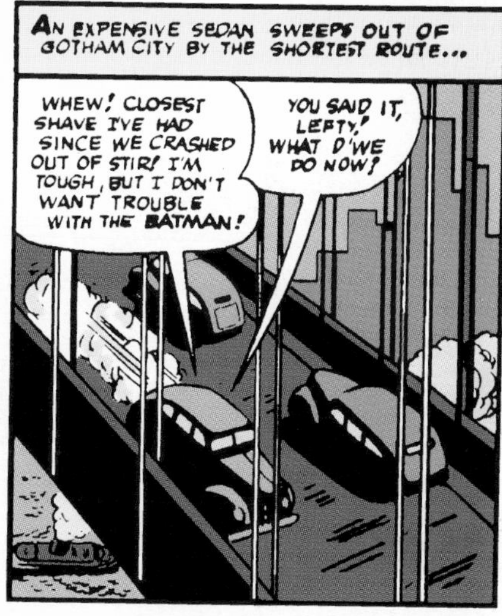
AN EXPENSIVE SEDAN SWEEPS OUT OF GOTHAM CITY BY THE SHORTEST ROUTE...
WHEW! CLOSEST SHAVE I'VE HAD SINCE WE CRASHED OUT OF STIR! I'M TOUGH, BUT I DON'T WANT TROUBLE WITH THE BATMAN!
YOU SAID IT, LEFTY! WHAT D'WE DO NOW?

WE STAY AWAY
ROM THE BIG TOWNS
TILL THE HEAT IS
FF! WE'LL PLAY
HE STICKS---COUNTY
AIRS AND STUFF LIKE
THAT---AND PICK
P WHAT JACK WE
CAN!
LIKE WE DID BEFORE! EH?

AND SO IT IS THAT TWO DAYS LATER, IN THE HOME OF BRUCE WAYNE AND HIS YOUNG WARD DICK GRAYSON...
THAT WASN'T A BAD HUNCH OF MINE, DICK! HERE'S WHERE WE PICK UP THE TRAIL OF OUR FRIENDS AGAIN!
THE ONES WHO SLUGGED US? WHAT A BREAK!

Con Men Flee County Fair in Unionville
RECOGNIZED BY A POLICEMAN, TWO CONFIDENCE MEN-LEFTY GORAN AND SLATS MACER-ESCAPED FROM THE UNIONVILLE COUNTY FAIR LAST NIGHT BEFORE THEY COULD BE ARRESTED. IT WAS SAID BY
Report
Exclusive:
5

BUT, BRUCE, HOW'LL WE FIND THEM?
THEY'RE PLAYING THEIR OLD RACKETS AROUND THE COUNTY FAIRS---AND THE ONLY OTHER FAIR IN THE VICINITY IS IN A VILLAGE CALLED MEADOWVALE!

A CAR OF WEIRD DESIGN AND BLINDING SPEED STREAKS ALONG A HIGHWAY MOMENTS LATER ---THE BATMOBILE...
MEADOWVALE HERE WE COME!

MEANWHILE, ALL IS GAIETY AND BRIGHTNESS AT THE MEADOWVALE COUNTY FAIR...
I'M GONNA SPEND MY NICKEL ON THE MERRY-GO-ROUND!
AW, COME AN' RIDE ON THE FERRIS WHEEL WITH ME!
STUPENDOUS!!!
PETRIFIED GIANT
EDUCATIONAL
COME
ADULTS ONLY
BETTY
LIVESTOCK HALL

WELL---ALMOST ALL...
REMEMBER---BABY FACE, TUG, DIPPY--- IF THERE'S ANY TROUBLE, YOU MEN START A FIGHT SO WE CAN GET AWAY IN THE EXCITEMENT!
GOTCHA, BOSS!

THUS BEGINS A BUSY DAY FOR TWO WHO ARE MASTERS IN THE ART OF EXTRACTING MONEY FROM THE GULLIBLE...
YOU LOSE AGAIN, MY FRIEND---BUT YOU CAN'T LOSE FOREVER! ALL YOU HAVE TO DO IS GUESS WHICH SHELL THE PEA IS UNDER!
WAALL, RECKON I CAN RISK ANOTHER FIVE DOLLARS!
LEMME TRY FOR TEN DOLLARS, WILL YUH?

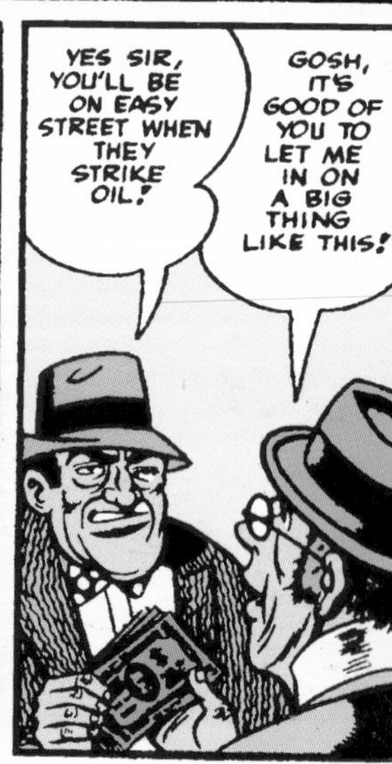
YES SIR, YOU'LL BE ON EASY STREET WHEN THEY STRIKE OIL!
GOSH, IT'S GOOD OF YOU TO LET ME IN ON A BIG THING LIKE THIS!

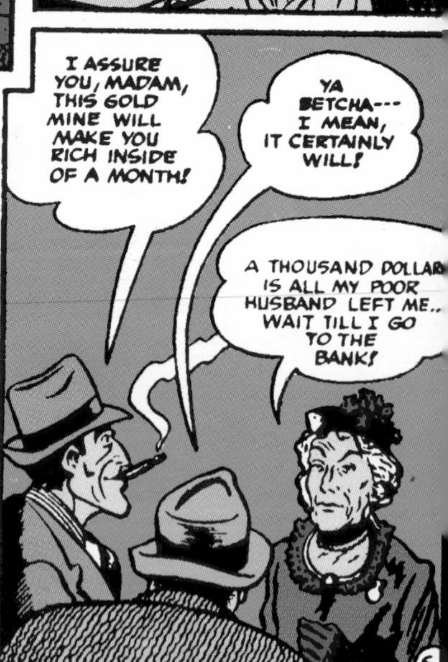
I ASSURE YOU, MADAM, THIS GOLD MINE WILL MAKE YOU RICH INSIDE OF A MONTH!
YA BETCHA---I MEAN, IT CERTAINLY WILL!
A THOUSAND DOLLAR IS ALL MY POOR HUSBAND LEFT ME.. WAIT TILL I GO TO THE BANK!
6

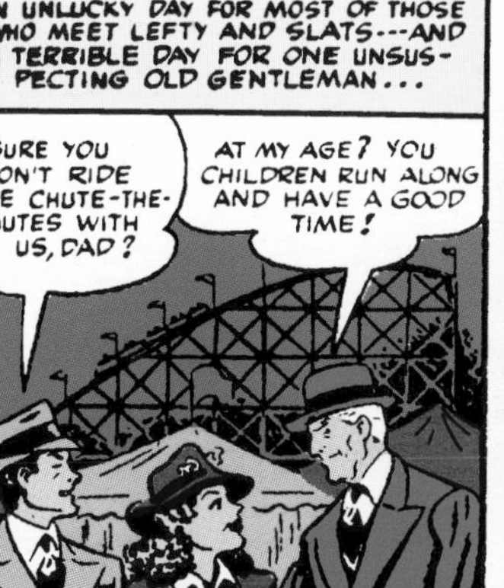
N UNLUCKY DAY FOR MOST OF THOSE WHO MEET LEFTY AND SLATS---AND A TERRIBLE DAY FOR ONE UNSUS-PECTING OLD GENTLEMAN...
SURE YOU ON'T RIDE E CHUTE-THE-HUTES WITH US, DAD?
AT MY AGE? YOU CHILDREN RUN ALONG AND HAVE A GOOD TIME!

FIRE EAT
MAN
LOOK, SLATS--- DO YOU SEE WHAT I SEE?
HUH?... WELL, I'LL BE HANGED IF IT AIN'T OUR OLD PAL!

ORGE BARROW! NCY MEETING OLD COLLEGE CHUM HERE!

PUT HER THERE, BUDDY!
LEFTY! SLATS! I'D HOPED NEVER TO SEE YOU TWO AGAIN! DON'T SPEAK TO ME!

YA WOULDN'T WANT US TO TIP OFF THE COPS ABOUT HOW YA LEFT PRISON WITHOUT GRADUATIN', WOULD YA?
YOU---YOU WOULDN'T DO THAT! YOU MADE ME GO WITH YOU WHEN MY SENTENCE WAS NEARLY OVER!

LOOKS LIKE YOU'RE QUITE A RESPECTABLE CITIZEN IN THESE PARTS! GOT A BANK ACCOUNT, TOO, I'LL BET!
PLEASE DON'T GIVE ME AWAY! I'VE LIVED AN HONEST LIFE! AND THERE'S MY SON---AND THE GIRL HE'S GOING TO MARRY--

OKAY, PAL--- WE WON'T TURN YA IN! NOT IF YA ET UP TWENTY GRAND TO KEEP US QUIET!
TWENTY THOUSAND DOLLARS! WHY, I COULDN'T RAISE A FRACTION OF THAT!

WELL, SEE HOW MUCH YA CAN DIG UP, AN' WE'LL TELL YA IF IT'S ENOUGH!
WE'LL GIVE YA TWO HOURS!
I--I'LL SEE ABOUT IT!

POOR GEORGE BARROW... WHAT A PROBLEM...
IF I LET THEM START BLACK-MAILING ME, THEY'LL KEEP IT UP FOR THE REST OF MY LIFE... BUT IF I DON'T, I'LL RUIN OTHER LIVES BESIDES MY OWN!
7

YOU LOOK ILL, MR. BARROW!
WRONG? NO, NOTHING'S WRONG! I'M A LITTLE TIRED, THAT'S ALL...
YES, DAD--- IS ANYTHING WRONG?
BLACKMAIL, THE MOST DESPICABLE OF ALL CRIMES... AND YET GEORGE BARROW FINDS HIMSELF HELPLESS TO ESCAPE IT...
I WAS GOING TO GIVE IT TO JIMMY AND MARY TO HELP THEM START HOUSEKEEPING... BUT IF MY PAST EVER CAME TO LIGHT, THEY'D NEVER EVEN MARRY!
NATIONAL
BANK
FIVE HUNDRED DOLLARS... IT'S EVERY PENNY I HAVE IN CASH! IT'LL HAVE TO DO!
OH, IT'LL DO---FOR A DOWN PAYMENT!
LISTEN! WE FOUND OUT YOUR KID'S GOIN' TO MARRY THE JUDGE'S DAUGHTER! IF YOU WANT THAT TO HAPPEN, YOU GET SOME MORE CASH!
BUT WHERE CAN I GET IT?
THERE THEY ARE!
WHAT DO WE CARE WHERE YA GET IT? BORROW FROM THE JUDGE! MORTGAGE YOUR HOUSE! ROB THE BANK!
BUT NOW THE TRICKSTERS ARE DUE FOR A SURPRISE... AS CLOAKED SHAPES STALK THEM WITH THE RELENTLESSNESS OF JUSTICE...
SH-H-H-H, ROBIN--- NO NOISE! IT'LL GIVE THEM A JOLT WHEN THEY SEE US RIGHT BEHIND THEM!
I'LL SEE THAT THEY GET THE JOLT!
YA GET THAT CASH OR ELSE---
YI-I-I-I-I!
OR ELSE WHAT, LITTLE MAN?
THE BATMAN HELP!
TUG! BABYFACE! DIPPY!
WE HAVE A LITTLE BUSINESS TO FINISH! REMEMBER?
START SOMETHIN' QUICK!
8

NDER COVER OF THE EXCITEMENT, EORGE BARROW BEATS A STEALTHY RETREAT...
I'LL GO TO THE IVESTOCK SHOW... OSE MYSELF IN THE CROWDS...
I'M RETURNING THE HEADACHES YOU GAVE US!
ENCORE! ENCORE!
SUDDENLY...
UGH
WHO'S SCARED O' TH' BIG, BAD BATMAN?
I CAN HANDLE THIS KID WITH ONE ARM!
A KNEE FOR AN EYE...
HEY, DON'T MAKE ME SORE!
...AND A FIST FOR A TOOTH!
THTOP IT! NOW YOU'RE MAKIN' ME LITHP!
... WHILE A BATTLE OF GIANTS RAGES THE LENGTH OF THE MIDWAY...
WHO NVITED OU TO THIS RAWL?
MAYBE I'M SCARED O' HIM, AFTER ALL!
OW!
TWO BADLY FRIGHTENED CONFIDENCE MEN SEEK A HIDING PLACE...
WHERE'LL WE GO?
TO THE LIVESTOCK SHOW! WE'LL LOSE OURSELVES IN THE MOB!
GET UP THERE AND DO YOUR STUFF, HANDSOME!
AN' NOW, LADIES AN' GENTS, LEMME PRESENT JO-JO THE DOG-FACED BOY!
9

WHA---? WHO---?
SO THAT'S THE DOGFACED BOY!
GOSH, AIN'T HE UGLY?
RING THE BELL AN' GET A CIGAR!
TRY YOUR LUCK, BIG BOY!
BONG
ONE CIGAR FOR THE LITTLE FELLA!
GIVE IT TO MY PAL---ON ME!
OLD DOC SMITH'S INDIAN BLOOD BITTERS for MAN OR BEAST
AND I GUARANTEE THIS SUPER TONIC WILL CURE--- HUH? WHAT'S THIS?
A PATIENT FOR YOU, DOC! YOU'LL HAVE TO DECIDE WHETHER HE'S MAN OR BEAST!
I KNOW YOU--- YOU'RE THE BATMAN AND ROBIN! SAY, THEM MEN YOU WERE FIGHTING RAN INTO THE LIVESTOCK SHOW!
THANKS, SONNY!
THE DYNAMIC DUO PLANS A STRATEGIC ATTACK...
THEY'LL HAVE GUNS, AND IF THEY SHOOT, THEY'LL ENDANGER OTHERS... WE'LL HAVE TO TAKE THEM BY SURPRISE!
JUST SO WE TAKE THEM!
LIVESTOC
3
I CAN SEE THEM, STANDING BY THAT LADDER!
WE'LL SWING DOWN ON MY SILK ROPE!

UT LEFTY AND SLATS HAVE ALSO BEEN DEVISING A STRATEGY...
AN' IF THEY SHOW UP, WE'LL SHOOT OFF OUR UNS AN' STAMPEDE HE CATTLE! WE'LL GO UP THIS LADDER--- BUT THEY'LL BE TRAMPLED TO DEATH!
THAT'S OKAY BY ME!
AND AS LUCK WOULD HAVE IT, DISCOVERY FOILS THE BATMAN'S PLAN...
HERE THEY COME NOW--- SWINGIN' ON A ROPE!
OKAY... START SHOOTIN'--- AND CLIMB FAST!
THEY'VE STAMPEDED THE CATTLE! PEOPLE WILL BE KILLED!
OUR FIRST JOB WILL BE TO STOP THAT! EVER RIDE HERD WITH A BULL FOR A HORSE, ROBIN?
BANG
BANG
BANG
GHTNING WITS AND SUPERBLY TRAINED USCLES RESPOND INSTANTLY TO THE NEW EMERGENCY...
WOW! OT MUCH CHOICE AMONG THEM!
YOU'LL HAVE TO STEER THEM BY THEIR HORNS, SO PICK THE BIGGEST PAIR OF HANDLEBARS IN RANGE!
GOT TO HEAD THE OTHERS BACK BEFORE THEY GET TO THE CROWDS!
HOPE I DON'T GET SEASICK!
E PLUNGING BEAST, EXPERTLY GUIDED, TURNS A CORE BACK INTO THEIR STALLS...
HOW ARE YOU DOING, PARDNER?
A-A-A-ALL R-RIGHT, I-I-I-I G-GUESS!
11

AND WHEN THE TERRIFIED CATTLE ARE QUIETED DOWN...
MR. BATMAN, I'M JUDGE WATTS! YOU'VE SAVED A LOT OF LIVES!
I'M THE MAYOR! I'LL SEE THAT YOU'RE REWARDED!
EXCUSE ME, GENTLEMEN--- ROBIN AND I HAVEN'T FINISHED OUR JOB YET!
BUT THE END OF THE JOB IS NOT FAR AWAY, FOR AN OLD MAN HAS DECIDED THAT JUSTICE IS MORE IMPORTANT THAN HIS OWN INTERESTS...
THEY DID IT DELIBERATELY, THE RATS! I WON'T LET THEM GET AWAY WITH IT, EVEN IF THEY DO EXPOSE ME!
THE OLD GOAT DOUBLE-CROSSED US!
OH, WHY DIDN'T I LEAD AN HONEST LIFE?
THIS WILL ONLY TAKE A MINUTE!
BUT I'LL ENJOY EVERY SECOND OF IT!
YOU'VE LIVED A PIGGISH LIFE, SO YOU OUGHT TO FEEL AT HOME THERE!
OINK
OINK!
OINK
AT LAST YOU'RE GETTING THE POINT, LEFTY!
OW-OOOOOOOO
SO FINALLY THE EXPOSURE HE HAS DREADED FOR OVER TWENTY YEARS COMES TO GEORGE BARROW, ESCAPED CONVICT...
OKAY---WE GO TO PRISON--- BUT BARROW GOES WITH US! HE ESCAPED WITH US BACK IN NINETEEN-TWENTY! HE'S A THIEF!
IT'S TRUE...
12

TWENTY-TWO YEARS AGO I WAS OUT OF A JOB AND HUNGRY... I FOUND A NECKLACE--- AND ALTHOUGH I KNEW I SHOULDN'T HAVE, I PAWNED IT! THEY ARRESTED ME, ACCUSED ME OF STEALING IT, GAVE ME A YEAR'S SENTENCE...

I OVERHEARD LEFTY AND SLATS PLANNING TO ESCAPE... THEY WERE AFRAID I WOULD TELL, AND FORCED ME TO GO WITH THEM AGAINST MY WILL ... AND ONCE OUTSIDE I WAS AFRAID THE WARDEN WOULDN'T BELIEVE MY STORY!

I CAN'T EXPECT YOU TO MARRY ME NOW! I'M GOING TO SEE THIS THING THROUGH WITH MY DAD!
JIMMY BARROW, DON'T YOU DARE TRY TO BREAK OUR ENGAGEMENT! I'M STICKING WITH YOU---AND WITH YOUR FATHER, TOO!

DON'T LOOK SO DOWNHEARTED, NEIGHBOR! YOU'VE MADE FRIENDS SINCE YOU CAME TO LIVE IN MEADOWVALE... AND THEY WON'T LET A MAN DOWN!
I-I DON'T KNOW WHAT TO SAY!

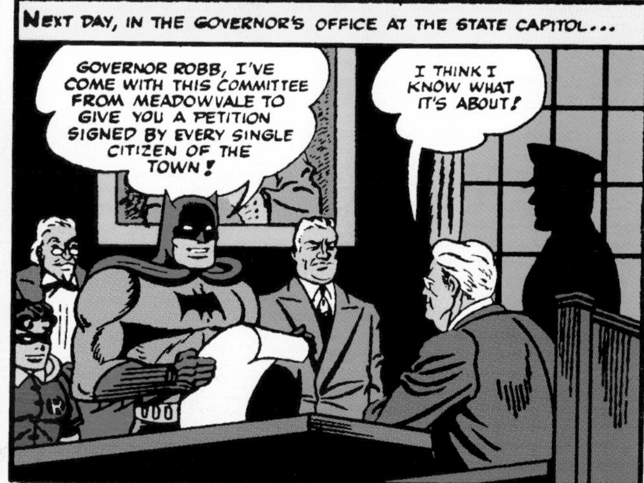
NEXT DAY, IN THE GOVERNOR'S OFFICE AT THE STATE CAPITOL...
GOVERNOR ROBB, I'VE COME WITH THIS COMMITTEE FROM MEADOWVALE TO GIVE YOU A PETITION SIGNED BY EVERY SINGLE CITIZEN OF THE TOWN!
I THINK I KNOW WHAT IT'S ABOUT!

ND WHEN THE BATMOBILE RACES BACK TO THE SLEEPY VILLAGE, FAR AHEAD OF THE OTHERS, ITS ERRAND IS LESS GRIM THAN USUAL...
I HURRIED BACK BECAUSE I THOUGHT YOU MIGHT IKE TO SEE THESE! FOR YOU, JIMMY AND MARY, A LICENSE TO MARRY! ND FOR YOU, MR. BARROW--- A PARDON, SIGNED BY THE GOVERNOR!
A PARDON? GOLLY...
MR. BATMAN, YOU'RE THE MOST WONDERFUL MAN ON EARTH! NEXT TO JIMMY, THAT IS...

WHY DIDN'T I STAY FOR THE WEDDING? WELL, ROBIN, WEDDINGS ARE SENTIMENTAL---AND YOU KNOW I'M THE MOST UNSENTIMENTAL PERSON IN THE WORLD!
OH, YEAH?
THE END
13

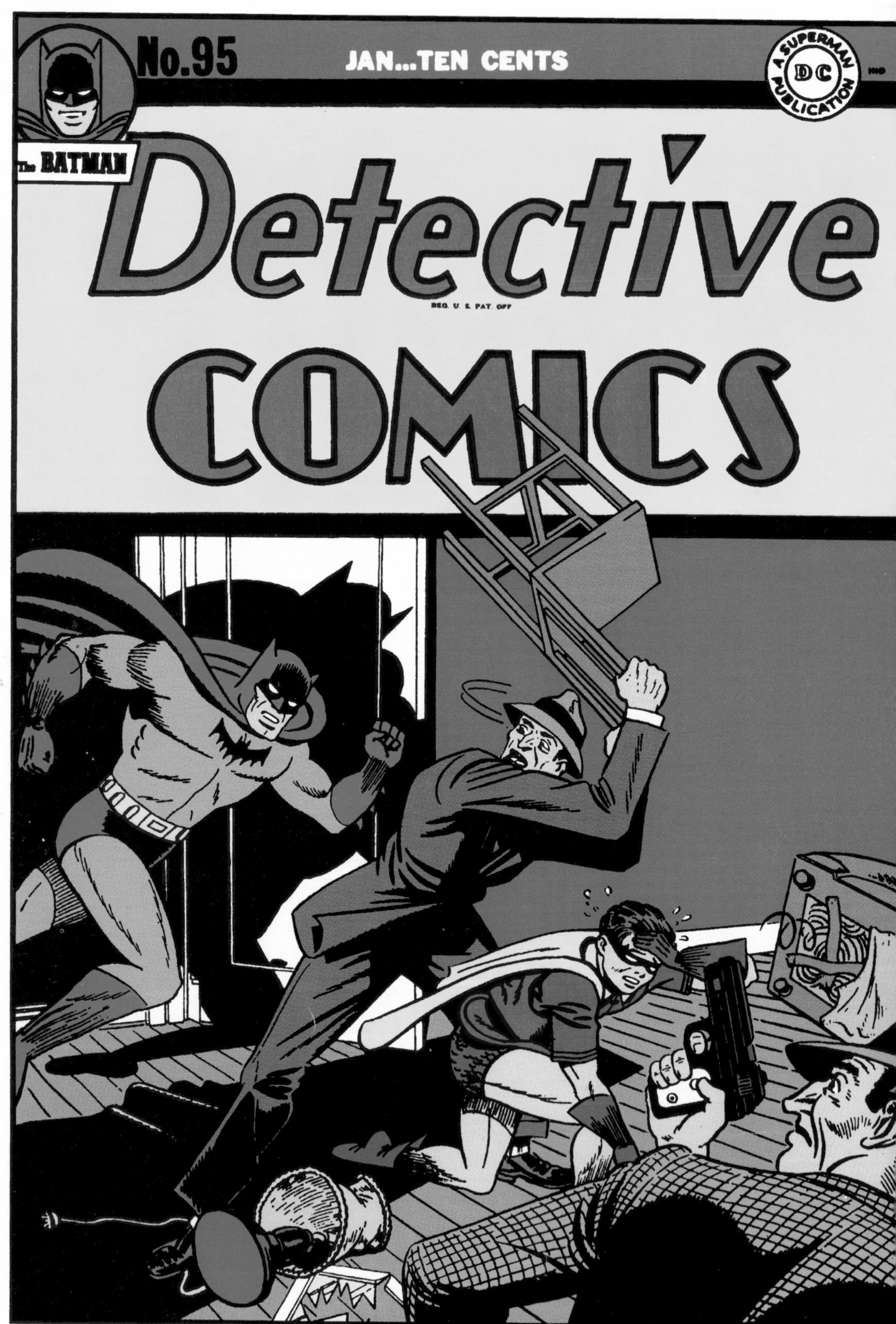
No.95
JAN...TEN CENTS
A SUPERMAN DC PUBLICATION
The BATMAN
Detective
REG. U. S. PAT. OFF
COMICS

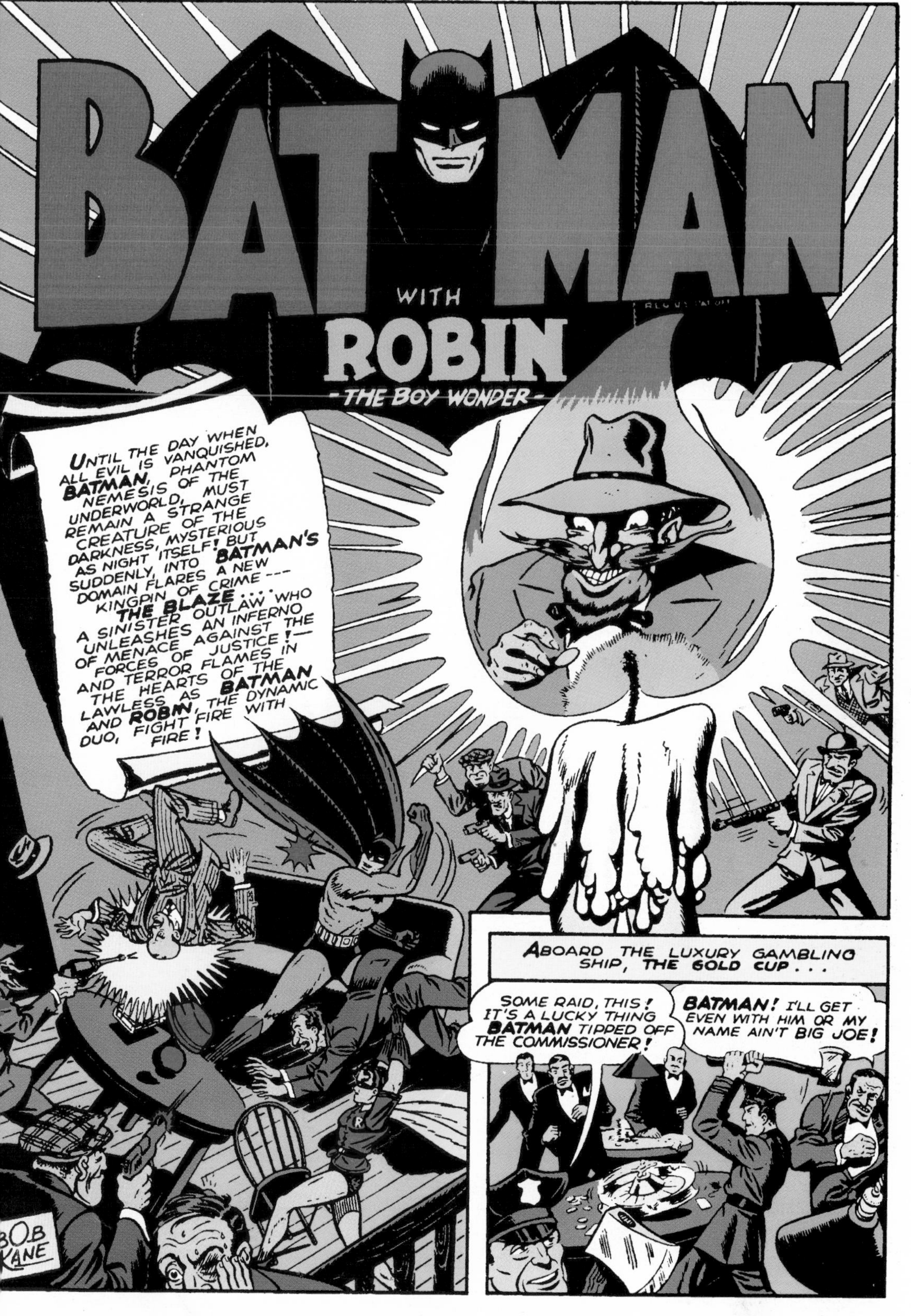
BATMAN
WITH
ROBIN
-THE BOY WONDER-
UNTIL THE DAY WHEN ALL EVIL IS VANQUISHED, BATMAN, PHANTOM NEMESIS OF THE UNDERWORLD, MUST REMAIN A STRANGE CREATURE OF THE DARKNESS, MYSTERIOUS AS NIGHT ITSELF! BUT SUDDENLY, INTO BATMAN'S DOMAIN FLARES A NEW KINGPIN OF CRIME --- THE BLAZE... A SINISTER OUTLAW WHO UNLEASHES AN INFERNO OF MENACE AGAINST THE FORCES OF JUSTICE!— AND TERROR FLAMES IN THE HEARTS OF THE LAWLESS AS BATMAN AND ROBIN, THE DYNAMIC DUO, FIGHT FIRE WITH FIRE!
BOB KANE
ABOARD THE LUXURY GAMBLING SHIP, THE GOLD CUP...
SOME RAID, THIS! IT'S A LUCKY THING BATMAN TIPPED OFF THE COMMISSIONER!
BATMAN! I'LL GET EVEN WITH HIM OR MY NAME AIN'T BIG JOE!

AT THE OFFICE OF ED RAFFERTY, PRESIDENT OF THE ACE PROTECTIVE ASSOCIATION..

YOUR RACKETEERING DAYS ARE OVER, RAFFERTY! **BATMAN** SUPPLIED US WITH ENOUGH EVIDENCE TO LAND YOU A SENTENCE AS LONG AS YOUR ARM!

BATMAN! BOY WOULD I LIKE TO TAKE HIM FOR A RIDE!

AND AT THE HIDEOUT OF RED BABBITT, THE TRI-STATE BANK ROBBER.. TEAR GAS TACTICS DRIVE A RAT OUT OF HIS NEST!

ALL RIGHT... I GIVE UP... COUGH! COUGH!

YOU'D BETTER SURRENDER, RED.... OR WE'LL BLAST YOU INTO THE NEXT STATE!

ANOTHER FEATHER IN **BATMAN'S** CAP, CORNERING THIS KILLER FOR US! HE CERTAINLY PROVES THAT CRIME DOESN'T PAY!

ROUND-UP TIME! AND DESPERADO AFTER DESPERADO IS SNARED IN THE MESHES OF THE **BATMAN'S** DRAGNET!

BATMAN ENDS

EVENING BLADE

BATMAN CRUSHES CRIME CZARS

The Star

EXTRA

BATMAN ENDS CRIME WAVE!

A FEW DAYS LATER, AND THE MOTLEY HORDE OF CRIMINALS ARE HERDED ABOARD A SPECIAL TRAIN, TO BEGIN THEIR LAST JOURNEY!

STEP LIVELY, MUGGS! THE TRAIN PULLS OUT IN A MINUTE!

TAKE YOUR LAST LOOK, PAL. IT'S GOODBYE BROADWAY!

AND UP FRONT, AS THE ASSISTANT ENGINEER STARTS TO BOARD THE TRAIN... A CRUEL BLOW FROM BEHIND FELLS HIM TO THE GROUND...

SORRY.. BUT I MEAN BUSINESS!

WHISTLES SHRIEKING, THE MIGHTY TRAIN ROCKETS THRU THE NIGHT... AND SUDDENLY VEERS OFF SHARPLY ONTO A NEW SET OF TRACKS BESIDE THE MAIN ROAD...

INTO THE WOODS PLUNGES THE TRAIN, FOLLOWING THE STRANGE DETOUR. FINALLY, THE HISS OF AIR BRAKES.. AND THE TRAIN STOPS!

HERE I AM, MEN! RIGHT ON SCHEDULE! YOU KNOW WHAT TO DO!
RIGHT, BOSS!
WATCH OUR SMOKE!

THE GRIM GHOULS OF GANGDOM BOARD THE TRAIN....
LAST STOP! EVERYBODY OFF!
NO YOU DON'T!

ANYBODY ELSE WANT TO MEET MY CHOPPER?

LAW AND LAWLESSNESS CLASH IN DEADLY COMBAT..

SHOOT TO KILL, MEN! BUT DON'T AIM AT THE PRISONERS!

O-O-O-F!

LATER... AFTER THE SMOKE OF BATTLE...

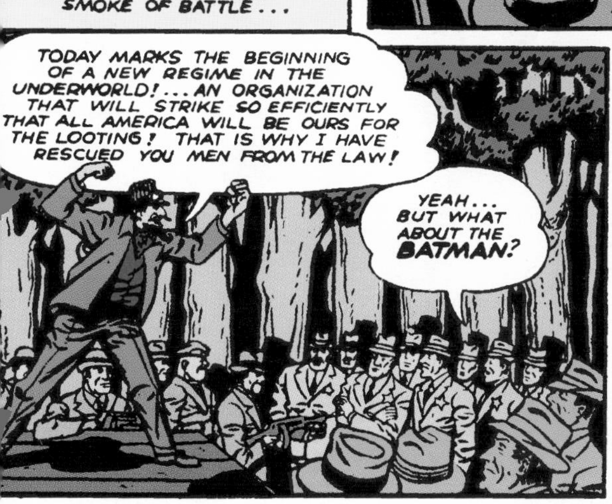

TODAY MARKS THE BEGINNING OF A NEW REGIME IN THE UNDERWORLD!... AN ORGANIZATION THAT WILL STRIKE SO EFFICIENTLY THAT ALL AMERICA WILL BE OURS FOR THE LOOTING! THAT IS WHY I HAVE RESCUED YOU MEN FROM THE LAW!
YEAH... BUT WHAT ABOUT THE BATMAN?

THE BATMAN... HE WILL BE DESTROYED LIKE A MOTH BY MY FLAME! OUR FIRST JOB WILL BE TO SET A TRAP FOR THE GREAT BATMAN! LISTEN...

THE NEXT DAY... AND COMMISSIONER GORDON RECEIVES A VISITOR
ALLOW ME TO INTRODUCE MYSELF.. I AM BARON VON PELTZ. TONIGHT I CELEBRATE MY BIRTHDAY--BUT MY ENEMIES HAVE SWORN TO KILL ME AT MIDNIGHT. I WOULD LIKE TO HAVE YOUR FAMOUS BATMAN PROTECT ME!
BATMAN PROTECT YOU... IMPOSSIBLE! HE'S NO ORDINARY DETECTIVE... HE ACCEPTS ONLY SPECIAL CASES! MY POLICE CAN GUARD YOU!
MAYBE I AM UNDULY ALARMED.. BUT I'M PREPARED TO DONATE A CHECK FOR $10,000. TO THE POLICE BENEFIT FUND IF YOU CAN GET BATMAN TO HELP ME!
WELL, I CAN'T MAKE ANY PROMISES.. BUT I'LL TRY AND PERSUADE HIM. IT'S LUCKY FOR YOU I'M SEEING BATMAN AT THE POLICE GRADUATION EXERCISES TONIGHT!
OUTSIDE THE POLICE STATION, THE "BARON" REMOVES HIS MONOCLE, LAUGHS SATANICALLY...
AT MIDNIGHT, IT WILL BE THE BATMAN VERSUS BLAZE.... AND I KNOW WHO WILL BE THE VICTOR! HA..HA..
MEANWHILE, IN THE APARTMENT OF BRUCE WAYNE AND YOUNG DICK GRAYSON, WHO ARE IN REALITY, THE BATMAN AND ROBIN... THE BOY WONDER!
SEEMS STRANGE-- PUTTING ON THESE THINGS WHEN WE'RE NOT ON A CASE! I FEEL AS IF WE WERE ON A BUSMAN'S HOLIDAY!
RIGHT! THIS IS ONE TIME WE DON'T HAVE TO WORRY ABOUT DODGING BULLETS!
MOMENTS LATER, TWO CLOAKED FIGURES RACE LITHELY THRU THE DARKNESS...
THE PAIR SOON REACH THEIR DESTINATION.. A VAST ASSEMBLY ROOM WHERE ONE HUNDRED POLICE ROOKIES ATTEND GRADUATION EXERCISES!
MEMBERS OF THE CITY'S FINEST.. I GIVE YOU THE NATION'S GREATEST CRIME-CRUSHERS. BATMAN AND ROBIN!
HURRAY... BATMAN!
BRAVO!
AS ONE HUNDRED PAIRS OF EYES LOOK ON, THE TORNADO TEAM PERFORM A SERIES OF JIU-JITSU FEATS!
THIS IS REALLY SIMPLE WHEN YOU KNOW HOW!
AND NOW, BATMAN WILL CONCLUDE HIS PERFORMANCE BY A DEMONSTRATION OF HIS ABILITY AT MAKE-UP AND DISGUISE!
4

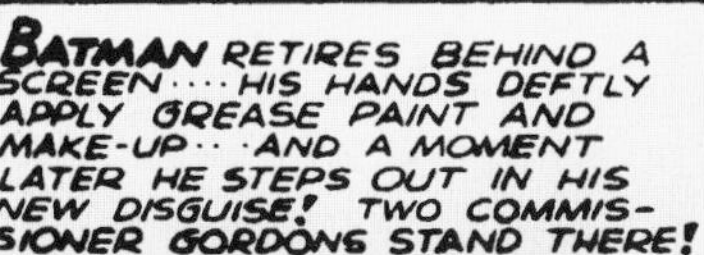

BATMAN RETIRES BEHIND A SCREEN.... HIS HANDS DEFTLY APPLY GREASE PAINT AND MAKE-UP.. AND A MOMENT LATER HE STEPS OUT IN HIS NEW DISGUISE! TWO COMMISSIONER GORDONS STAND THERE!

I CAN'T BELIEVE MY EYES!
IT'S A MIRACLE!

LATER.... THE COMMISSIONER CONCLUDES THE CEREMONIES BY BESTOWING A SPECIAL HONOR ON BATMAN!
WE WANT YOU TO ACCEPT THIS DIAMOND-STUDDED BATMAN BADGE AS A TOKEN OF OUR RESPECT!
THANKS... I REALLY DON'T KNOW WHAT TO SAY! THANKS AGAIN!

AFTERWARDS.
AND SO I TOLD VON PELTZ I'D TRY AND PERSUADE YOU TO BE AT HIS PLACE AT MIDNIGHT. HERE'S HIS ADDRESS.
GLAD TO OBLIGE! I'M ALL DRESSED UP WITH NO PLACE TO GO ANYWAY!

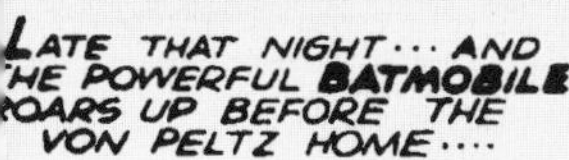

LATE THAT NIGHT... AND THE POWERFUL BATMOBILE ROARS UP BEFORE THE VON PELTZ HOME....

THE WHOLE THING'S PROBABLY A FALSE ALARM, ROBIN! YOU WAIT OUT HERE AND STUDY YOUR MULTIPLICATION TABLES MEANWHILE!
SAVE ME A PIECE OF THE BIRTHDAY CAKE, PAL!

INSIDE THE VAST BARONIAL HALL.
IT WAS GOOD OF YOU TO COME, BATMAN. MAYBE THE WHOLE THING IS JUST A SILLY PRANK... BUT I FEEL BETTER WITH YOU HERE!
IF TROUBLE POPS, I'LL BE READY!

IT IS ONLY WHEN ONE'S BIRTHDAY COMES THAT ONE REALIZES HOW QUICKLY THE YEAR HAS PASSED BY!.... WOULD YOU CARE FOR A SLICE OF MY CAKE?
I SURE WOULD!
HAPPY

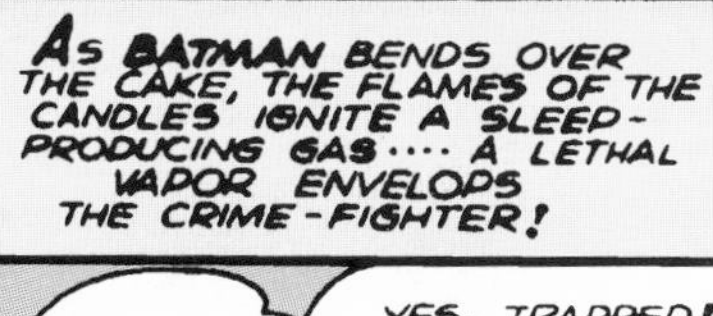

AS BATMAN BENDS OVER THE CAKE, THE FLAMES OF THE CANDLES IGNITE A SLEEP-PRODUCING GAS.... A LETHAL VAPOR ENVELOPS THE CRIME-FIGHTER!

I'M GETTING DROWSY. TRAPPED..
YES. TRAPPED! TRAPPED BY A FLAME! THAT'S WHY THEY CALL ME THE BLAZE!

THE SENSE-NUMBED BATMAN LASHES OUT FUTILELY...
FOOL TO THINK YOU CAN SNUFF OUT THE BLAZE! I HELD MY BREATH WHILE I LIT THE CANDLES!
5

A WORD FROM THE SINISTER CRIME-LEADER..... AND HIS TUXEDOED HENCHMEN UNCOIL INTO ACTION..
ALL RIGHT, MEN! THAT STEEL-MESH NET... IT OUGHT TO HOLD THE BATMAN... THE POOR FISH! HA HA!
COMING, BOSS!
A CABLE IS ATTACHED TO THE STEEL NET... AND THE UNCONSCIOUS BATMAN IS HOISTED INTO MID-AIR..
YES, SIR BOYS THE BATMAN'S OPERATIONS ARE.. SHALL WE SAY.. TEMPORARILY SUSPENDED ?
I CAN HARDLY WAIT TO SEE HIS FACE WHEN HE COMES TO!
A FEW MINUTES LATER..
MY HEAD.. FEELS LIK A BALLOON WHAT HAPPENED. .OHHH. I'M TRAPPED!
TAUNTING LAUGHTER ROLLS UP TO BATMAN'S EARS.. THE MOCKING SCORN OF THE NATION'S LEADING PUBLIC ENEMIES!
REMEMBER ME, BATMAN? I'M RED BABBITT. YOU SENT ME UP FOR LIFE.. BUT FROM NOW ON IT'S THE LIFE OF RILEY FOR ME! HA HA!
YOU GOT ME A TICKET FOR THE HOT SEAT, CHUM! SORRY. BUT I WON'T BE USING IT!
NOW YOU'RE CAUGHT IN A DRAGNET AIN'T IT A LAUGH !
THOSE RATS MEAN BUSINESS. I'VE GOT TO DO SOMETHING ..FAST!
AND NOW MEN, HOW SHALL WE EXECUTE OUR FRIEND? ANY SUGGES-TIONS?
TOMMY-GUN !
NAW... BURN HIM ALIVE !!
STEEL WIRE! NO CHANCE OF BREAKING THIS. THE ONLY THING THAT CAN CUT THRU IS DIAMOND! DIAMOND.. THAT'S IT.. MY BADGE!
QUICKLY, SURREPTITIOUSLY, BATMAN REMOVES HIS DIAMOND BADGE, RUBS ITS KEEN-FACETED EDGE ACROSS ONE OF THE WIRE STRANDS..
I'M USING THIS BADGE SOONER THAN I THOUGHT!
6

BACK AND FORTH... BACK AND FORTH ACROSS THE STEEL WIRE HE DRAWS THE SUPER-HARD GEM... UNTIL...
SUCCESS! AND NOW TO REPEAT THE STUNT!
SNAP
DESPERATELY BATMAN RACES AGAINST TIME... STRAND AFTER STRAND IS SAWED THROUGH... AND THEN...
WELL, BATMAN... I'M GOING TO BURN YOU UP... WITH THIS ACETYLENE TORCH!
SORRY... BUT I'M ALLERGIC TO FLAME!
THE NEMESIS OF THE UNDERWORLD SLIDES THRU THE OPENING HE HAS CUT IN THE MESH NET... KICKS OUT!
SEE WHAT I MEAN?
THE BATMAN'S LOOSE! GET HIM!
THE HUMAN PENDULUM SWINGS THRU THE AIR LIKE A SWEEPING SCYTHE !!
ROBIN WILL NEVER FORGIVE ME FOR BEING OUT OF THIS!
HAPPY BIRTHDAY!
AND HERE ARE THE RETURNS OF THE DAY!
7

OUTSIDE, ROBIN, THE BOY WONDER, HEARS THE STACCATO GUN-SHOTS...
GUNFIRE! THAT SOUNDS LIKE MY CUE!

SOME BIRTHDAY PARTY! MIND IF I CRASH?
NICE GOING, ROBIN!

THIS'LL STOP THAT LITTLE WILDCAT!
THE CABLE SEVERED... THE STEEL MESH DESCENDS ON ROBIN..
HEY... WHAT'S THIS...
AND A MOMENT LATER THE BLAZE LASHES OUT WITH A CRUEL BLOW...
NEXT TIME DON'T ATTEND BIRTHDAY PARTIES UNLESS YOU'RE INVITED!
ALL RIGHT, BATMAN! SURRENDER... OR YOUR LITTLE BOY BLUE PAL GETS A TASTE OF THIS FLAME-GUN!
I GUESS THIS IS YOUR ROUND.. COME AND TAKE ME!
FROM THE FRYING PAN INTO THE FIRE... HOW'LL I GET OUT OF THIS SPOT?
8

BATMAN TALKS SWIFTLY, DESPERATELY STALLING FOR PRECIOUS MOMENTS... SIMULTANEOUSLY, HE USES THE TOE OF ONE FOOT TO EASE THE BOOT OFF THE OTHER...
THEN, A SPLIT SECOND LATER, THE BLACK-CLAD CRIME-SMASHER KICKS OUT...AND THE RELEASED SHOE SPEARS THRU THE AIR LIKE A DEADLY MISSILE!
ANOTHER POINT FOR MY SIDE!
SUDDENLY, THE SHRILL SCREAM OF POLICE SIRENS CLEAVES THRU THE AIR...
I THINK THIS EVENS THE SCORE!
BUT AS THE BATMAN LUNGES IN, A TREACHEROUS BLOW FROM BEHIND FELLS THE CRIME-CRUSHER...
THE COPPERS! THEY HEARD THE SHOOTING! LET'S GET OUT OF HERE! THE BACK ENTRANCE!
BATMAN! BATMAN! SPEAK TO ME!
EEEEEEEEEEEEE
UP ABOVE, ON THE WINDOW LEDGE, A SMALL FIGURE SURVEYS THE TUMULTUOUS SCENE BELOW...
HERE GOES NOTHING!
THE BAND OF OUTLAWS SCATTER FROM THE HOUSE LIKE FRIGHTENED RATS!
NOT A MOMENT TO LOSE, BOYS! RED, YOU TAKE THAT CAR! RAFFERTY, YOU TAKE THE OTHER!
OKAY, BLAZE, AND WATCH THEM COPPERS SWALLOW OUR EXHAUST!
EEEEEEEEE

DOWN PLUMMETS THE LAUGHING BOY WONDER IN AN AMAZING ACROBATIC LEAP.....
FIRST DOWN— GOAL TO GO!
AAGH—
BUT A CRUEL, CRUSHING BLOW FROM BEHIND FELLS THE GALLANT YOUTH....
THIS'LL STOP THE WILDCAT!
KEEP HIM IN THE CAR! THE COPPERS WON'T DARE SHOOT AT US FOR FEAR OF HURTING THE KID!
AND AS THE GETAWAY CARS ROCKET OFF, HIDDEN EXHAUST PIPES SPURT DENSE CLOUDS OF BLACK SMOKE...
THAT'S WHAT I CALL PERFECT CAMOU-FLAGE!
BY THE TIME THAT SMOKE CLEARS WE'LL HAVE LOST THEM!
PD
SMOKE GETS IN THEIR EYES! HA, HA! TO THE WATERFRONT HIDEOUT, BOYS!
RIGHT, BOSS! NO WONDER YOU CALL YOURSELF THE BLAZE — AFTER THE WAY YOU FIGHT 'EM WITH FIRE AND SMOKE!
AT THE WATERFRONT HIDE-OUT... A RAMSHACKLE WAREHOUSE WHOSE ROTTING TIMBERS BULK GLOOMILY IN THE EERIE MOONLIGHT...
HERE WE ARE, MEN!
THIS PLACE GIVES ME THE CREEPS.. NO ONE'S BEEN INSIDE FOR MONTHS!
THE FLICKERING RAYS OF A SEARCHLIGHT CAST EERIE SHADOWS AS ROBIN'S LIMP FIGURE IS DRAGGED ACROSS THE DUST-CAKED FLOOR OF THE WAREHOUSE..
MAYBE I'M GETTING OLD (COUGH, COUGH) BUT THIS BRAT SEEMS TO WEIGH A TON! AND THIS HEAVY DUST DON'T HELP MY PIPES NONE! (COUGH, COUGH)
SHUT UP! WE'RE ONLY STAYING HERE UNTIL TOMORROW AFTER-NOON!
MILES AWAY.... AND A NERVE-WROUGHT BATMAN KEEPS AN ALL-NIGHT VIGIL IN COMMISSIONER GORDON'S OFFICE...
I TELL YOU, COMMISSIONER, IF THEY SO MUCH AS HARM A HAIR OF ROBIN'S HEAD, I'LL GET THEM.... IF I HAVE TO SEARCH EVERY RAT-HOLE IN THE COUNTRY!
DON'T WORRY, BATMAN. ROBIN CAN TAKE CARE OF HIMSELF!

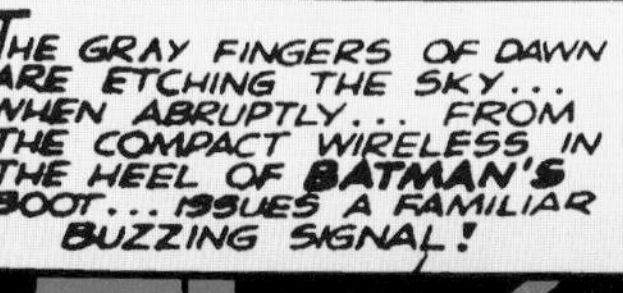
THE GRAY FINGERS OF DAWN ARE ETCHING THE SKY... WHEN ABRUPTLY... FROM THE COMPACT WIRELESS IN THE HEEL OF BATMAN'S BOOT... ISSUES A FAMILIAR BUZZING SIGNAL!

COMMISSIONER! WAKE UP! ROBIN'S ALIVE... HE'S SIGNALLING ME!
HUH... I MUST HAVE DOZED OFF... WHAT'S UP?

A MOMENT LATER, ROBIN'S S.O.S. FLASHES TO BATMAN'S WAITING EARS...
ROBIN! WHERE ARE YOU!
CAN'T TALK... AM AT WAREHOUSE ON PIER 8...

AND AT THE WAREHOUSE..
TRYING TO TIP OFF YOUR PAL, THE BATMAN, EH? WELL, YOU WON'T BE ABLE TO USE THAT GADGET OF YOURS AGAIN!
SMASH!

BUT THE BATMAN HAS HEARD ENOUGH! EBON CLOAK UNFURLED BEHIND HIM, THE NEMESIS OF CRIME SWINGS DOWN TO THE STREET BELOW ON SILKEN CORD...
HOLY COW! IT'S THE BATMAN!
MILK CO

OFF INTO THE DISTANCE ROARS THE BATMOBILE, LIKE A RUNAWAY METEOR!
DOESN'T THAT GUY EVER SLEEP? WHAT A MAN!

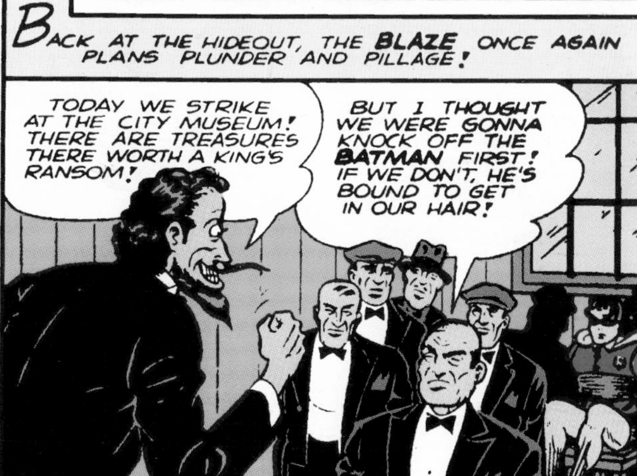
BACK AT THE HIDEOUT, THE BLAZE ONCE AGAIN PLANS PLUNDER AND PILLAGE!
TODAY WE STRIKE AT THE CITY MUSEUM! THERE ARE TREASURES THERE WORTH A KING'S RANSOM!
BUT I THOUGHT WE WERE GONNA KNOCK OFF THE BATMAN FIRST! IF WE DON'T, HE'S BOUND TO GET IN OUR HAIR!

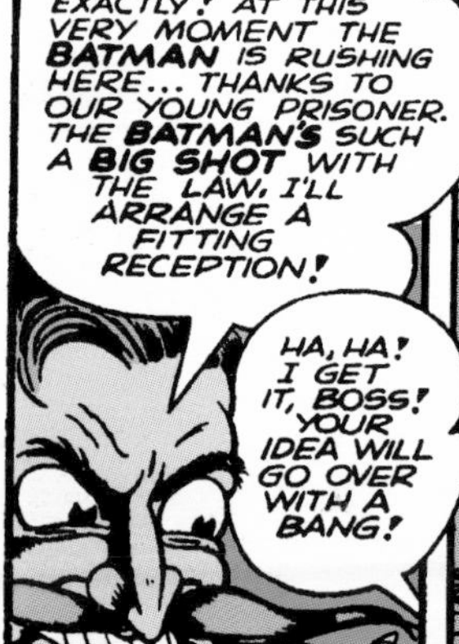
EXACTLY! AT THIS VERY MOMENT THE BATMAN IS RUSHING HERE... THANKS TO OUR YOUNG PRISONER. THE BATMAN'S SUCH A BIG SHOT WITH THE LAW, I'LL ARRANGE A FITTING RECEPTION!
HA, HA! I GET IT, BOSS! YOUR IDEA WILL GO OVER WITH A BANG!

MOMENTS LATER, THE VICIOUS VANDALS VANISH INTO THE MISTY MORN... AND PRESENTLY THE BLACK-CLOAKED CRIME-FIGHTER CRASHES IN UPON THE SCENE..
SIT TIGHT, ROBIN! I'LL HAVE YOU LOOSE IN A JIFFY!

SUDDENLY... AS THE ACE MANHUNTER LUNGES IN TO FREE HIS COMRADE IN COMBAT... THE BOY WONDER KICKS OUT BRUTALLY !!
HEY!

HMM.... NOW WHY DID ROBIN DO THAT... AND JUST WHEN I WAS TRYING TO UNTIE HIM! THERE MUST BE A REASON!

A MOMENT LATER BATMAN COUNTERS FOR THE SAVAGE KICK WITH AN EQUALLY MAD ACTION...
ONE GOOD TURN DESERVES ANOTHER, PAL... AND OUT OF THE WINDOW AND INTO THE WATER YOU GO!
WHAT STRANGE MOTIVE LIES BEHIND THIS WILD BYPLAY BETWEEN THE TWO FRIENDS??...

AND NOW BATMAN ARROWS INTO THE WATER DIVING AFTER THE HELPLESS BOY WONDER..

BENEATH THE SURFACE OF THE WATER BATMAN'S NIMBLE FINGERS FLASH INTO ACTION, FREEING ROBIN OF HIS BONDS....

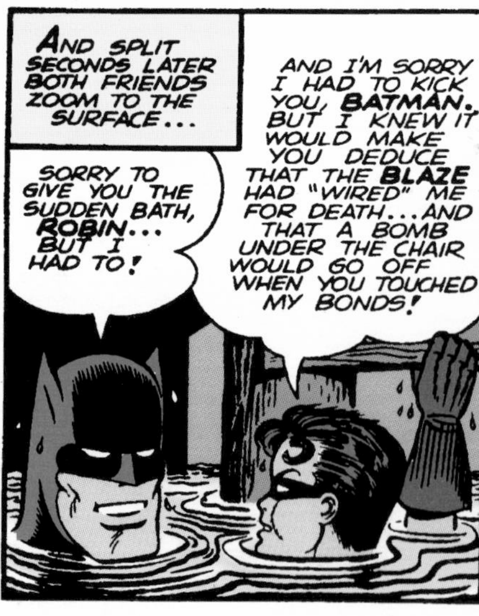
AND SPLIT SECONDS LATER BOTH FRIENDS ZOOM TO THE SURFACE...
SORRY TO GIVE YOU THE SUDDEN BATH, ROBIN... BUT I HAD TO!
AND I'M SORRY I HAD TO KICK YOU, BATMAN. BUT I KNEW IT WOULD MAKE YOU DEDUCE THAT THE BLAZE HAD "WIRED" ME FOR DEATH...AND THAT A BOMB UNDER THE CHAIR WOULD GO OFF WHEN YOU TOUCHED MY BONDS!

WATER-SOAKED AND USELESS, THE DEADLY BOMB THAT WAS TO HAVE ENDED THE CAREERS OF BATMAN AND ROBIN RESTS BENEATH THE SEA....

THAT AFTERNOON.... AT THE CITY MUSEUM....
I'D LIKE TO DONATE THESE MUMMY CASES TO YOUR MUSEUM.
YES...WE FOUND THEM IN ONE OF THE EGYPTIAN PYRAMIDS ON OUR LAST EXPEDITION!
I CAN HARDLY WAIT TO OPEN THEM!

A MODERN TROJAN HORSE!
THEY'RE NOT MUMMIES... THEY'RE GANG-STERS!
YES... THE BEST IN THE TOWN! AND THEY'RE COLLECTORS, TOO!
YEAH... WE WANT TO COLLECT SOME OF THE TREASURES IN THIS PLACE!

SUDDENLY...RINGING ACROSS THE FLOOR COME THE MOCKING TONES OF THE DYNAMIC DUO!
SORRY TO BURN YOU UP, BLAZE—BUT YOU'LL HAVE TO COLLECT ME FIRST!
AND DON'T FORGET ROBIN!
BATMAN! RUSH HIM, MEN!

WEIRD BATTLE IN THE HALL OF FOSSILS!
THIS MASTODON ISN'T COMPLAINING... SO WHY SHOULD YOU?

WHIRLWIND ACTION...WINDMILL FISTS FLYING!
KEEP 'EM FLYING!
OOF

DOUBLE...
PLAY!

LATER
I'M NOT HAPPY!
THESE BONES... THEY GIMME THE CREEPS... LOOK LIKE BARS!
YES, BOYS... AND YOU'LL BE LOOKING THRU IRON BARS REAL SOON!
MORAL—IT DOESN'T PAY TO HAVE A SKELETON IN THE CLOSET!
BOB KANE
13

No. 96
BACK THE 6TH WAR LOAN!
A SUPERMAN DC PUBLICATION
The BATMAN
Detective
REG. U. S. PAT. OFF.
COMICS
FEB.
10c.

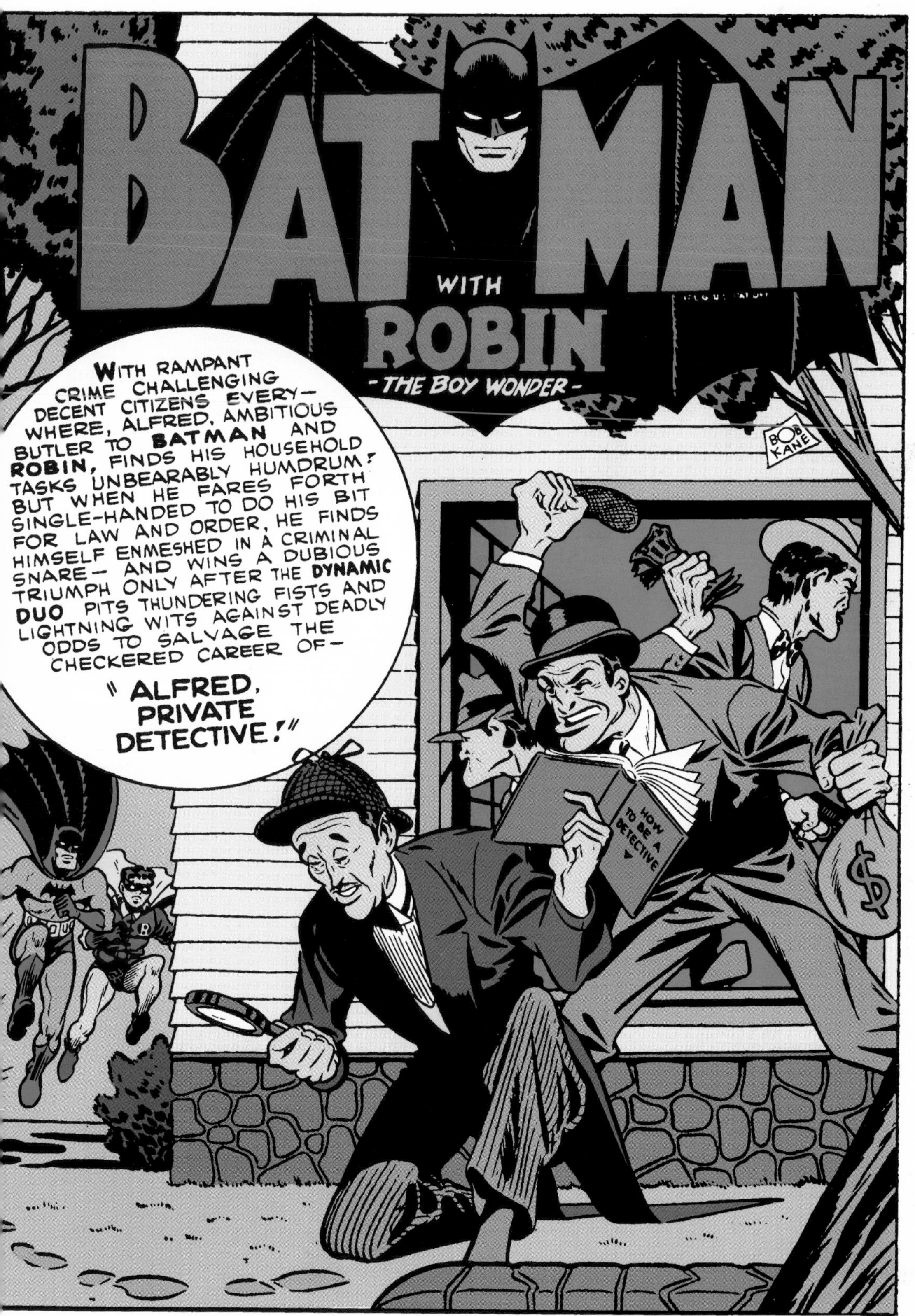
BATMAN
WITH
ROBIN
-THE BOY WONDER-
BOB KANE
WITH RAMPANT CRIME CHALLENGING DECENT CITIZENS EVERY-WHERE, ALFRED, AMBITIOUS BUTLER TO BATMAN AND ROBIN, FINDS HIS HOUSEHOLD TASKS UNBEARABLY HUMDRUM! BUT WHEN HE FARES FORTH SINGLE-HANDED TO DO HIS BIT FOR LAW AND ORDER, HE FINDS HIMSELF ENMESHED IN A CRIMINAL SNARE-- AND WINS A DUBIOUS TRIUMPH ONLY AFTER THE DYNAMIC DUO PITS THUNDERING FISTS AND LIGHTNING WITS AGAINST DEADLY ODDS TO SALVAGE THE CHECKERED CAREER OF--
"ALFRED, PRIVATE DETECTIVE!"
HOW TO BE A DETECTIVE
$

A PLEADING VOICE IS RAISED IN THE HOME OF BRUCE WAYNE, WEALTHY YOUNG MAN-ABOUT-TOWN..
CAWN'T I GO WITH YOU ON TONIGHT'S PROWL, SIR, IN HONOR O' FINISHIN' MY MAIL ORDER COURSE IN CRIMINOLOGY?
SORRY, ALFRED— ONE DOESN'T LEARN ALL THERE IS TO KNOW ABOUT CROOKS BY MAIL!

THEN THERE'S THIS LITTLE VOLUME WHICH I'VE PERUSED TILL I KNOW IT BY HEART, SIR!
HOW TO BE A DETECTIVE IN ONE EASY LESSON
NOR FROM BOOKS, EITHER, ALFRED!
DON'T FEEL BADLY, ALFRED! YOU'VE HELPED US MANY TIMES, AND WILL AGAIN—BUT TONIGHT WE'RE AFTER STONEY PETERS!
AND HE BOSSES THE MOST DANGEROUS GANG OF THIEVES IN GOTHAM CITY!

FORGIVE ME, MR. WAYNE AND MAWSTER DICK! MIGHT I AWSK A FAVOR BEFORE YOU GO?
OF COURSE! ANYTHING AT ALL!

I'VE A MONTH'S HOLIDAY DUE, AND YOU SAID I MIGHT TAKE IT ANY TIME! WOULD IT INCONVENIENCE YOU IF I SHOULD START TONIGHT?
TONIGHT?... WHY CERTAINLY, START TONIGHT IF YOU WANT TO! BUT WHERE WILL YOU GO?

I'D RAWTHER NOT SAY PRECISELY, BEGGIN' YOUR PARDON... BUT I'M ANXIOUS TO VISIT A CERTAIN CITY NEARBY!
WE'LL HAVE TO HURRY, BATMAN! IT'S ALMOST TIME!
ALL RIGHT, ALFRED! HAVE A GOOD TIME! AND IF THERE'S ANY TROUBLE, OR YOU NEED MONEY, WIRE ME IMMEDIATELY!

IN ITS UNDERGROUND GARAGE, THE POWERFUL BATMOBILE AWAITS THE DYNAMIC DUO...

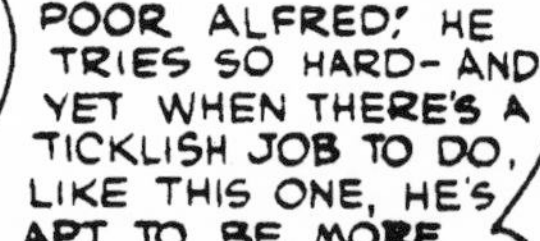
POOR ALFRED! HE TRIES SO HARD- AND YET WHEN THERE'S A TICKLISH JOB TO DO, LIKE THIS ONE, HE'S APT TO BE MORE BOTHER THAN HELP!

I HOPE WE DIDN'T HURT HIS FEELINGS ... PROBABLY A MONTH'S CHANGE OF SCENERY WILL DO HIM GOOD!
2

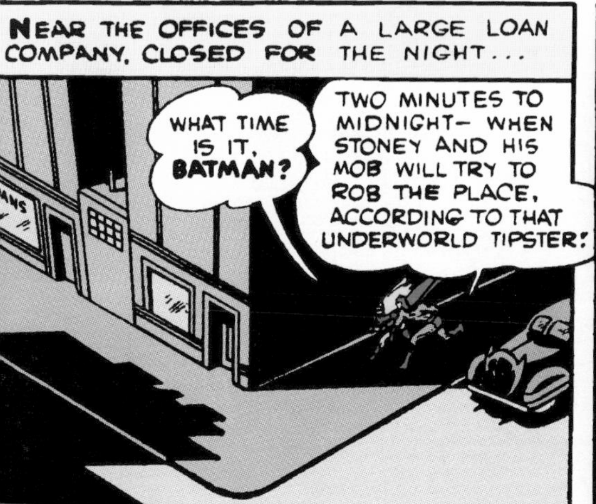
NEAR THE OFFICES OF A LARGE LOAN COMPANY, CLOSED FOR THE NIGHT...
WHAT TIME IS IT, BATMAN?
TWO MINUTES TO MIDNIGHT— WHEN STONEY AND HIS MOB WILL TRY TO ROB THE PLACE, ACCORDING TO THAT UNDERWORLD TIPSTER!

BACK IN THIS DOORWAY! WE'LL WAIT TILL THEY ACTUALLY START TO BREAK IN BEFORE WE TACKLE THEM!
ON THE DOT!

A HARD-BOILED AND EXPERT BAND OF THIEVES PREPARES FOR ACTION...

ALL RIGHT, YOU GUYS! THERE'S SUPPOSED TO BE FORTY GRAND IN THE SAFE! FINGERS, GO TO WORK ON THIS DOOR!
I'LL OPEN IT WITHOUT A TINKLE FROM DA ALARM SYSTEM, STONEY!

THERE— WHA'D I TELL YA!
GOT YOUR SAFE-CRACKIN' TOOLS, EEL?... NOW IF ONLY BATMAN DON'T SHOW UP TO SPOIL THIS JOB, LIKE HE DID THE LAST ONE...

SUDDENLY...
SORRY TO DISAPPOINT YOU, STONEY— BUT WE COULDN'T RESIST THE TEMPTATION!
YIIIIII!
IT'S THEM!
THIS TIME YOU WON'T FIND IT SO EASY TO GET AWAY!

YOU'RE GOING TO SPEND A LONG TIME BEHIND DOORS YOU CAN'T OPEN, FINGERS!
HERE'S WHERE I SETTLE THINGS FOR GOOD!
TSK, TSK! AIMING AT THE STARS AGAIN!
3

A GALLANT BATTLE IS ENDED BY THE CRASH OF A PISTOL SHOT!
THAT'LL TEACH YA TO BUTT INTO OTHER PEOPLE'S BUSINESS!
BATMAN! THEY'VE GOT HIM!

NICE WORK, STONEY!
SHUT UP AN' LET'S GET OUTA HERE BEFORE THAT SHOOTIN' BRINGS THE COPS!
BATMAN! WAKE UP! SAY SOMETHING!

FOR A MINUTE I THOUGHT HE'D KILLED YOU!
JUST A FLESH WOUND... KNOCKED ME OUT FOR A MINUTE!... SO THE RATS GOT AWAY AGAIN!

BUT WE'LL GET THEM, ROBIN — IF WE HAVE TO FOLLOW THEM ALL OVER THE COUNTRY!
SAY IT AGAIN — AND THEN I'LL GET YOU TO A DOCTOR!

MEANWHILE, IN THE HIDEOUT OF STONEY PETERS AND HIS GANG, A MOMENTOUS CONFERENCE IS TAKING PLACE...

BUT WHADDA WE GOTTA LAM FOR, STONEY? IF HE'S WOUNDED, HE WON'T BOTHER US FOR A LONG TIME — AN' IF HE'S DEAD, HE WON'T NEVER BOTHER US!

YOU FOOL! IF HE'S DEAD, THE COPS WILL MAKE THIS TOWN TOO HOT TO HOLD ANY OF US — AND IF HE ISN'T, BATMAN WILL NEVER REST TILL HE'S SENT US ALL TO THE BIG HOUSE!

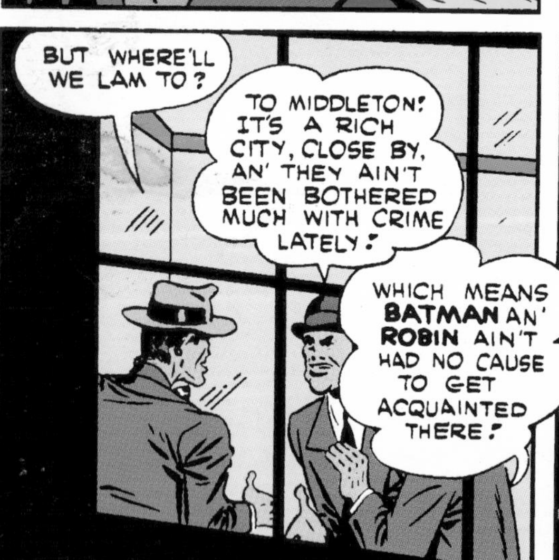

BUT WHERE'LL WE LAM TO?
TO MIDDLETON! IT'S A RICH CITY, CLOSE BY, AN' THEY AIN'T BEEN BOTHERED MUCH WITH CRIME LATELY!
WHICH MEANS BATMAN AN' ROBIN AIN'T HAD NO CAUSE TO GET ACQUAINTED THERE!

MIDDLETON, DID STONEY SAY? WELL, WELL — WHAT A COINCIDENCE!
SO THIS IS MIDDLETON. WHERE I WILL SHOW THE MAWSTERS — BLESS 'EM — THAT ALFRED IS A BETTER SLEUTH THAN THEY SUSPECT!
4

PRESENTLY THE CITIZENS OF MIDDLETON ARE MADE AWARE OF A NEW ENTERPRISE IN THEIR MIDST...
ETON GAZETTE
Alfred Beagle
PRIVATE DETECTIVE
SHADOWING
SLEUTHING
DEDUCTION
INDUCTION
GRADUATE CUM LAUDE OF HIVES CRIMINOLOGICAL ORRESPONDENCE SCHOOL
INFORMATION DISCREETLY DEVELOPED! Alfred BEAGLE PRIVATE DETECTIVE
CROOKS CAUGHT CHEAP ALFRED BEAGLE PRIVATE DETECTIVE
NOW ALL I HAVE TO DO IS WAIT FOR MY FIRST CASE — AND THIS MAY BE IT!
KNOCK KNOCK
COME IN!
A CLIENT — AND WHAT A CLIENT!
ME, I'M PETE STONE, AN' I THINK A CERTAIN BANKER IN THIS BURG IS PLANNIN' TO ROB HIS OWN BANK! HIS NAME IS J.C. WILLIS!
I SEE, SIR! YOU WISH ME TO SHADOW HIM AND REPORT HIS EVERY MOVEMENT, I PRESUME?
DAT'S DA IDEA! FIND OUT EVERYT'ING HE DOES, AN' REPORT TOMORRA NIGHT TA DA HOUSEBOAT OFF-
NIX, FINGERS! ... BRING YOUR REPORT TO THE SHACK AT THE END O' PIER 69, DOWN AT THE RIVERFRONT!
YOU MAY DEPEND ON ME, SIR!
SO LATER...
J.C. WILLIS DOESN'T LOOK LIKE A BOUNDER - BUT YOU NEVER CAN TELL!
A NICE HOME, I MUST SAY! I'LL JUST TAKE A LOOK ABOUT THE GROUNDS!
WHAT'S THIS?
EH?... NICE DOGGIE! ... OH, COME NOW- I WASN'T MEANIN' NO HARM!
GRRRR!
5

HUNTER AND HUNTED MEET!
HELP! MURDER! OH-H-H...
ER— OUCH!

POLICE! HELP!
MY WORD! I'D BEST RETIRE FOR A BREATHIN' SPELL!
GGRRRR!

NEVERTHELESS, UNDAUNTED BY OBSTACLES, ALFRED PERSISTS IN HIS ASSIGNMENT— AND IN DUE TIME PRESENTS A LENGTHY REPORT TO HIS CLIENT...
DESPITE THE MOST ASSIDUOUS WATCHFUL-NESS, SIR, I FAILED TO FIND ANY INDICATION OF FELONIOUS INTENT, AND—
OKAY, CHUM, OKAY! HERE'S FIFTY SMACKERS! NOW SCRAM!

LISSEN AT THIS! "SUBJECT LEAVES HOME DAILY AT 8:30 A.M., RETURNS AT 6 P.M. FOR DINNER EXCEPT TUESDAYS WHEN HE ATTENDS LODGE MEETING AND SERVANTS HAVE NIGHT OFF..." AN' THIS IS TUESDAY!
STONEY, YA'RE A GENIUS, GETTIN' A DUMB PRIVATE COPPER TA DIG UP ALL DA INFO IN ADVANCE FOR US!

NEXT MORNING, NEWS HEADLINES FILL ALFRED WITH DEEP MISGIVINGS!
WHAT-O- THE WILLIS HOME!.. IT'S A HORRIBLE THOUGHT— BUT I WONDER IF PETER STONE MIGHT HAVE BEEN PULLIN' MY LEG!
NEWS
EXPERT BURGLAR GANG ROBS BANKER'S HOME!

AND HIS CONSCIENCE DRIVES HIM, IN FEAR AND TREMBLING, TOWARD THE OFFICE OF THE MAN HE SO RECENTLY SHADOWED!
I-ER- MUST SEE MR. WILLIS IMMEDIATELY ABOUT THE BURGLARY AT HIS HOME!
FOLLOW ME!
6

SIR, I FELT I HAD TO EXPLAIN THAT—
YOU!... HOLD HIM, GUARD, WHILE I CALL THE POLICE!
I'VE GOT HIM!
GUARD

MEANWHILE, NEWS OF THE BURGLARY REACHES THE WAYNE RESIDENCE IN GOTHAM CITY..

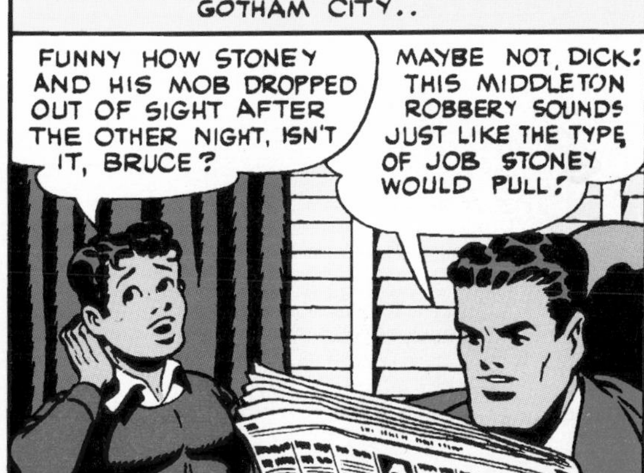
FUNNY HOW STONEY AND HIS MOB DROPPED OUT OF SIGHT AFTER THE OTHER NIGHT, ISN'T IT, BRUCE?
MAYBE NOT, DICK! THIS MIDDLETON ROBBERY SOUNDS JUST LIKE THE TYPE OF JOB STONEY WOULD PULL!

NEXT STOP MIDDLETON, EH?
YOU BET! DIDN'T WE AGREE TO GET STONEY IF WE HAD TO FOLLOW HIM ALL OVER THE COUNTRY?

LATER, IN THE OFFICE OF THE MIDDLETON CHIEF OF POLICE...
NICE OF YOU TO OFFER TO HELP OUT, BATMAN! WE'VE ALREADY GOT ONE SUSPECT WE'RE PRETTY SURE OF— A MAN WHO SPIED ON WILLIS, PRETENDING TO BE A PRIVATE DETECTIVE!
MIND IF WE TAKE A LOOK AT HIM?

WHY, IT'S—
SH-H-H-H!
BLESS ME, BATMAN AND ROBIN!...ULP! AT LEAST, YOU RESEMBLE PICTURES I'VE SEEN OF THEM!...

BELIEVE ME, SIRS, I'M INNOCENT AS A NEWBORN BABE! I WAS RUNNIN' A DETECTIVE AGENCY, AND A MAN NAMED PETER STONE — AN UNCOUTH SORT OF FELLOW— SAID WILLIS WAS A CROOK AND HIRED ME TO—
PETER STONE, EH? DID HE GIVE YOU ANY ADDRESS?
7

HE SEEMED TO HAVE HEADQUARTERS IN A SHACK AT PIER 69, IN THE RIVERFRONT DISTRICT!
WELL, MY GOOD MAN, WE'LL SEE WHAT WE CAN DO!
IF YOU ASK ME, HE LOOKS MIGHTY GUILTY!

POOR ALFRED! WITH HIS LAST HOPES OF IMPRESSING HIS FAMOUS EMPLOYERS GONE GLIMMERING, HIS THOUGHTS PLUMB THE DEPTHS OF DESPAIR!
SUCH HUMILIATION! SUCH SHAME! I WOULDN'T CARE IF THEY SENT ME TO PRISON FOR LIFE!
WAKE UP, BEAUTIFUL! THE DETECTIVES WANT TO TEST YOUR REFLEXES!

WAIT HERE! THE DETECTIVES WILL BE UP IN A MINUTE!
YES SIR!

A HALF-FORGOTTEN INCIDENT GNAWS AT ALFRED'S MIND AS HE AWAITS QUESTIONING...
IF ONLY BATMAN FINDS THE RAWSCALS AT THE DOCK! ...BUT WAIT A MINUTE! BEFORE PETER STONE MENTIONED THE SHACK ON THE DOCK, THE OTHER ONE SAID— I'VE GOT IT!

A HOUSEBOAT! THAT MUST BE THEIR REAL HIDEOUT! I MUST GET WORD TO BATMAN AND MAWSTER ROBIN RIGHT AWAY! I DISLIKE TO CRAWL OUT THE WINDOW LIKE A COMMON CRIMINAL, BUT—

HALT OR WE'LL SHOOT!
I'LL APOLOGIZE TO THE POLICEMEN UPON MY RETURN!
8

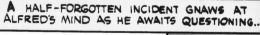

HALT!
BANG
BANG!
OH, DEAR! EVEN IF THEY DON'T KILL ME, THEY'RE CERTAIN TO BE PREJUDICED WHEN I COME BACK TO EXPLAIN!

AT THIS MOMENT, ON PIER 69...
ROBIN, THERE'S NOTHING INSIDE THAT SHACK BUT JUNK! PETER STONE—OR STONEY PETERS—WOULDN'T GIVE ALFRED HIS RIGHT ADDRESS! BUT PERHAPS IF WE GET OUT OF SIGHT AND KEEP OUR EYES OPEN...

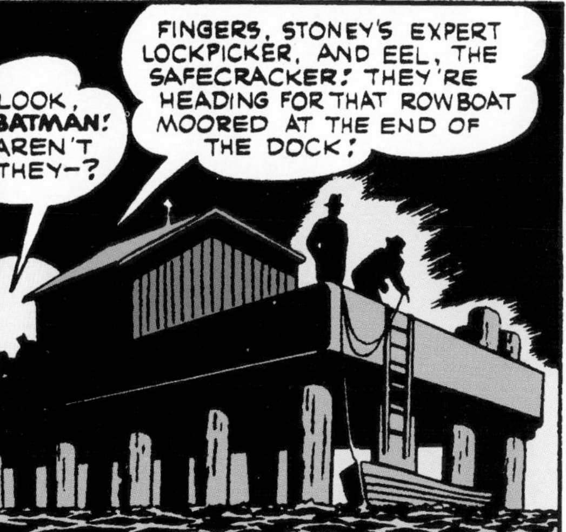
LOOK, BATMAN! AREN'T THEY—?
FINGERS, STONEY'S EXPERT LOCKPICKER, AND EEL, THE SAFECRACKER! THEY'RE HEADING FOR THAT ROWBOAT MOORED AT THE END OF THE DOCK!

THEY'RE HEADING FOR THAT HOUSEBOAT!
AND SO ARE WE—BUT WE'LL SWIM FOR IT!

VE'LL WAIT IERE FOR FURTHER EVELOPMENTS, EH?
IF WE DON'T NAB STONEY, ALFRED MAY BE IN JAIL A LONG TIME! WE'VE GOT TO GET A CONFESSION FROM THE REAL CRIMINALS!

MINUTES LATER..
NOW TO FIND THE REAL HIDEOUT!
9

LOOK, STONEY-THAT DUMB DETECTIVE! I THOUGHT THEY'D LOCKED HIM UP!
I'LL TEACH HIM TO SNOOP AROUND HERE!
WHAT-O — A HOUSEBOAT! IF I SHOULD CAPTURE THE VILLAINS SINGLE-HANDED, IT WOULD BE A FEATHER IN MY CAP...

WHAT'LL WE DO-TOSS HIM IN DA DRINK?
NO — WE'LL TAKE HIM TO THE HOUSEBOAT AND FIND OUT HOW MUCH HE TOLD THE COPS ABOUT US!

PRESENTLY...
IT'S ALFRED! BUT HOW COULD THEY GET HIM, IF HE WAS IN JAIL?
I DON'T KNOW-BUT KNOWING STONEY, I THINK WE'D BETTER RESCUE ALFRED WITHOUT DELAY!

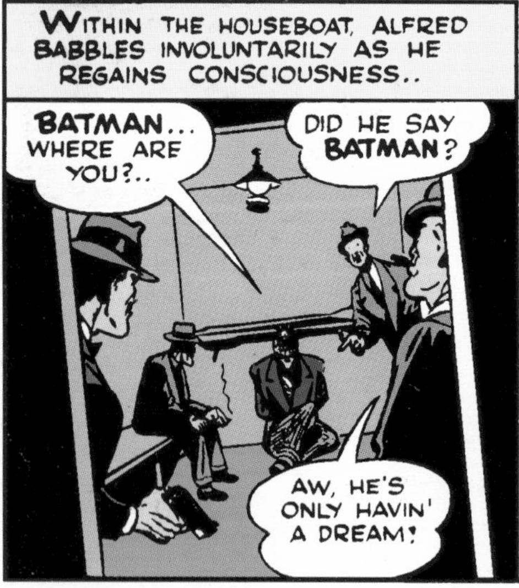
WITHIN THE HOUSEBOAT, ALFRED BABBLES INVOLUNTARILY AS HE REGAINS CONSCIOUSNESS..
BATMAN... WHERE ARE YOU?..
DID HE SAY BATMAN?
AW, HE'S ONLY HAVIN' A DREAM!

THE NEXT INSTANT...
I'M AFRAID YOU LADS ARE HEADING FOR A SHIPWRECK!
BATMAN! NICE OF YOU TO DROP IN!

DROP IN A LITTLE DEEPER, WHY DON'T YOU?
HEY!
I CAN'T DECIDE! AFTER I SHOOT YA, SHALL I SINK YA IN THE RIVER, OR BURN YA UP WITH THE HOUSEBOAT?
OH, DEAR! I'VE SIMPLY GOT TO DO SOMETHING!
YOU CAN'T GET AWAY WITH IT, AND YOU KNOW IT!

TENSE WITH DESPERATION, ALFRED FORCES HIMSELF ERECT...
IT DOESN'T MATTER IF THEY KILL ME — AS LONG AS THEY DON'T DO IT BEFORE I CAN GET A GRIP ON THIS OAR AND START SWINGIN'....
ABRUPTLY...
TAKE THAT — MURDERERS — BOUNDERS — RUFFIANS!
WHAT'S GOIN' ON?
YOU'RE JUST IN TIME, EEL!

THIS IS WHERE EEL MEETS HEEL!
WHAT'S THE IDEA, BATMAN — STEALING MY GAG STUFF?
NERVOUS, STONEY? YOU'RE NOT SHOOTING AS STRAIGHT AS YOU WERE THE OTHER NIGHT!
11

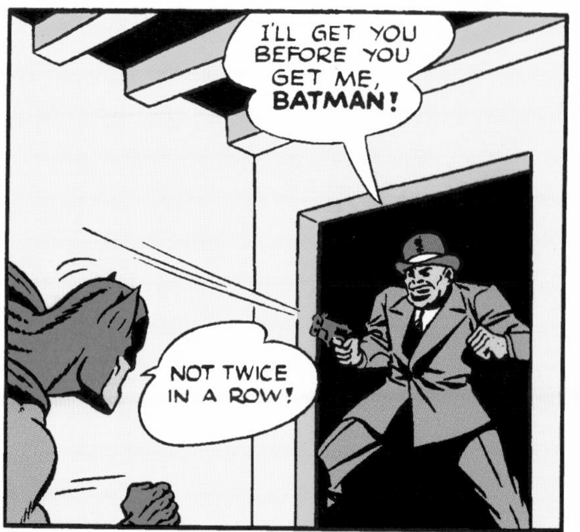
I'LL GET YOU BEFORE YOU GET ME, BATMAN!
NOT TWICE IN A ROW!

GIVE UP?

LATER, AT POLICE HEADQUARTERS...
YES- PRIVATE DETECTIVE BEAGLE NOT ONLY LED US TO STONEY AND HIS PALS, BUT SAVED OUR LIVES WHEN WE CRASHED IN TO CAPTURE THEM!
REALLY, GENTLEMEN, IT WAS NOTHIN'! I ONLY DID MY DUTY AS I SAW IT!

ANOTHER EVENING, IN GOTHAM CITY...
I SHOULD CERTAINLY SAY I SHOWED 'EM, ALL RIGHT, ALL RIGHT!
GOTHAM NEWS
PRIVATE DETECTIVE SAVES LIVES OF BATMAN, ROBIN; HELPS SMASH ROBBER RING!

YOUR FIGHTIN' TOGS, MR. WAYNE AND MAWSTER DICK! AND NOW- SINCE I HAVE PROVED BEYOND QUESTION MY QUALIFICATIONS AS A NEMESIS O' CRIMINALS-
YES, ALFRED?
12

WHERE DO WE GO TONIGHT?
The END

No.97
MAR...TEN CENTS
A SUPERMAN DC PUBLICATION
BATMAN
Detective
COMICS

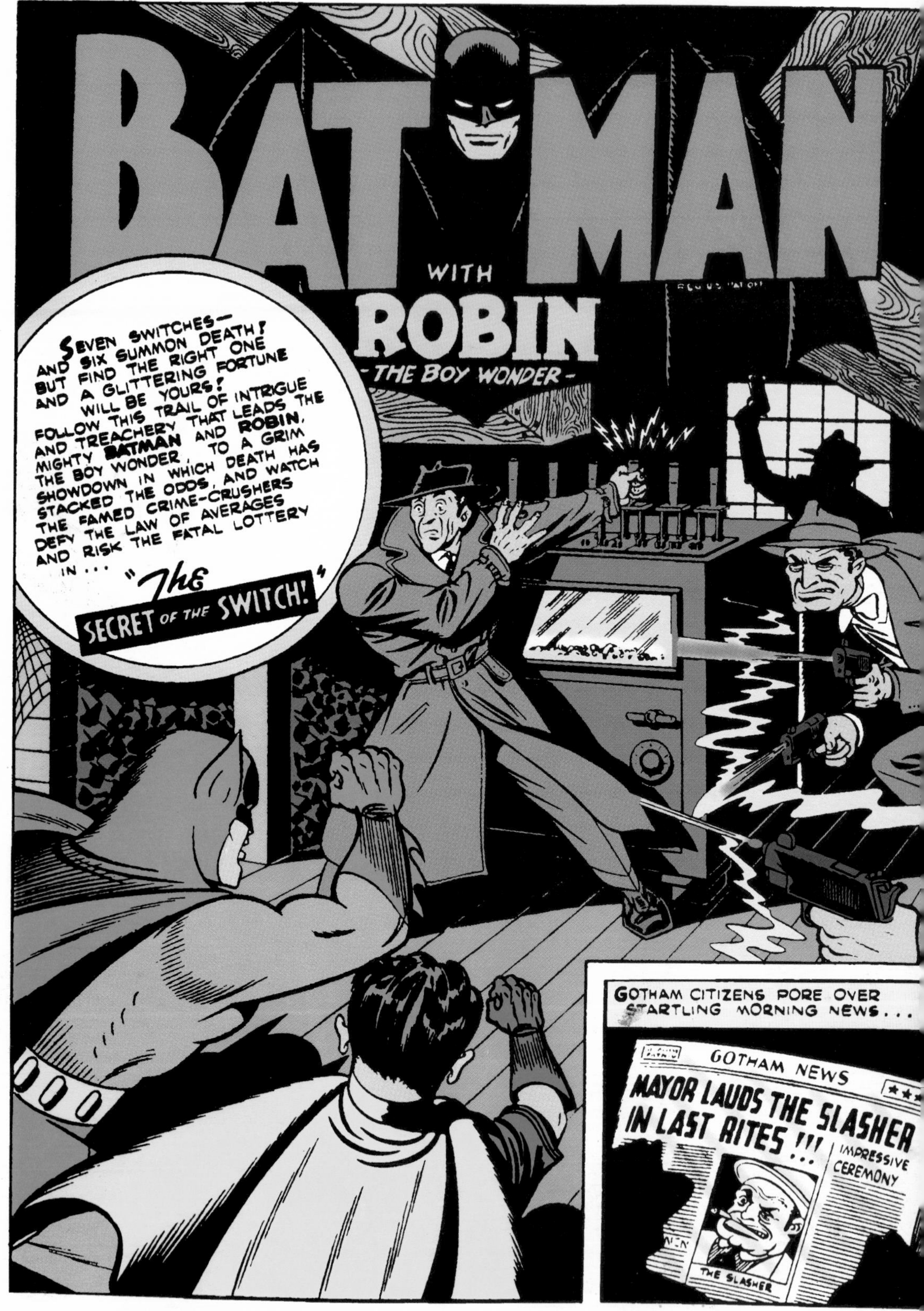
BATMAN
WITH
ROBIN
-THE BOY WONDER-
SEVEN SWITCHES— AND SIX SUMMON DEATH! BUT FIND THE RIGHT ONE AND A GLITTERING FORTUNE WILL BE YOURS! FOLLOW THIS TRAIL OF INTRIGUE AND TREACHERY THAT LEADS THE MIGHTY BATMAN AND ROBIN, THE BOY WONDER, TO A GRIM SHOWDOWN IN WHICH DEATH HAS STACKED THE ODDS, AND WATCH THE FAMED CRIME-CRUSHERS DEFY THE LAW OF AVERAGES AND RISK THE FATAL LOTTERY IN...
"THE SECRET OF THE SWITCH!"
GOTHAM CITIZENS PORE OVER STARTLING MORNING NEWS...
GOTHAM NEWS
MAYOR LAUDS THE SLASHER IN LAST RITES !!!
IMPRESSIVE CEREMONY
THE SLASHER

WHAT'S THIS?— WAS NOT THE SLASHER A RUTHLESS CRIMINAL, ONE OF GOTHAM CITY'S WORST CITIZENS? WHY, THEN, SUCH GLOWING OBITUARIES FOR THE MAN THE **BATMAN** HAD PUBLICLY SWORN TO GET? ONLY TWENTY-FOUR HOURS EARLIER...

IN A SINISTER WATERFRONT DIVE, THE **BATMAN** AND **ROBIN** MEET OSCAR THE WEASEL—
BUT WHY ARE YOU TIPPING ME OFF TO THE SLASHER'S HIDEOUT?
THE SLASHER WON'T LEMME PULL OUT, SEE? I WANNA GO STRAIGHT!
I'LL STILL HOLD ON TO MY WATCH!

CHECKING THE WEASEL'S TIP-OFF, THE CRIME FIGHTERS APPROACH THE MASTER CROOK'S LAIR...
WE'D BE CRAZY TO TRUST THAT LITTLE RAT!
YES — WE'D BETTER WATCH OURSELVES! IT MIGHT BE A TRAP!

AT'S FUNNY— HE DOOR'S NOT OCKED! I DON'T LIKE THIS...
LOOKS LIKE WE'RE EXPECTED... -WATCH OUT FOR THE BRASS BAND!

BUT OMINOUS SILENCE SHROUDS THE HOUSE!
BEHIND THAT CURTAIN-- THAT'S THE ONLY PLACE WE HAVEN'T SEARCHED!
I SMELL TROUBLE!

HOLY SMOKE!
WHAT IS IT?

UICIDE! CAN'T ELIEVE IT!
LOOK—THERE'S A NOTE ON THE WINDOW SHADE!

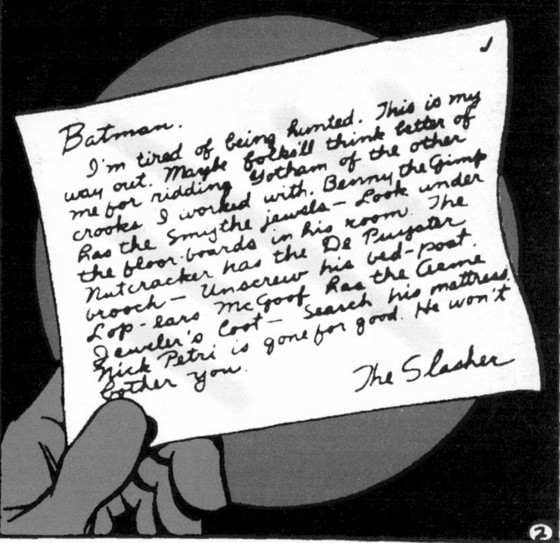
Batman.
I'm tired of being hunted. This is my way out. Maybe folks'll think better of me for ridding Gotham of the other crooks I worked with. Benny the Gimp has the Smythe jewels—Look under the floor-boards in his room. The Nutcracker has the De Puyster brooch—Unscrew his bed-post. Lop-ears McGoof has the Acme Jeweler's Loot—Search his mattress. Nick Petri is gone for good. He won't bother you.
The Slasher

2

AFTER THIS I'LL BELIEVE IN MIRACLES! BUT FIRST, LET'S FIND OUT IF ALL THIS IS TRUE!
IF IT IS— IT MEANS THE END OF THE WORST CRIMINAL COMBINE IN GOTHAM CITY!

MINUTES LATER - IN THE APARTMENT OF BENNY THE GIM
NOW LISTEN, BATMAN— YOU AIN'T GOT NOTHIN' ON ME!
NO? WE'LL SOON FIND OUT! PULL UP THOSE FLOOR-BOARDS, ROBIN!

TRY ARGUIN' WIT DIS, YOU BIG— OOF!
LOOKS LIKE I WON THE ARGUMENT!

HERE'S THE STUFF, ALL RIGHT!

HEAVE-HO!
HEY— I JUST HAD DIS SUIT PRESSED!
YOU DON'T HAVE TO DRESS UP FOR THE WARDEN!
POLICE DEPT.

CONTINUING THE SWIFT ROUND-UP THE DYNAMIC DUO PAYS A CRASH VISIT TO JOE THE NUTCRACKER...
AWRK! WHO SQUEALED ON ME?
A LITTLE GHOST TOLD US!
THIS IS ONE CASE WHERE ICE GETS A FELLOW IN A HOT SPOT!

AND FINALLY, THE THIRD GOTHAM GANGSTER DROPS IN AT POLICE HEADQUARTERS...
I DEMAND A LAWYER!
HE'S ALL YOURS, SERGEANT!

LATER— IN COMMISSIONER GORDON'S OFFICE...
I WONDER WHERE PETRI DISAPPEARED TO? AND WHERE'S THE LOOT FROM THE JOBS THEY PULLED TOGETHER?
THE GANG MUST HAVE DISPOSED OF THE LOOT LONG AGO! ANYWAY, WE'RE RID OF A DANGER-OUS CRIMINAL COMBINE! GOTHAM CITY OWES THE SLASHER A NICE SEND-OFF!
3

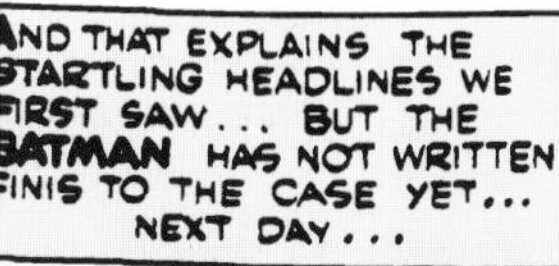
AND THAT EXPLAINS THE STARTLING HEADLINES WE FIRST SAW... BUT THE BATMAN HAS NOT WRITTEN FINIS TO THE CASE YET... NEXT DAY...

FUNNY THING ABOUT SLASHER'S DOG! WONDER WHAT HAPPENED TO IT? THOSE TWO WERE. INSEPARABLE!
CAN'T IMAGINE ANYONE HE'D GIVE IT TO! NOBODY COULD HAVE WANTED THAT FIERCE BEAST!

YOU'RE RIGHT! NOBODY ELSE COULD HAVE HANDLED THAT SAVAGE BRUTE! IT'S WISE TO CHECK THESE LITTLE THINGS! OSCAR THE WEASEL MIGHT KNOW WHERE THE DOG IS!
LET'S GO!

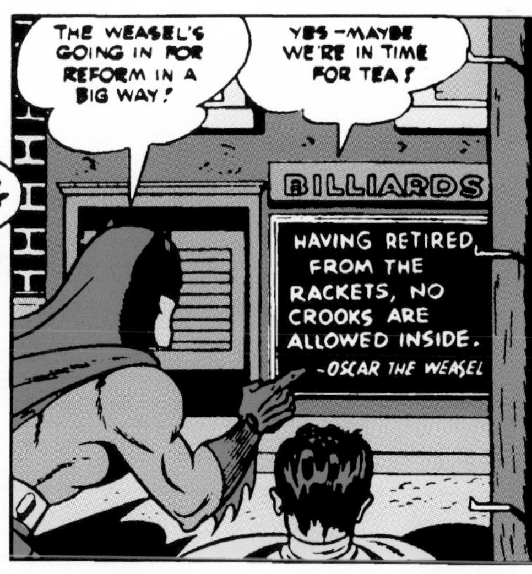
THE WEASEL'S GOING IN FOR REFORM IN A BIG WAY!
YES-MAYBE WE'RE IN TIME FOR TEA!
BILLIARDS
HAVING RETIRED FROM THE RACKETS, NO CROOKS ARE ALLOWED INSIDE.
-OSCAR THE WEASEL

HELLO, OSCAR-JUST DROPPED IN TO SEE HOW YOU WERE DOING! BY THE WAY-WHAT EVER BECAME OF SLASHER'S DOG?
THE MUTT?-WHY-ER-HE GAVE DAT TO A PAL O' HIS OVER AT THE AUTO WRECKER'S!

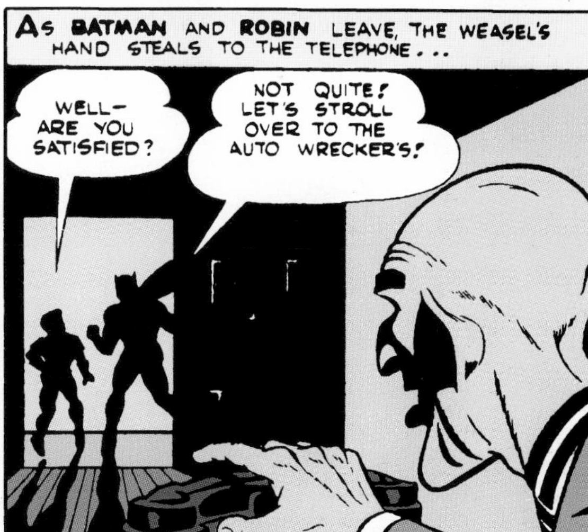
AS BATMAN AND ROBIN LEAVE, THE WEASEL'S HAND STEALS TO THE TELEPHONE...
WELL-ARE YOU SATISFIED?
NOT QUITE! LET'S STROLL OVER TO THE AUTO WRECKER'S!

DIS IS OSCAR, BOSS! HE'S ON HIS WAY! HE DONE JUST LIKE YOU TOLD ME HE WOULD!
NICE GOIN', OSCAR! WE'RE ALL SET AT THIS END!

IGNORANT OF THE TRAP THAT AWAITS THEM, BATMAN AND ROBIN ARRIVE AT THE JUNK-YARD...
THAT'S FUNNY-THERE'S NO ONE AROUND! WHERE'S THE DOG?
MAYBE IT'S TIED UP IN THE SHACK DURING BUSINESS HOURS!
4

GET HIM, FANG!

CAT-LIKE, THE BATMAN LEAPS FOR COVER!
THAT WAS CLOSE- GOT TO THINK FAST! STRANGE, THAT DOG OBEYING ANOTHER MASTER SO SOON!
DON'T GET SO HOT UNDER THE COLLAR, FIDO!
GET HIM, BOYS!
GRRRRRR

MAYBE I CAN BORROW A STUNT FROM THE INDIANS!
COME ON OUT, BATMAN! YER A COOKED GOOSE!

THIS IS THE PAY-OFF, BATMAN!
TIRES 1.00
THIS IS GETTING TOUGH! WHAT'S THE BATMAN UP TO?

STEEL MUSCLES BEND THE IMPROVISED BOW...
I HOPE THIS WORKS!

AND THE STEEL SHAFT FINDS ITS TARGET!

A RINGER!
5

WHAT PRETTY TEETH!
THE BETTER TO BITE YOU WITH— WATCH OUT!

CHEW ON THIS, FIDO!
E-E-E-YIPE!

NO USE, ROBIN— WE'LL NEVER CATCH THOSE CROOKS NOW!
RRRRIIIINNGGGGG
THE PHONE— INSIDE THE SHACK!
ZOOM

I'LL ANSWER IT! MIGHT BE A LEAD TO WHO THOSE THUGS WERE!

I JUST CHECKED THAT SCHEDULE FOR YOU, SIR! THE 5:10 FROM BRANDYWINE WILL BE IN ON TIME!
R.R. STATION MASTER
ER— THANKS!

EVIDENTLY OUR MYSTERIOUS FRIEND IS EXPECTING SOMEONE ON THE 5:10! WHAT PUZZLES ME, THOUGH, IS HOW HE GOT SO FAMILIAR WITH SLASHER'S DOG!
MAYBE WE OUGHT TO GO TO THE STATION FOR OUR ANSWER!

NO—FIRST WE'RE GOING TO CHECK THE ROOM WHERE SLASHER KILLED HIMSELF! I'M GETTING A LITTLE CURIOUS ABOUT THAT SUICIDE!
6

BACK AT THE SCENE OF THE SUICIDE...
DOESN'T SEEM TO BE ANYTHING OF IMPORTANCE AROUND...
WHAT'S THIS QUEER GADGET?

LOOKS LIKE THE RECEIVING END OF A BURGLAR ALARM! LET'S TRACE IT AND SEE WHERE IT'S CONNECTED!
IT GETS WACKIER AND WACKIER! WHAT WOULD A CROOK WANT WITH A BURGLAR ALARM!

THAT'S STRANGE! IT LEADS TO THE ROOF!
MAYBE SLASHER RIGGED IT UP TO KEEP HIMSELF FROM CRACKING HIS OWN SAFE!

THIS IS GETTING MORE AND MORE MYSTERIOUS! WHERE CAN IT LEAD!
IT'S A CINCH IT'S NOT BEING USED FOR A CLOTHES LINE!

IT RUNS INTO THE OLD TAYLOR HOUSE! BUT— NOBODY'S LIVED THERE FOR YEARS!
YES, IT'S SUPPOSED TO BE HAUNTED!

THE DUST ON THE FLOOR HASN'T BEEN DISTURBED FOR A LONG TIME! WHY SHOULD THE SLASHER HAVE CONNECTED A BURGLAR ALARM TO THIS OLD PLACE!
MAYBE THE CHAP WITH THE DOG COULD TELL US THAT! DO YOU THINK HE'LL BE AT THE STATION?

WE'LL GO THERE LATER! LOOK— THERE'S THE WIRE AGAIN! IT RUNS BEHIND THE WALL HERE!
PERHAPS THERE'S A SECRET PANEL!
7

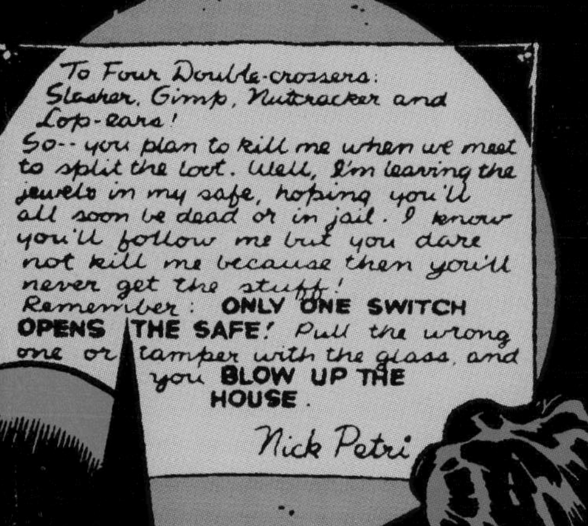

To Four Double-crossers:
Slasher, Gimp, Nutcracker and Lop-ears!
So-- you plan to kill me when we meet to split the loot. Well, I'm leaving the jewels in my safe, hoping you'll all soon be dead or in jail. I know you'll follow me but you dare not kill me because then you'll never get the stuff!
Remember: **ONLY ONE SWITCH OPENS THE SAFE!** Pull the wrong one or tamper with the glass, and you **BLOW UP THE HOUSE**.
Nick Petri

AYBE HE'S THE E BEHIND ALL S! MAYBE HE EALLY KILLED E SLASHER, ADE IT LOOK KE SUICIDE. D TIPPED F THE COPS THE HERS!

THAT'S POSSIBLE, ROBIN—BUT I DON'T THINK IT'S THE ANSWER! BUT THAT SUICIDE, I'M CONVINCED, WAS FAKED!

YOU MEAN OUR MYSTERIOUS ATTACKER WAS THE SLASHER HIMSELF!

RIGHT! THAT'S WHY THE DOG RESPONDED SO READILY! THE SLASHER MUST HAVE GOT HIS FACE FIXED UP BY A PLASTIC SURGEON! THE FELLOW WE FOUND DEAD—PROBABLY SOME HOBO—WAS KILLED AND HIS FACE CHANGED TO LOOK LIKE SLASHER'S!

8

SUDDENLY...
IT MUST BE PETRI WHO IS COMING IN ON THAT TRAIN! WHICH MEANS THE SLASHER SHOULD BE HERE SOON TO MEET- HUH?
YOU'RE TOO SMART, BATMAN! REACH!
TRAINED MUSCLES RESPONDING SWIFTLY, THE BATMAN'S TOE LASHES OUT...
CHOKE- SPLUTTER- MY EYES! I'M BLIND!
ASHES TO ASHES- YOU'RE SUPPOSED TO BE DEAD, REMEMBER?

HOW ABOUT A SHINER TO LIGHT YOUR WAY?
WATCH OUT!

THIS'LL CUT YOU DOWN TO YOUR RIGHT SIZE, BRAT!
AND THIS OUGHT TA GIVE YOU A HEADACHE!

THEY'RE OKAY, BOSS! WE TOOK CARE OF 'EM!
YEAH- LUCKY YOU HAD US POSTED IN DIFFERENT PLACES!
OW- I WUZ HIT BY A TRAIN!

DUMP 'EM BEHIND THE COAL BIN, BOYS! I GOT A SPECIAL WAY OF FINISHING THESE PESTS WHEN WE SETTLE WITH PETRI!
I HEAR SOMEBODY COMING!

IDE—QUICK! HAT MUST BE PETRI!
OH, BOY-I KIN FEEL DEM BEEOOTIFUL JOOLS BOININ' MY POCKETS RIGHT NOW!
I'M GONNA BUY ME ONE O' DEM FANCY CREAM-COLORED ROADSTERS!

UNAWARE OF THE LURKING THREAT BEHIND THE COAL BIN, A SHADOWY FIGURE STEALS SOFTLY INTO THE BASEMENT AND GLIDES TOWARD THE SAFE...
AT LAST, MY PATIENCE IS REWARDED! I SHALL BE RICH BEYOND MY WILDEST DREAMS!

O WE UMP HIM OW, BOSS?
NO, YOU FOOL! WAIT TILL HE PULLS THE RIGHT SWITCH!
WHAT A SET-UP! I'M GONNA GET ME TWO ROADSTERS!

AND SO, AFTER TWO LONG YEARS, NICK PETRI'S EAGER, TREMBLING HAND PULLS DOWN THE SECRET SWITCH!

GREEDY FINGERS DIP INTO THE GLITTERING HOARD...
AH, HOW BEAUTIFUL THEY LOOK! AND THEY'RE MINE! ALL MINE!

A FAINT SOUND BETRAYS THE MENACE APPROACHING NICK PETRI...
SO WE MEET AGAIN, EH, PETRI? AND THIS IS THE PAY-OFF! I HAD SOMEBODY TAILING YOU ALL THE TIME... THAT'S HOW I KNEW WHEN YOU'D SHOW UP!
W-WHO ARE YOU?
10

WHO AM I? HA, HA! YOUR OLD PAL, THE SLASHER! NEVER THOUGHT I'D BE READING ABOUT MY OWN FUNERAL! DIDYA SEE WHAT DE MAYOR SAID ABOUT ME? HO, HO! ME—A GHOST WHAT'S SOON GONNA LAY HIS HANDS ON A MILLION CLAMS!

I'VE DONE THIS OFTEN IN MY DREAMS!
AAAGH!

CRAZED WITH GREED, THE CROOKS DO NOT NOTICE A LOW MOAN FROM THE COAL BIN...
OOW— MY HEAD! GOT TO WAKE UP THE BATMAN!

BATMAN— COME OUT OF IT!
ROBIN— ARE YOU ALL RIGHT?

NOW'S OUR CHANCE!
WORKED JUST AS I PLANNED! THE BIGGEST HAUL OF MY CAREER!
I'LL BE THE ROCKYFELLER OF DE POOL-ROOMS!

SWIFT AND SURE, THE TWIN AVENGERS LEAP INTO ACTION!
I CAN RETIRE NOW— WHA! THEY'RE CONSCIOUS!
DIS TIME YER A DEAD PIGEON, BATMAN!

SPEAKING OF BIRDS, CROW OVER THIS!
THIS'LL SEND YA FLYIN'!
ROBIN'S A TOUGH BIRD, TOO!
11

BUT, HEEDLESS OF THE WARNING, BATMAN ADVANCES TOWARD THE DESPERATE CROOK!

THIS IS MY LAST WARNING! STAND BACK!

HE'LL DO IT, BATMAN! STOP!

No.98
NEEDS YOUR SUPPORT!
A SUPERMAN DC PUBLICATION
The BATMAN
Detective
APRIL
TEN CENTS
COMIC

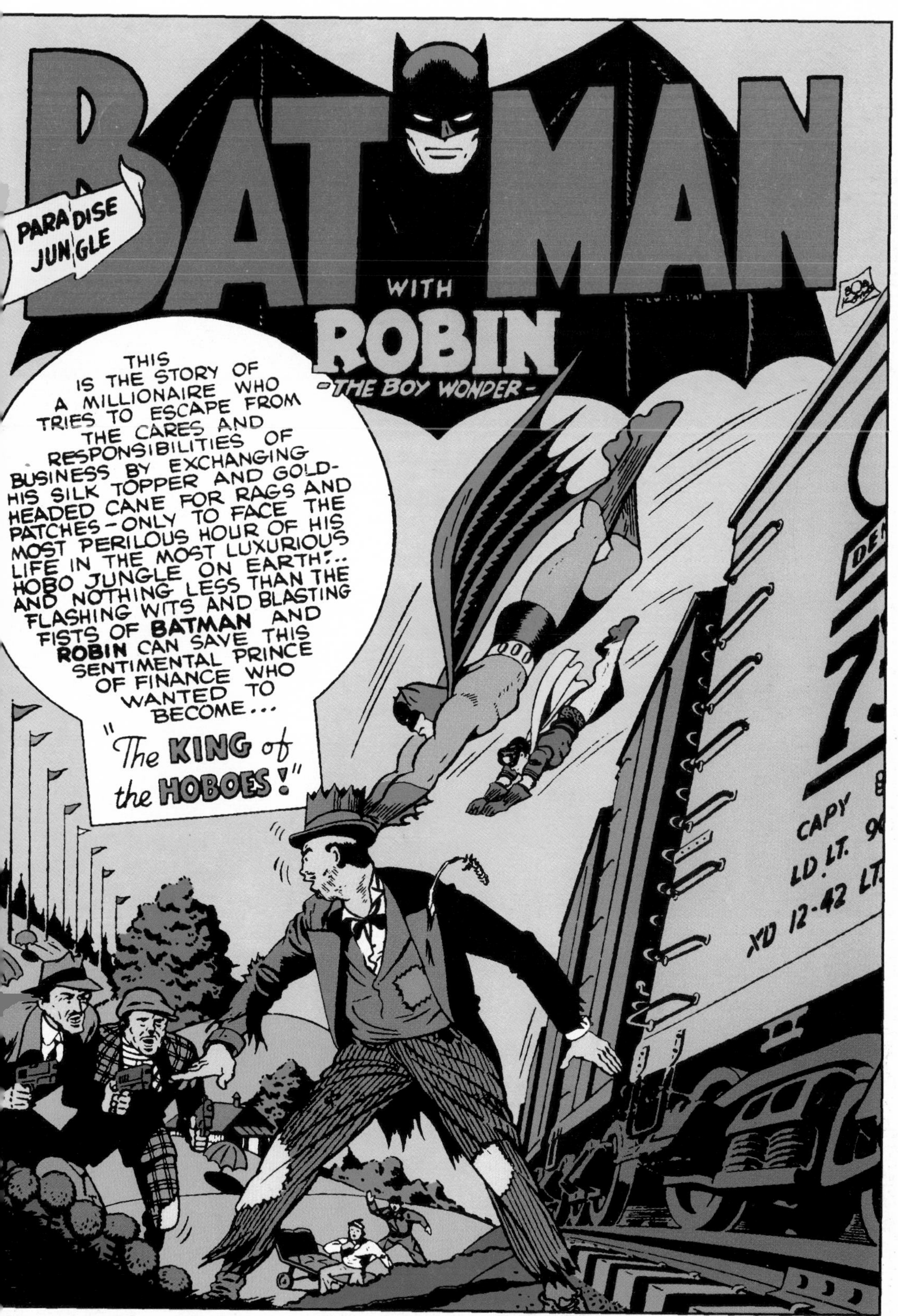
PARADISE JUNGLE
BATMAN
WITH
ROBIN
-THE BOY WONDER-
THIS IS THE STORY OF A MILLIONAIRE WHO TRIES TO ESCAPE FROM THE CARES AND RESPONSIBILITIES OF BUSINESS BY EXCHANGING HIS SILK TOPPER AND GOLD-HEADED CANE FOR RAGS AND PATCHES-ONLY TO FACE THE MOST PERILOUS HOUR OF HIS LIFE IN THE MOST LUXURIOUS HOBO JUNGLE ON EARTH!.. AND NOTHING LESS THAN THE FLASHING WITS AND BLASTING FISTS OF BATMAN AND ROBIN CAN SAVE THIS SENTIMENTAL PRINCE OF FINANCE WHO WANTED TO BECOME...
"The KING of the HOBOES!"
CAPY
LD. LT.
XD 12-42 LT.

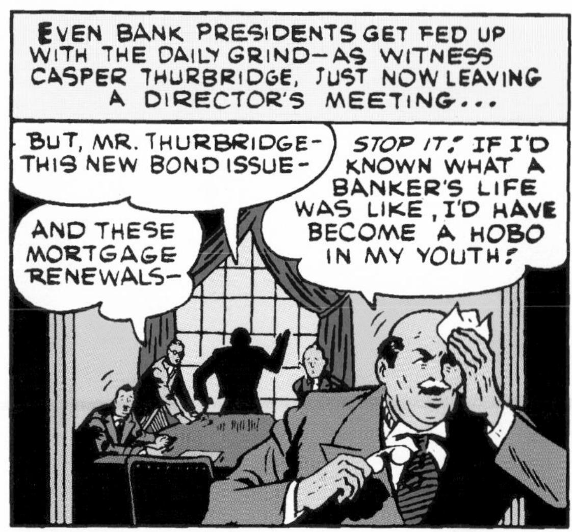
EVEN BANK PRESIDENTS GET FED UP WITH THE DAILY GRIND—AS WITNESS CASPER THURBRIDGE, JUST NOW LEAVING A DIRECTOR'S MEETING...
BUT, MR. THURBRIDGE- THIS NEW BOND ISSUE-
AND THESE MORTGAGE RENEWALS-
STOP IT! IF I'D KNOWN WHAT A BANKER'S LIFE WAS LIKE, I'D HAVE BECOME A HOBO IN MY YOUTH!

FATEFUL WORDS- FOR A MOMENT LATER
WORRY—WORRY— NOTHING BUT WORRY!
I SAID, COULD YA KINDLY SPARE A FEW PENNIES FOR A GENT IN DISTRESS T'ROUGH NO FAULT OF HIS OWN!
EH?...

OF COURSE, MY GOOD MAN- BUT FIRST WALK WITH ME IN THE PARK AND TALK ABOUT ANYTHING EXCEPT BUSINESS! YOU DON'T KNOW HOW I ENVY YOU!
HUH?.. YOU ENVY ME— FRISCO FRED, WHAT AIN'T HAD A SQUARE MEAL IN T'REE MONT'S?

MEALS! BAH! HUNGER WOULD BE A DELIGHT COMPARED WITH TAXES, INTEREST, CONTRACTS- A MILLION DETAILS OF BUSINESS IN WHICH I'M NOT THE LEAST INTERESTED!
CHEE— I NEVER KNEW BEIN' RICH WAS AS BAD AS ALL DAT!

FOR YEARS I'VE DREAMED OF CHUCKING IT ALL FOR THE CAREFREE LIFE OF A KNIGHT OF THE ROAD!
AN' FOR YEARS I'V WISHED I COULD DRES UP SWELL LIK YOU AN' CARR A REAL BANKROLL—JUS ONCE!

AIN'T IT FUNNY, YOU WISHIN' YOU WAS ME, AN' ME WISHIN' I WAS YOU?
FUNNY? IT'S MIRACULOUS! WHY CAN'T I LEAVE MY BANK IN THE HANDS OF MY TWELVE VICE-PRESIDENTS AND TAKE A VACATION WITH YOU, NOT TELLING ANYONE-?

THEN, WHEN WE CAME BACK, I COULD GIVE YOU A GOOD JOB, AND—
ME, A REAL BANKER? IF YOU'RE KIDDIN'- STOP! I COULDN BEAR IT!

STRANGE AND
ONTRADICTORY
RE THE AMBITIONS
OF MEN! THE
OOR DREAM OF
ICHES, WHILE THE
VEALTHY OFTEN
YEARN FOR A
IMPLER LIFE
HAN THE CARES
F BUSINESS AND
SOCIETY WILL
PERMIT!...

AND THERE ARE
SOME...

...LIKE SILVERS SILKE, WHOSE ONE DESIRE IS TO PROFIT AT THE EXPENSE OF OTHERS!...
CASPER THURBRIDGE, THE BANK PRESIDENT! MAYBE THIS IS THE BREAK I'VE BEEN LOOKING FOR!

A WEEK PASSES—AND LATE ONE NIGHT...
ARE WE GOING TO TAKE A LOOK AT THURBRIDGE'S HOUSE AGAIN TONIGHT, BATMAN?
YES, ROBIN! TONIGHT AND EVERY NIGHT, TILL SOMETHING TURNS UP TO EXPLAIN HIS STRANGE DISAPPEARANCE!

THERE IT IS—AND APPARENTLY IT HASN'T BEEN USED OR OPENED SINCE HE VANISHED!

BUT EVEN AT THAT MOMENT, BEHIND THE CLOSED SHUTTERS OF THE BANKER'S MANSION...
EASY, SOAPY! DON'T LET THAT OXYACETYLENE FLAME GO THROUGH AND BURN UP WHAT'S INSIDE!
ARE YOU TRYIN' TA TELL ME MY OWN BUSINESS, SILVERS?

AIN'T SEEN O MUCH UGH SINCE E BLEW UP T ARMORED RUCK!
THURBRIDGE SAID HE KEPT FIFTY GRAND HERE! IF THE COUNT'S RIGHT, YOU'VE GOT TEN GRAND COMING WHEN WE GET BACK TO THE JUNGLE, SQUINT—AND SOAPY GETS ANOTHER TEN!

AS THE ROBBERS DEPART...
NOT SO FAST, SILVERS! WE DON'T WANTA LOSE YA WHILE YA'RE LUGGIN' DA SWAG!
SH-H-H!
BATMAN—LOOK!
3

SUDDENLY...
WELL!
BATMAN!

I'VE GOT SOMETHING RIGHT HERE FOR YOU, BATMAN!
AND I'VE GOT SOMETHING FOR YOU!

LIKE IT?

YOUSE GUYS CAN'T WIN ALL DA TIME!
MAYBE NOT, CHUM—

—BUT SO FAR, WE HAVEN'T DONE TOO BADLY!
I'LL SHOW YOU GUYS A HOT TIME!

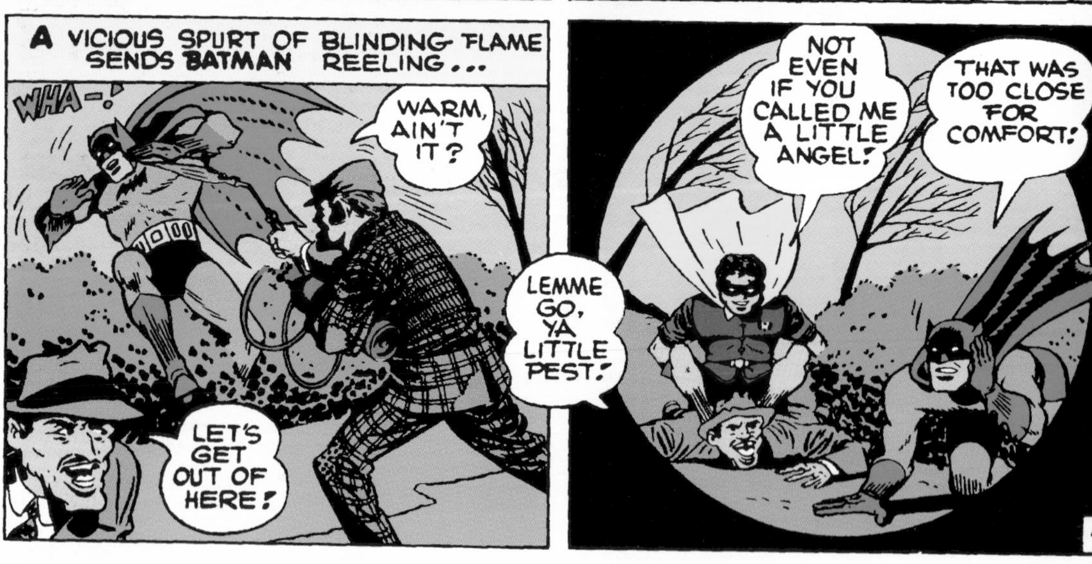
A VICIOUS SPURT OF BLINDING FLAME SENDS BATMAN REELING...
WHA—!
WARM, AIN'T IT?
LET'S GET OUT OF HERE!
LEMME GO, YA LITTLE PEST!
NOT EVEN IF YOU CALLED ME A LITTLE ANGEL!
THAT WAS TOO CLOSE FOR COMFORT!

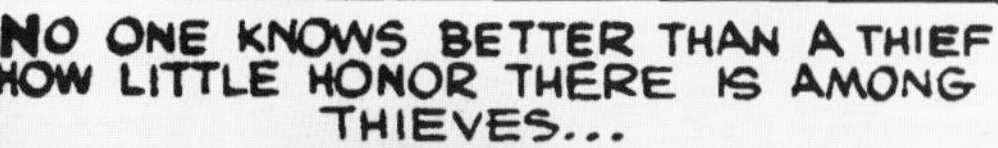

NO ONE KNOWS BETTER THAN A THIEF HOW LITTLE HONOR THERE IS AMONG THIEVES...

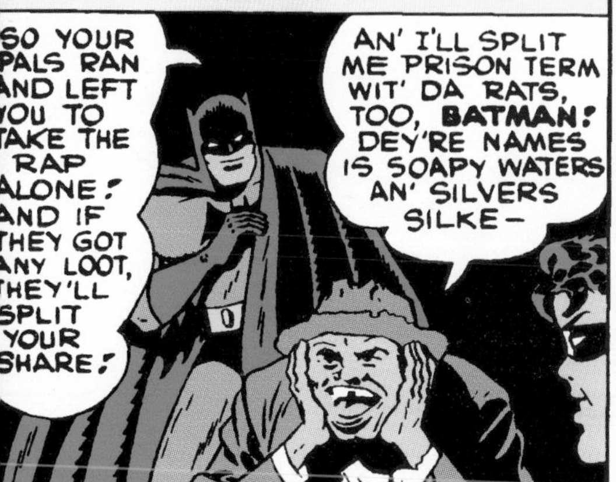

SO YOUR PALS RAN AND LEFT YOU TO TAKE THE RAP ALONE! AND IF THEY GOT ANY LOOT, THEY'LL SPLIT YOUR SHARE!
AN' I'LL SPLIT ME PRISON TERM WIT' DA RATS, TOO, BATMAN! DEY'RE NAMES IS SOAPY WATERS AN' SILVERS SILKE—

—AN' WE WERE GONNA HIDE OUT IN A FANCY HOBO PARK CALLED PARADISE JUNGLE! I DON'T KNOW WHERE IT IS, BUT—
A HOBO JUNGLE, EH?

LATER, IN THE BRUCE WAYNE HOME, ALFRED, THE BUTLER, RELUCTANTLY HELPS HIS MASTERS CHANGE INTO COSTUMES OF WHICH HE DOES NOT APPROVE...

BEGGIN' YOUR PARDON, SIRS—BUT YOU CAWN'T ACTUALLY INTEND TO WEAR THOSE HORRIBLE GARMENTS IN PUBLIC!
DON'T WORRY, ALFRED! THEY'LL BE THE LATEST STYLE WHERE WE'RE GOING!
BESIDES, WE'RE WEARING OUR FIGHTING TOGS UNDERNEATH!

AND STILL LATER, AS A LONG FREIGHT TRAIN RUMBLES THROUGH THE OUTSKIRTS OF GOTHAM CITY...

CAREFUL, FELLA! THIS IS DANGEROUS BUSINESS!
IF IT WASN'T, IT WOULDN'T BE HALF AS MUCH FUN!

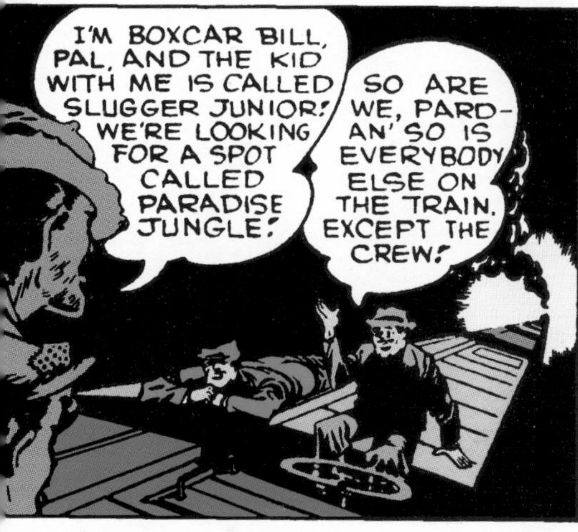

I'M BOXCAR BILL, PAL, AND THE KID WITH ME IS CALLED SLUGGER JUNIOR! WE'RE LOOKING FOR A SPOT CALLED PARADISE JUNGLE!
SO ARE WE, PARD— AN' SO IS EVERYBODY ELSE ON THE TRAIN, EXCEPT THE CREW!

WE'RE ANXIOUS TA GET THERE WHILE THERE'S STILL ROOM LEFT!
THEY SAY ALL THE HOBOES WHAT'S SEEN IT WANTA SETTLE THERE FOR LIFE!
IF IT'S THAT GOOD, MAYBE EVEN RICH FOLKS WILL BE FIGHTING TO GET IN!
5

PARADISE JUNGLE—A HOBO HAVEN SUCH AS NO ONE HAS EVER SEEN BEFORE—WHOSE FAME HAS ALREADY, IN A FEW DAYS, SPREAD FAR AND WIDE AMONG THE BRETHREN OF THE ROAD! ... THE LONG TRAIN RUMBLES THROUGH THE NIGHT, BEARING THE DISGUISED **BATMAN** AND **ROBIN** AMONG OTHER UNINVITED PASSENGERS—AND SHORTLY AFTER SUNRISE A GREAT SHOUT GOES UP!..

WHEE! WE'RE THERE!
I CAN HARDLY WAIT!
WELCOME KNIGHTS OF THE ROAD TO PARADISE JUNGLE 1 MI. AHEAD!!

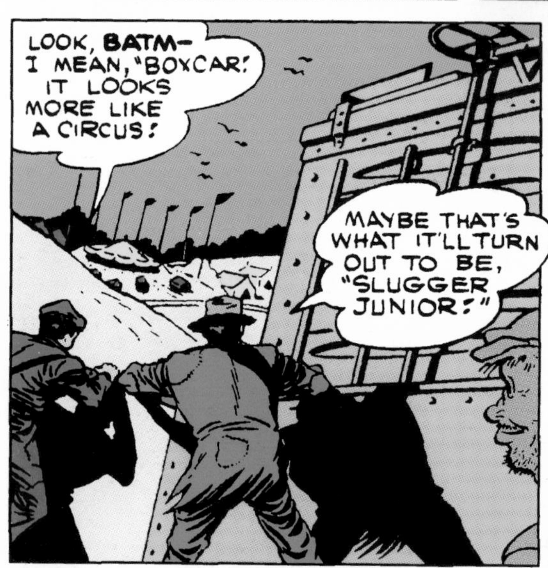
LOOK, BATM— I MEAN, "BOXCAR!" IT LOOKS MORE LIKE A CIRCUS!
MAYBE THAT'S WHAT IT'LL TURN OUT TO BE, "SLUGGER JUNIOR!"

THIS WAY, 'BOES! EVERYBODY'S WELCOME, AN' EVERYT'ING IS FREE!
CHEE—LIKE DA BIG ROCK CANDY MOUNTAINS! YIPPEEE!
REFR HMENTS

PINCH ME, "BOXCAR," I THINK I'M DREAMING!
FREE CANDY
COMMISSARY HANDOUTS FREE!
I'M BUSY PINCHING MYSELF!

'BOES, MEET CASPER DA COASTER—KING O' PARADISE JUNGLE, AN' MAYBE SOME DAY KING O' DA HOBOES EVERYWHERE!
MAKE YOURSELVES AT HOME, MY FRIENDS!
IT'S CASPER THURBRIDGE I'M BEGINNING TO UNDERSTAND
6

ME, I'M FRISCO FRED, RIGHT-HAND MAN FOR ME PAL CASPER! NY OFFICIAL BUSINESS A GOT, YA CAN TAKE T UP WIT' ME FIRST!
MAYBE WE'D BETTER FIND OUT WHAT THIS IS ALL ABOUT FROM THE ELEGANT FRISCO, EH?

TAILOR SHOP
YOU BRING THE BUTTON-WE SEW ON THE PANTS -FREE!!
ME, I'M DA GUY WHAT BROUGHT CASPER DA COASTER HERE! HE WAS WALKING DOWN A STREET IN GOTHAM CITY, ALL DRESSED UP AN' MISERABLE, AN'—
THEN PARADISE JUNGLE WAS YOUR IDEA?

AT GUY IN DA HAMMOCK RODE IT' US IN DA SAME SIDE-DOOR ULLMAN! HE SOLD CASPER N DA IDEA O' FIXIN' P DIS PLACE!
WHY, IT'S—
HOLD IT, SLUGGER!

CASPER HAD A MONEY-BELT FULLA CASH, AN' HE SPENT IT ALL FIXIN' UP DIS JOINT! DEN DIS GUY—SILVERS IS HIS NAME— GOT HIM T'NKIN' HE OUGHTTA FIX UP A WHOLE CHAIN O' JUNGLES LIKE DIS ACROSS DA COUNTRY!

CASPER SAID HE HAD CASH IN DA BANK AN' FIFTY GRAND IN A WALL SAFE AT HOME—BUT HE WASN'T GONNA GET IT FOR AWHILE, ON ACCOUNT HIS PALS'D T'INK HE WAS CRAZY IF DEY KNEW WHAT HE WAS UP TO!
HMM...

ELL CASPER HE WON'T AVE TO WORRY ABOUT E CASH FROM HIS ALL SAFE! SILVERS ROUGHT IT HERE TO HIM!
OH, BOY!

DIDN'T YOU, SILVERS?
HEY! WHAT'S GOIN' ON?
7

YOU DO GET AROUND, DON'T YOU?
IF IT ISN'T OUR OUR OLD FRIEND, THE TORCH-BEARER!
HUH?
NEAT THINKING, SLUGGER JUNIOR!
MOVE OVER— AND COOL OFF!
OOPS! RIGHT IN A BED OF NETTLES!
YIIIII!
CEASE! STOP IT! VIOLENCE IS NOT PERMITTED IN PARADISE JUNGLE!
SORRY, YOUR MAJESTY- BUT THIS MONEY IS THE RESULT OF CONSIDERABLE VIOLENCE DONE BY THESE TWO GENTLEMEN TO THE WALL SAFE IN YOUR HOME IN GOTHAM CITY!
MONEY?..MY WALL SAFE?... I REMEMBER MENTIONING IT TO HIM—BUT—
SLUGGER JUNIOR AND I WERE PASSING YOUR PLACE WHEN WE SAW THESE TWO RUN OUT, AFTER A SCRAP WITH BATMAN! YOU CAN READ ABOUT THE ROBBERY IN THE NEWSPAPERS!
IT MUST BE TRUE... I REMEMBER THIS THOUSAND-DOLLAR BILL WITH THE INK-STAIN ON THE CORNER!
BUT-BUT I WAS JUST BRINGING THE DOUGH TO YOU, SO WE COULD USE IT FOR-
NO USE LYING. I SEE IT ALL NOW!
WH-WHAT HAPPENED?
GET OUT, AND DON'T COME BACK! YOU'RE LUCKY I'M NOT TURNING YOU OVER TO THE AUTHORITIES!
I STILL DON'T UNDERSTAND WHAT HAPPENED!
WAIT, FELLA! WE'RE GOING AFTER THEM— BUT NOT AS BOXCAR BILL AND SLUGGER JUNIOR!
8

NCE BEYOND THE MITS OF PARADISE JUNGLE...
REN'T YOU ISE TO WHO THOSE EDDLERS ERE, SOAPY- HE BIG ELLA ND THE KID?
YA MEAN- BATMAN AN' ROBIN? CHEE- WE'RE LUCKY WE GOT OUTA THERE AT ALL!

LUCKY, NOTHING! I COULD HAVE TAKEN OLD THURBRIDGE FOR HALF A MILLION AT LEAST- AND MAYBE I WILL YET!
YA MEAN- WE'RE GOIN' BACK? NOT ME- NOT WHILE DEM TWO BUNDLES O' DYNAMITE IS STILL AROUND!
245

OH, THEY WON'T BE THERE! SEE- THEY'RE COMING AFTER US NOW, AS I THOUGHT THEY WOULD!
OOHH!.. WHAT ARE WE STANDIN' HERE FOR?...

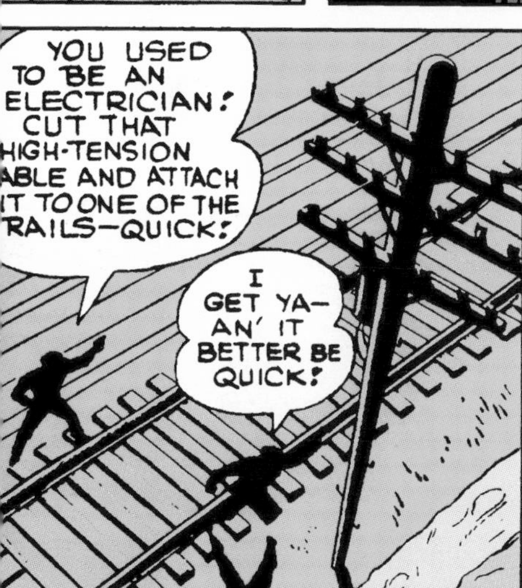
YOU USED TO BE AN ELECTRICIAN! CUT THAT HIGH-TENSION ABLE AND ATTACH IT TO ONE OF THE RAILS-QUICK!
I GET YA- AN' IT BETTER BE QUICK!

ONCE MORE WEARING THE CAPED UNIFORMS THAT HAVE STRUCK TERROR TO THE HEARTS OF COUNTLESS CRIMINALS, THE DYNAMIC DUO SIGHTS THE ENEMY...
THERE THEY ARE-BUT WHAT ARE THEY DOING?
PROBABLY TRYING TO GET THAT MOTOR-SCOOTER STARTED FOR THEIR GETAWAY!

ND CHARGES!
OME ON! E'RE READY FOR YOU!
CAREFUL, ROBIN! THEY'VE GOT SOME TRICK UP THEIR SLEEVES!
YAAA! WHO'S A-SCARED O' DA BIG, BAD BATMAN?

SUDDENLY...
HAW, HAW, HAW! JUST LIKE DA ELECTRIC CHAIR-ONLY YA TAKE IT STANDIN' UP!
9

JOLTED INTO UNCONSCIOUSNESS BY THE POWERFUL CURRENT, **BATMAN** AND **ROBIN** ARE LASHED TO THE RAILROAD SCOOTER...

A NEW WAY O' TAKIN' TROUBLE-MAKERS FOR A RIDE—EH, SILVERS!

SHUT UP AND GET THAT THING STARTED! THE WESTERN LIMITED WILL COME THROUGH ON THIS TRACK IN TEN MINUTES!

A GASOLINE MOTOR SPUTTERS...A TINY CAR MOVES OVER SHINING RAILS, GATHERING SPEED IN A SPINE-TINGLING RACE TOWARD DEATH.. AND WHEN CONSCIOUSNESS RETURNS TO **BATMAN**...

HUH?.. I'M TIED—AND WE'RE MOVING FAST!... ROBIN!

SCANT MINUTES MEASURE THEIR CHANCES...

ROBIN'S STILL UNCONSCIOUS AND—**GREAT SCOTT!** A PASSENGER TRAIN COMING STRAIGHT FOR US!

A HAND-OPERATED SWITCH! IF ONLY I CAN REACH THE TOOLBOX— AH—THE ROPE IS LOOSENING A LITTLE!...
THE SWITCH TURNS!.. BUT IS THERE TIME?
IF ONLY WE MAKE IT, I CAN WORK MY WAY OUT OF THESE ROPES IN A MINUTE OR TWO...

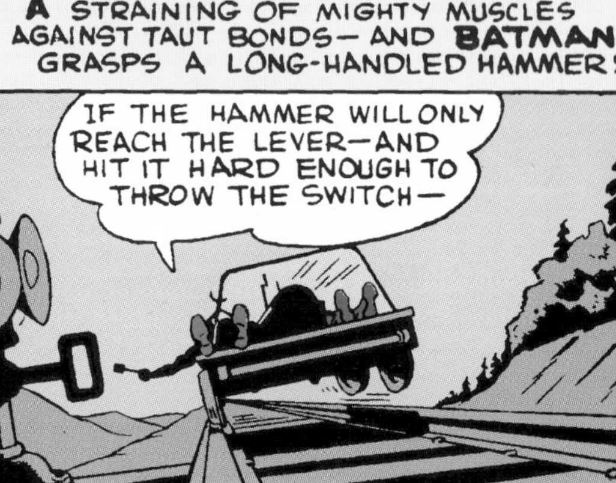

A STRAINING OF MIGHTY MUSCLES AGAINST TAUT BONDS—AND BATMAN GRASPS A LONG-HANDLED HAMMER!
IF THE HAMMER WILL ONLY REACH THE LEVER—AND HIT IT HARD ENOUGH TO THROW THE SWITCH—

IN THE NEXT SPLIT SECOND..

MEANWHILE, THE EXILES HAVE RETURNED TO PARADISE JUNGLE TO DAZZLE WITH ELOQUENT LIES THE WITS OF NEWCOMERS, WHO KNOW LITTLE OR NOTHING OF THE TRUTH OF THE MATTER...

YOU SAW 'EM YOURSELVES, GRABBIN' THE DOUGH I WAS GOING TO USE TO MAKE THINGS NICER HERE! IT WAS ME STARTED PARADISE JUNGLE—AND CASPER THE COASTER IS TRYING TO TAKE THE CREDIT—AND THE CASH!

HE'S THE ONE OUGHTTA BE KICKED OUT!

LIKE MANY ANOTHER KING BEFORE HIM, CASPER IS FRIGHTENED AND BEWILDERED AT THE APPROACH OF AN ANGRY MOB...
ARE YA GONNA LET DA RAT GET AWAY WIT IT?
WE'LL DUMP HIM IN DA CREEK!
GENTLEMEN! WH-WHAT'S THE TROUBLE?
NO!
WE LL RIDE HIM ON A RAIL!

REMEMBERING THAT LYNCHINGS HAVE GROWN OUT OF JUST SUCH SMALL BEGINNINGS AS THIS, THE SELF-STYLED KING OF THE HOBOES KNOWS REAL TERROR FOR THE FIRST TIME IN HIS LIFE!

WE'LL LOCK HIM IN A REFRIGERATOR CAR!

JUST TIE HIM UP—AND LEAVE HIM TO SOAPY AN' ME!

WE'LL LYNCH HIM!

NO! NO! I ONLY WANT TO BE YOUR FRIEND!

BUT THE NEXT INSTANT...
WHAT'S THIS? REBELLION IN PARADISE JUNGLE?
BATMAN AND ROBIN!
IT'S DEM—OR GHOSTS!

YOU CAN CRACK A SAFE—BUT I CAN CRACK A JAW!
COME ON, YOU GUYS! WE CAN HANDLE EM!
NUTTIN' DOIN'! WHATEVER SIDE BATMAN IS ON IS DA RIGHT SIDE—AN' DAT'S OUR SIDE TOO!

THIS TIME I'LL GET YOU!
HUH?...
BATMAN—LOOK OUT!
11

THANKS, ROBIN!
DON'T MENTION IT, BATMAN!

SILVERS AND SOAPY ARE COMMON THIEVES- AND YOU'VE LET THEM MAKE PLAIN, ORDINARY FOOLS OF YOU!
DAT'S WHAT I BEEN TRYIN' TA TELL 'EM, BATMAN!

AS FOR CASPER THE COASTER - HE'S A MILLIONAIR WHO WANTED TO GIVE YO SOME OF THE COMFORTS AND LUXURIES YOU'VE MISSED, IN RETURN FOR YOUR FRIENDSHIP!
AN' SEE HOW YA TREATED HIM! HE OUGHTTA WASH HIS HANDS O' DA LOT O' YA!

NO, FRISCO! THEY DIDN'T KNOW HOW IT WAS! I'M GOING AHEAD WITH THE PARADISE JUNGLES PROJECT- BUT AFTER THIS EXPERIENCE, PERHAPS I'D BETTER DO IT FROM MY OFFICE IN THE BANK!
HOORAY FOR CASPER DA COASTER!

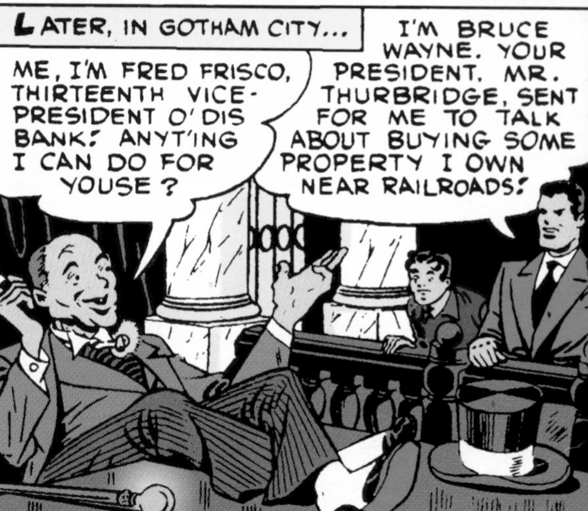
LATER, IN GOTHAM CITY...
I'M BRUCE WAYNE. YOUR PRESIDENT, MR. THURBRIDGE, SENT FOR ME TO TALK ABOUT BUYING SOME PROPERTY I OWN NEAR RAILROADS!
ME, I'M FRED FRISCO, THIRTEENTH VICE-PRESIDENT O' DIS BANK! ANYT'ING I CAN DO FOR YOUSE?

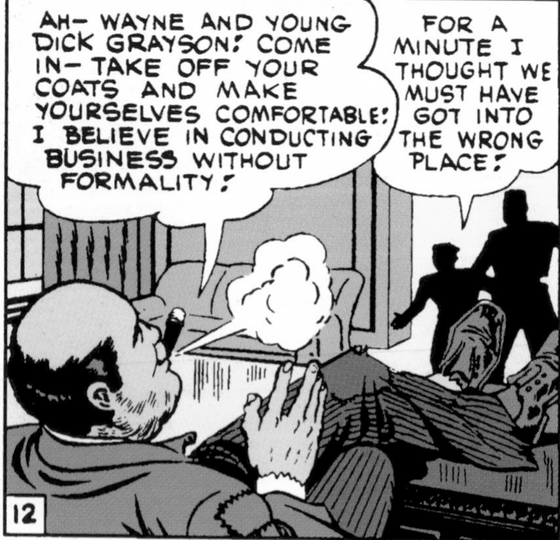
AH- WAYNE AND YOUNG DICK GRAYSON! COME IN- TAKE OFF YOUR COATS AND MAKE YOURSELVES COMFORTABLE! I BELIEVE IN CONDUCTING BUSINESS WITHOUT FORMALITY!
FOR A MINUTE I THOUGHT WE MUST HAVE GOT INTO THE WRONG PLACE!
12

YOU SEE, I'VE ALWAYS HAD A SOFT SPOT IN MY HEART FOR HOBOES! AND I THOUGHT, IF I COULD BUY YOUR PROPERTY TO USE FOR-
DON'T SAY IT! LET ME GUESS! AND YOU CAN HAVE IT AT YOUR OWN PRICE, MR. THURBRIDGE!
MAYBE WE CAN SPEND OUR VACATIO THERE, EH, BRUCE
THE END

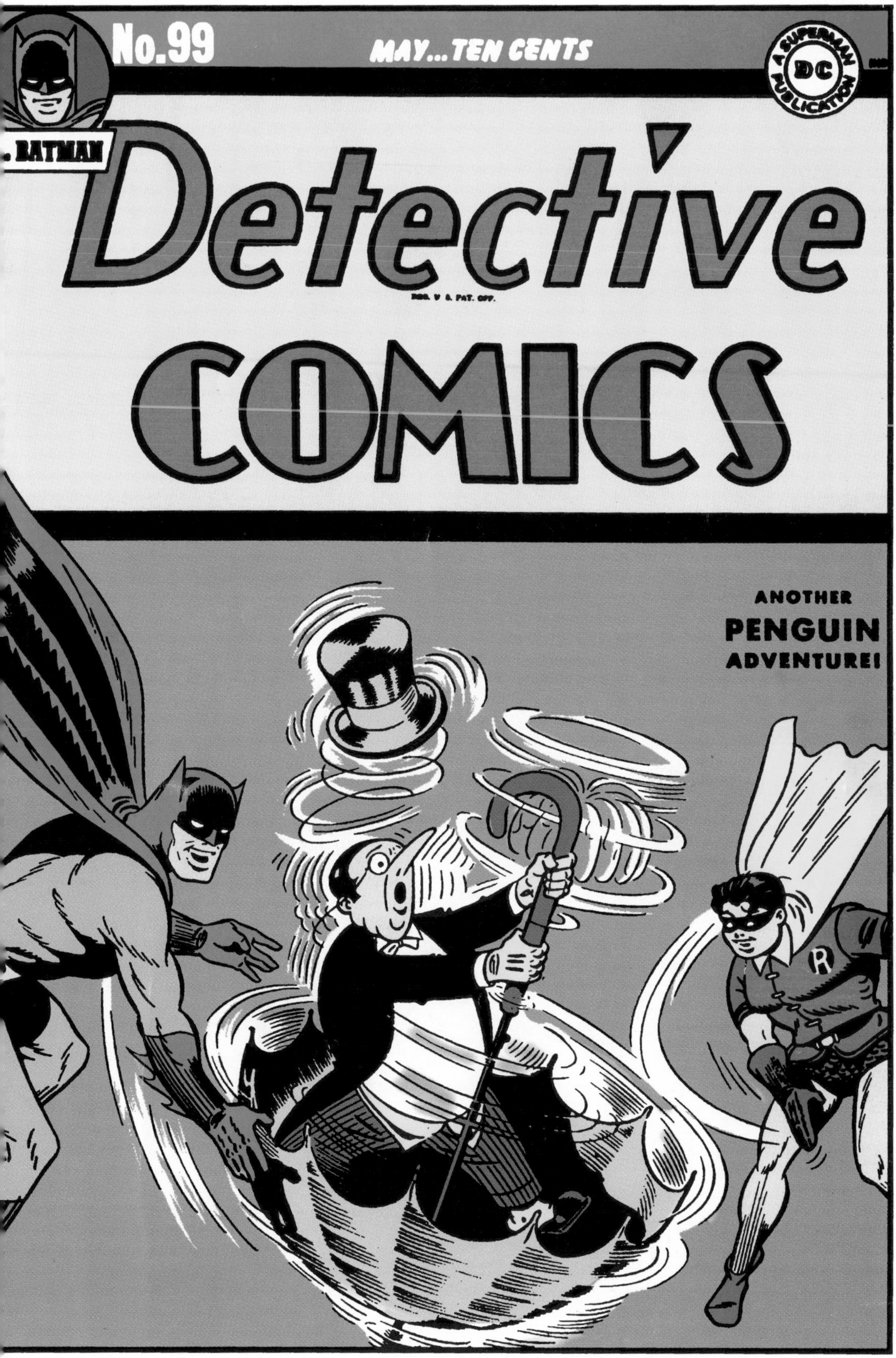

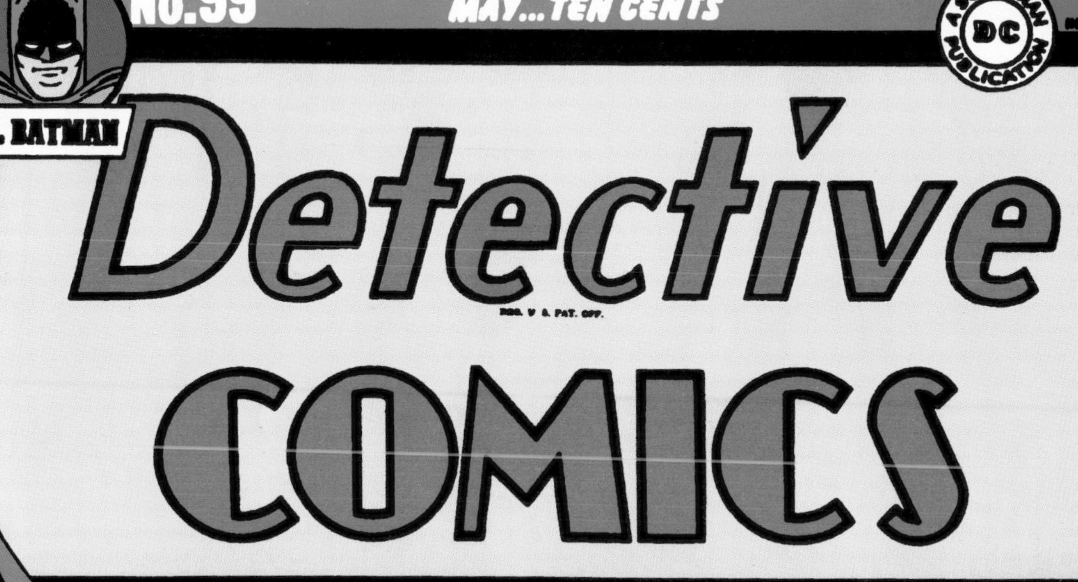
No.99
MAY...TEN CENTS
A SUPERMAN PUBLICATION
DC
BATMAN
Detective
COMICS
ANOTHER
PENGUIN
ADVENTURE!

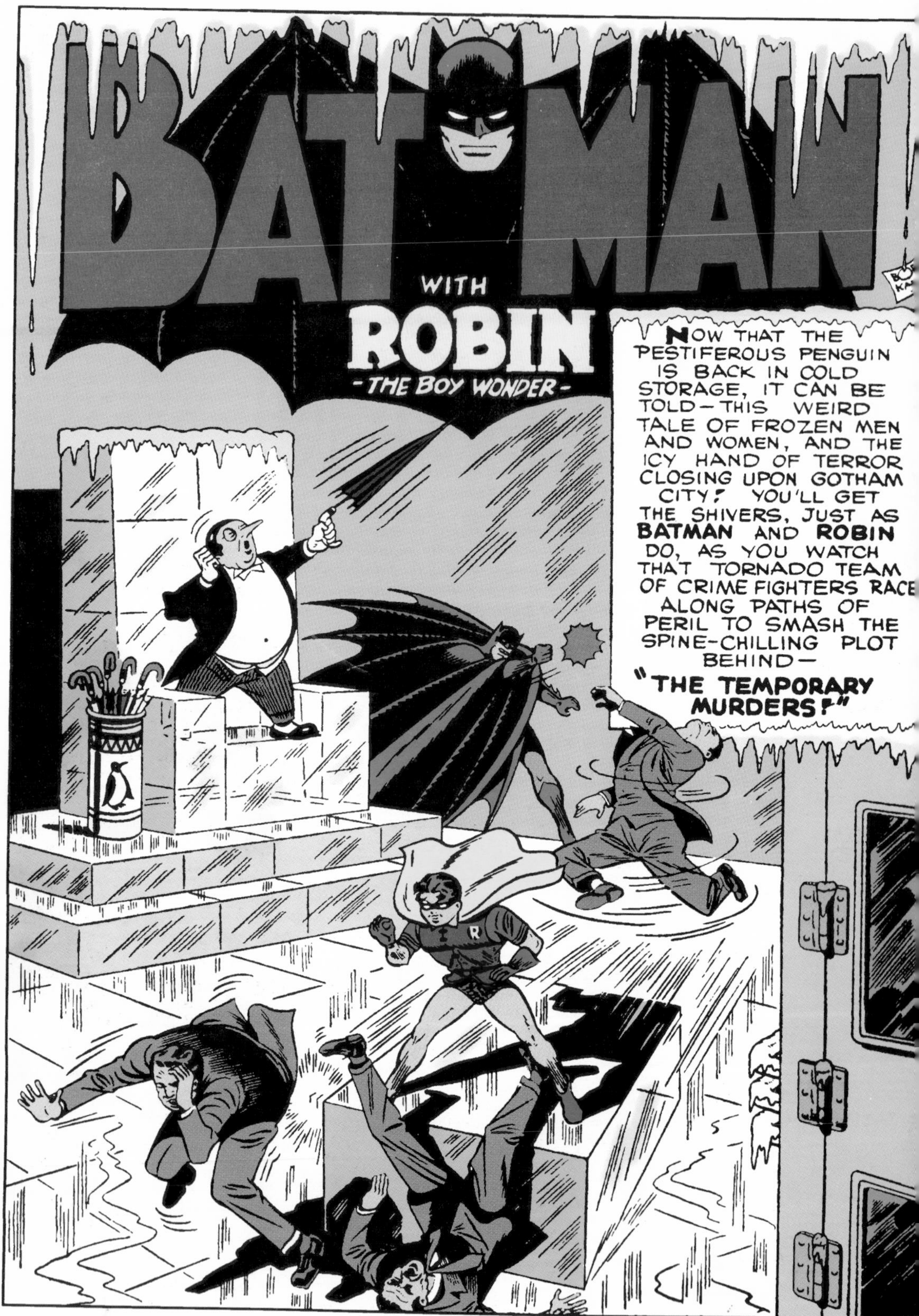
BATMAN
WITH
ROBIN
-THE BOY WONDER-
NOW THAT THE PESTIFEROUS PENGUIN IS BACK IN COLD STORAGE, IT CAN BE TOLD—THIS WEIRD TALE OF FROZEN MEN AND WOMEN, AND THE ICY HAND OF TERROR CLOSING UPON GOTHAM CITY! YOU'LL GET THE SHIVERS, JUST AS BATMAN AND ROBIN DO, AS YOU WATCH THAT TORNADO TEAM OF CRIME FIGHTERS RACE ALONG PATHS OF PERIL TO SMASH THE SPINE-CHILLING PLOT BEHIND—
"THE TEMPORARY MURDERS!"

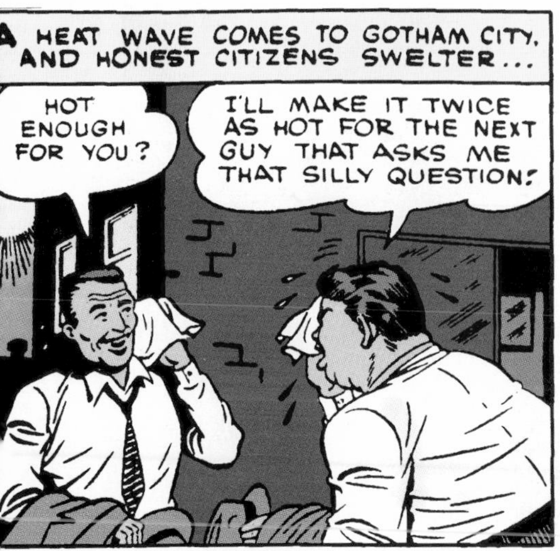
A HEAT WAVE COMES TO GOTHAM CITY, AND HONEST CITIZENS SWELTER...
HOT ENOUGH FOR YOU?
I'LL MAKE IT TWICE AS HOT FOR THE NEXT GUY THAT ASKS ME THAT SILLY QUESTION!

BUT LOOK AT THESE MEN!
BRRR! I BET IT'S WARMER AT THE NORTH POLE!
AN HOUR AGO YOU WERE SQUAWKIN' ABOUT THE HEAT, JIMJAM!
AT LAST. THE BOSS IS COMIN'!

OUR THIRD AND AST DELIVERY FOR ODAY IS READY, GENTLEMEN!
THAT'S GOOD, PENGUIN! IT'S COMFORTIN' TO KNOW SOMEBODY IS COLDER'N ME!
ORK!
ORKLE!

HANDLE IT CAREFULLY! IT'S BRITTLE, YOU KNOW!
ALL I NEED TO KNOW IS THAT IT'S WORTH FIFTY GRAND!
WE JUST LEAVE IT AT THE EXPRESS OFFICE, LIKE THE OTHERS, HUH?

HE PENGUIN, BIRD OF LL OMEN, CHORTLES APPILY AS HE LEAVES HE FRIGID ROOM...
HA, HA, HA! OF ALL HE CLEVER CRIMES MY GENIUS HAS ONTRIVED, THIS IS THE LEVEREST! RICHES ND POWER ARE JUST ROUND THE CORNER!

AND ENTERS A PALACE OF ICE, COLD AS THE HEART WITHIN HIM!
AND WHAT A HIDEOUT I'VE PICKED FOR MYSELF! IT'S FOOLPROOF, POLICE-PROOF— AND BATMAN-PROOF!
ORK!
2

ON THIS VERY DAY, BRUCE WAYNE ATTENDS A DIRECTORS' MEETING OF A SHIPPING COMPANY IN WHICH HE IS FINANCIALLY INTERESTED...
WHAT'S KEEPING ROGERS? HE'S NEARLY 40 MINUTES LATE!
MAYBE THE HEAT WAS TOO MUCH FOR HIM!
PRESENTLY...
WHAT'S THIS? YOU MEN WANT THE SHIPPING ROOM IN THE BASEMENT!
WRONG, BROTHER! OUR ORDERS WERE TO DELIVER THIS TO THE DIRECTOR'S ROOM!
SOMETHING ABOUT THE SIZE AND SHAPE OF THAT BOX GIVES ME A SHIVERY FEELING!

HURRY UP! I'M CURIOUS!
WHATEVER IS INSIDE IS PACKED IN SAWDUST!
I'LL TAKE A LOOK AT THIS NOTE THAT WAS TACKED TO THE BOX!
GREAT CAESAR! IT'S ROGERS— AND HE'S COLD AS ICE!
DEAD!
NOT NECESSARILY DEAD! LISTEN TO THIS!

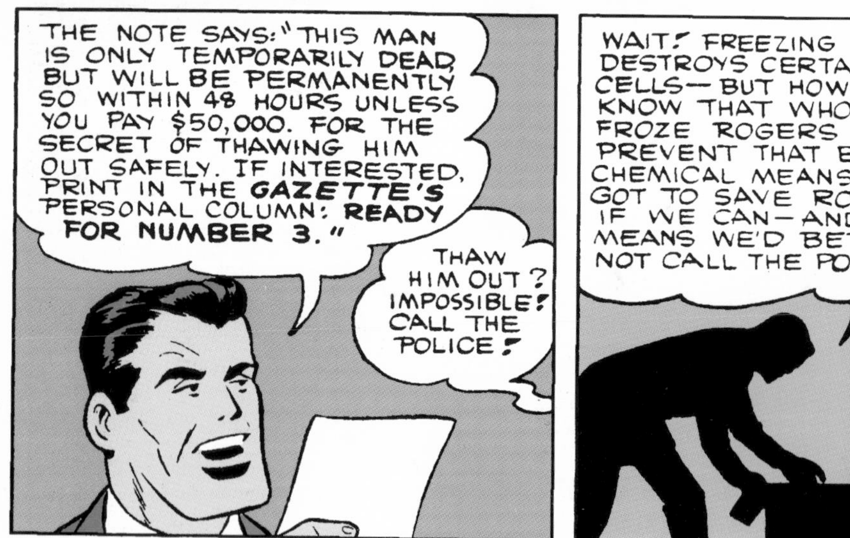
THE NOTE SAYS: "THIS MAN IS ONLY TEMPORARILY DEAD, BUT WILL BE PERMANENTLY SO WITHIN 48 HOURS UNLESS YOU PAY $50,000. FOR THE SECRET OF THAWING HIM OUT SAFELY. IF INTERESTED, PRINT IN THE GAZETTE'S PERSONAL COLUMN: READY FOR NUMBER 3."
THAW HIM OUT? IMPOSSIBLE! CALL THE POLICE!

WAIT! FREEZING USUALLY DESTROYS CERTAIN BLOOD CELLS— BUT HOW DO WE KNOW THAT WHOEVER FROZE ROGERS DIDN'T PREVENT THAT BY SOME CHEMICAL MEANS? WE'VE GOT TO SAVE ROGERS IF WE CAN— AND THAT MEANS WE'D BETTER NOT CALL THE POLICE!
YOU THINK THEY MIGHT SCARE OFF THE CROOKS AND WE'D NEVER LEARN THE SECRET, EH?
3

WAYNE IS RIGHT! WE'D BETTER PHONE THAT AD TO THE GAZETTE RIGHT AWAY!
I'LL PUT UP THE MONEY MYSELF IF NECESSARY!

MEANWHILE, IN OTHER SECTIONS OF THE CITY...
BETTY! MY LITTLE GIRL!
DON'T WORRY, MABEL! I'LL PHONE THE GAZETTE RIGHT AWAY, AND PAY A MILLION, IF I HAVE TO, TO SAVE HER!

OPERATOR, I WANT THE GAZETTE— IN A HURRY! IT'S A MATTER OF LIFE AND DEATH!

LATER, AT THE BRUCE WAYNE HOME...
NOTHING ON THE FRONT PAGE! BUT ON THE BACK PAGE, AMONG THE PERSONAL ADS—
LET ME SEE!
READY FOR NUMBER 1
READY FOR NUMBER 2
READY FOR NUMBER 3

THREE OF THEM— AND I KNOW ONLY ONE OF THE VICTIMS! WHAT WOULD YOU DO IN A CASE LIKE THIS, ALFRED?
ME, SIR? YOU FLATTER ME, AWSKING MY ADVICE! BUT—

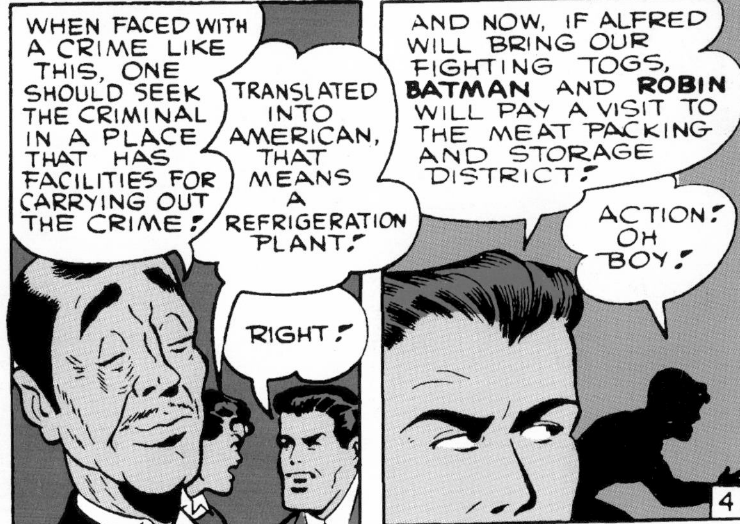
WHEN FACED WITH A CRIME LIKE THIS, ONE SHOULD SEEK THE CRIMINAL IN A PLACE THAT HAS FACILITIES FOR CARRYING OUT THE CRIME!
TRANSLATED INTO AMERICAN, THAT MEANS A REFRIGERATION PLANT!
RIGHT!
AND NOW, IF ALFRED WILL BRING OUR FIGHTING TOGS, BATMAN AND ROBIN WILL PAY A VISIT TO THE MEAT PACKING AND STORAGE DISTRICT!
ACTION! OH BOY!
4

THROUGH A RAGING STORM— THE FIRST BREAK IN THE HEAT WAVE — RACES THE STREAMLINED BATMOBILE!
TAKE A LOOK AT THOSE UMBRELLAS, ROBIN, AND SEE IF YOU CAN GUESS WHOM I SUSPECT OF THIS CRIME!
UMBRELLAS?.. THE PENGUIN OF COURSE! WHEN HE BROKE OUT OF PRISON A MONTH AGO, I WONDERED HOW SOON WE'D PICK UP HIS TRAIL!

COME TO THINK OF IT, PENGUINS ARE SUPPOSED TO THRIVE AT LOW TEMPERATURES!
PLENTY OF LOW TEMPERATURES AROUND HERE! NEARLY EVERY COLD STORAGE AN REFRIGERATION PLANT IS WITHIN THREE BLOCKS OF US!

OOPS! BEG PARDON!
THAT GOES DOUBLE!
WHAT-!

THE PENGUIN!
BATMAN AND ROBIN!
WHAT A PLEASANT SURPRISE!

SPEAKING OF SURPRISES— HERE'S ANOTHER!
LOOK OUT! A NET!

TA, TA! I HOPE YOU APPRECIATE MY INGENUITY IN LINING THAT FISH NET WITH FISH HOOKS!
DON'T STRUGGLE, ROBIN! THE MORE CAREFUL WE ARE, THE SOONER WE'LL GET RID OF THIS!
OUCH!..
5

MINUTES LATER...
HEW! I'M FULL OF CRATCHES!... AND I ON'T SUPPOSE WE'VE OT A CHANCE OF ATCHING UP WITH HE PENGUIN NOW!
YES WE HAVE! HE WAS CARRYING A PACKAGE OF SOME KIND OF WHITE POWDER, AND IT SPILLED AND LEFT A TRAIL!

THE QUICK-FREEZ COMPANY! IT'S BEEN OUT OF BUSINESS FOR SOME TIME, BUT ALL THE EQUIPMENT MUST HAVE BEEN LEFT IN THE BUILDING!
QUICK-FREEZ CO.
HE WENT IN HERE!

IT'S DARK!
WE'LL HAVE TO FEEL OUR WAY! A LIGHT WOULD WARN WHOEVER IS INSIDE!

IT'S COLD! WE SHOULD HAVE BROUGHT OVERCOATS!
IF THE PENGUIN HAS ANY HENCHMEN HERE, THE EXERCISE WILL WARM US UP!

SUDDENLY...
HEY! THE TEPS ARE OVERED WITH CE!... LOOK OUT!
A FINE TIME TO WARN ME!

H-HOW M-MUCH FARTHER?
ASK ME L-LATER!
6

ABOUT TIME YOU WERE GETTING HERE! I'VE BEEN WAITING NEARLY A QUARTER OF AN HOUR!
THE PENGUIN'S VOICE!
WONDER IF HE THINKS WE'RE SOMEONE ELSE?

LIGHTS FLASH UP, AND—
AFTER I DELIBERATELY LEFT THAT TRAIL TO GUIDE YOU, I SHOULD HAVE THOUGHT YOU'D BE MORE PROMPT!
IF I'D KNOWN YOU WERE WAITING FO US, I'D HAVE HURRIED, PENGUIN
WHEN WE TAKE YOU BACK TO PRISON, I'M GOING TO ASK THE WARDEN TO PUT FISH HOOKS IN YOUR MATTRESS!

PRISON! HA, HA! HOW DROLL! NOT WHILE I HAVE THIS TRUSTY UMBRELLA THAT THROWS A HEAT RAY!
A HEAT RAY WOULD BE WELCOME IN THIS PLACE!

BUT THE WILY PENGUIN AIMS HIS UMBRELLA NOT AT THE DYNAMIC DUO, BUT AT THE CEILING ABOVE THEM— AND AS THE RAY STRIKES..
OBSERVE HOW CAREFULLY I HAVE GUARDED MYSELF!
DUCK, ROBIN! THOSE ICICLES ARE GOING TO FALL!
BUT THERE ARE S MANY, THERE NO PLACE TO DUCK!

OH-H...
I'LL GET YOU FOR THAT, PENGUIN!
REALLY, I HAVE MY DOUBTS!

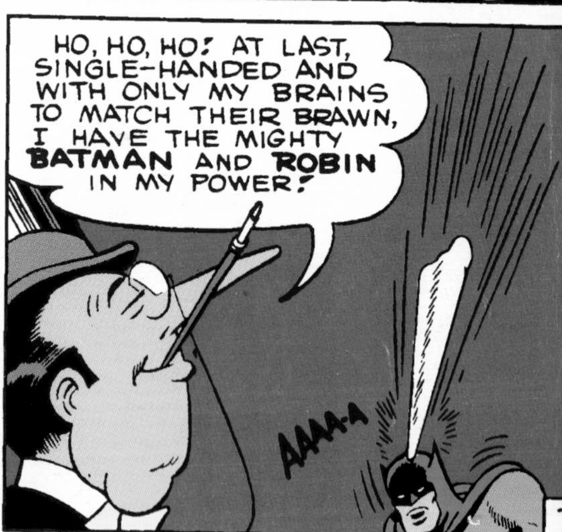
HO, HO, HO! AT LAST, SINGLE-HANDED AND WITH ONLY MY BRAINS TO MATCH THEIR BRAWN, I HAVE THE MIGHTY BATMAN AND ROBIN IN MY POWER!
AAAA-A

WHEN I FIRST CHOSE THIS DESERTED REFRIGERATOR PLANT AS A HIDEOUT, I KNEW THE MACHINERY WOULD COME IN HANDY!

THEY'VE BEEN ASSETS TO LAW AND ORDER LONG ENOUGH! FROM NOW ON, THEY'LL BE FROZEN ASSETS—AND NO SECRET FORMULA WILL EVER THAW THEM OUT!

NO USE TAKING CHANCES... I'LL TURN IT ON FULL POWER AND FINISH THEM QUICKLY!
DIUM
FULL

AND AS BATMAN REGAINS CONSCIOUSNESS...

W-WHAT-?
DON'T MIND THE COLD, BATMAN! YOU WON'T FEEL IT FOR MORE THAN TEN MINUTES OR SO!

I MUST LEAVE TO COLLECT $150,000. FOR THREE SACKS OF SALT, WHICH CERTAIN FOOLS WILL THINK IS A SECRET CHEMICAL FOR BRINGING THE DEAD BACK TO LIFE! HO, HO, HO!
YOU GRINNING LITTLE RAT!

AND SO, FAREWELL TO BATMAN AND ROBIN! I'LL MISS THE LITTLE GAMES OF HIDE-AND-SEEK WE USED TO PLAY—BUT I WAS GETTING TIRED OF BEING THROWN INTO PRISON ALL THE TIME!

LEFT ALONE WITH HIS UNCONSCIOUS COMPANION, THE MIGHTY WARRIOR SHIVERS HELPLESSLY IN HIS PRISON!

NEVER EXPECTED TO WIND UP THIS WAY, TURNING INTO A HUNK OF ICE... BUT IF THAT'S THE WAY IT HAS TO BE, I'M GLAD ROBIN DOESN'T KNOW ANYTHING ABOUT IT, POOR KID!

8

IF I HAD SOMETHING TO USE AS A LEVER, I MIGHT PRY ONE OF THOSE PIPES LOOSE!

BATMAN'S UTILITY BELT HAS STOOD HIM IN GOOD STEAD MANY TIMES—BUT NEVER BEFORE HAS ITS STRONG METAL BUCKLE BEEN CALLED UPON TO SUPPLY SUCH LEVERAGE AS THIS!

A FORLORN HOPE—BUT THERE'S NOTHING LIKE TRYING! WE'LL BOTH BE DEAD IN A FEW MINUTES, IF SOMETHING DOESN'T HAPPEN!

POWERFUL MUSCLES STRAIN TO THEIR UTMOST!

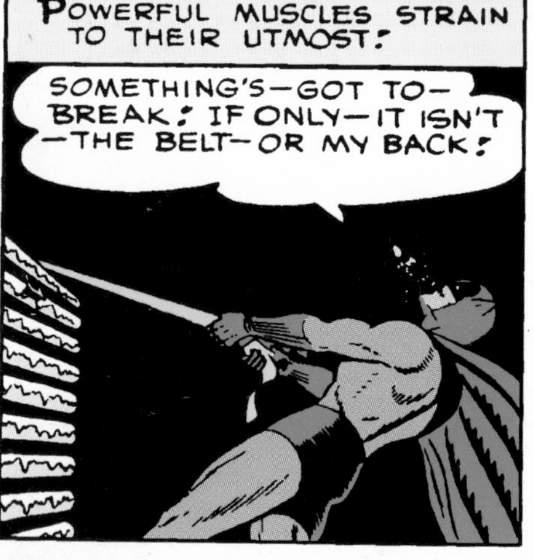

SOMETHING'S—GOT TO—BREAK! IF ONLY—IT ISN'T—THE BELT—OR MY BACK!

AND AT LAST...

THERE! NOW I'VE GOT TO WORRY ABOUT AMMONIA FUMES, WHICH WILL KILL QUICKER THAN COLD!

CAN'T—BREATHE! CAN'T EVEN—OPEN MY EYES!

HOLD YOUR BREATH, ROBIN! WE'LL BE OUT OF HERE IN A SECOND OR TWO!
WHAT—(GASP)—WHERE—?

THAT DOES IT! COME ON, ROBIN!

NO USE LEAVING THE MACHINERY RUNNING, TO FILL THE WHOLE PLACE WITH AMMONIA FUMES!
IF I NEVER SMELL THAT STUFF AGAIN, IT'LL BE TOO SOON!

WHAT ARE YOU LOOKING FOR, ANYWAY?
NOTHING THAT'S IN THIS CLOSET, ANYWAY!

IN ANOTHER PART OF THE BASEMENT OF THE REFRIGERATION PLANT...
THIS LOOKS AS IF IT MIGHT BE THE PLACE!
LOOKS LIKE THE DOOR TO A DUNGEON! YOU'RE NOT EXPECTING TO FIND PEOPLE LOCKED UP IN THERE ARE YOU?

BATMAN!
THANK GOODNESS— WE'RE SAVED FROM THAT AWFUL LITTLE MAN AND HIS GANGSTERS!
YOU SEE, ROBIN? NO SECRET PROCESS IS NEEDED TO BRING THE PENGUIN'S VICTIMS BACK TO LIFE!
BUT HOW DID YOU KNOW, BATMAN?

FOR ONE THING, THAT BOX SENT TO THE DIRECTORS' MEETING CONTAINED WHAT LOOKED SUSPICIOUSLY LIKE A WAX IMAGE— AND FOR ANOTHER THING, I DIDN'T THINK THE PENGUIN WOULD ACTUALLY RISK KILLING ANYONE— EXCEPTING US!
HE MADE MASKS OF OUR FACES! I DIDN'T KNOW WHAT FOR!

SINCE THE BOXES WERE SUPPOSED TO CONTAIN FROZEN PEOPLE— WHO WOULD DIE IF THEY WERE ALLOWED TO THAW OUT CARELESSLY— NO ONE WOULD DARE DISTURB THE SAWDUST OR MAKE TOO CLOSE AN EXAMINATION!
AND THE PENGUIN IS OUT RIGHT NOW— COLLECTING A FORTUNE FOR AS SIMPLE A TRICK AS THAT! BUT HE'LL BE COMING BACK...
10

A DAY'S WORK FOR $150,000! NOW DO YOU GENTLEMEN SEE WHAT I MEANT WHEN I SAID I COULD START FROM NOTHING AND BECOME RICH OVERNIGHT?
YEAH—ONLY DON'T FORGET, HALF THAT DOUGH GOES TO ME AND THE BOYS, TO SPLIT BETWEEN US!

AND NOW, AS FINAL PROOF OF MY GENIUS, I HAVE AN EVEN GREATER SURPRISE AWAITING YOU IN OUR HIDEOUT!

IF YOU CARE TO GLANCE INSIDE THE REFRIGERATOR, YOU WILL FIND TWO CHUNKS OF ICE THAT ONCE WERE THE BATMAN AND ROBIN—CAPTURED AND SUBDUED BY ME SINGLE-HANDED!
DON'T LOOK NOW, PENGUIN—BUT THE DOOR'S SMASHED!
THEY WALKED OUT ON YOU!

HOW EMBARRASSING!
WALK OUT? WE WOULDN'T THINK OF SUCH A THING!
YIIII! IT'S THEM!

THIS WILL STIFFEN YOU OUT QUICKER THAN ANY QUICK-FREEZING PROCESS!
I'M JUST WARMING UP!
GET THEM, BEEFY!

YOU'RE TOO SLOW ON THE TRIGGER, BEEFY! YOU MUST ASK THE WARDEN FOR A PISTOL SO YOU CAN PRACTICE WHEN YOU GET TO THE BIG HOUSE!
I'LL FIX YOU!

YOU'RE A DEAD PIGEON THIS TIME— BATMAN—AND NO FOOLING!
WHAT DOES THAT UMBRELLA DO — WHISTLE A TUNE?
THAT CAKE OF ICE...

IT FIRES EXPLOSIVE CARTRIDGES POWERFUL ENOUGH TO BLOW YOU IN HALF!
CAREFUL! IT MIGHT BACKFIRE!
THIS WEIGHS PLENTY, IF I CAN ONLY GET IT MOVING FAST ENOUGH!

THE NEXT INSTANT...
HOW'M I DOING!
YOU COULDN'T DO BETTER!
MY GRACIOUS!

IT SEEMS I'M NOT A DEAD PIGEON, AFTER ALL!
BUT IF YOU ASK ME, THE PENGUIN IS A GONE GOOSE!

OMETHING AS GONE WRONG!
GONE RIGHT, YOU MEAN! I'LL CALL THE POLICE TO SHOVEL YOU OUT AND TAKE YOU TO THE COOLER!
IF IT'S ANY COOLER THAN THIS, IT'LL KILL ME!

NEXT DAY, AT THE WAYNE HOME...
THIS IS INTERESTING, DICK! THE STORY SAYS ALL THREE OF THE PENGUIN'S VICTIMS RETURNED HOME, EACH WITH THE $50,000 COLLECTED FROM FRIENDS AND RELATIONS!
NOW I WONDER HOW THAT CAME ABOUT?
SINCE IT WAS I WHO SOLVED THE CASE BY STARTING BATMAN AND ROBIN ON THE RIGHT TRACK, MODESTY FORBIDS MY COMMENTING!
The END

No.100
JUNE...TEN CENTS
A SUPERMAN DC PUBLICATION
The BATMAN
Detective
REG U S PAT OFF
COMICS

BATMAN
WITH
ROBIN
-THE BOY WONDER-
OUT OF A BLACK NIGHT COMES THE SINISTER SPARKLE OF GEMS WORTH A KING'S RANSOM, TWISTING MEN'S MINDS INTO PATTERNS OF GREED AND TREACHERY— AND MURDER! AND ONCE AGAIN BATMAN AND ROBIN FLASH INTO ACTION, TRACING A DEAD MAN'S CLUE TO A WILD AND LONELY HEADLAND WHERE, WITH THE WIND'S MOAN AND THE OCEAN'S ROAR THUNDERING AN EERIE OBBLIGATO, THEY DARE FANTASTIC PERILS TO EXPLORE THE AMAZING SECRET BEHIND...
"THE CROW'S NEST MYSTERY!"
BOB KANE

NIGHT... A CALM SEA... AND THE LIGHTS OF A TRAMP FREIGHTER OFF A ROCKY COAST...

A FURTIVE ARM EXTENDS THROUGH A PORTHOLE—AND A SMALL LUMINOUS PARCEL IS TOSSED INTO THE WATER!

AS THE THROB OF THE SHIP'S PRO PELLER FADES INTO THE DISTANC A SECOND CRAFT EMERGES SILENTLY FROM THE DARKNES
SWING A LITTLE TO THE LEFT, BEN!
SWING, HE SAYS! AS IF I HADN'T BE SWINGIN' THESE OA ALL EVENIN', WHIL YOU BEEN TAKIN IT EASY!

ALL YOU GOTTA DO NOW IS AIM FOR THAT LIGHT!
WHADDYA MEAN, ALL! I'M GETTIN SICK OF DOIN' ALL THE HEAVY WORK, JORUM!
A TORTUOUS PASSAGE BETWEEN SHARK-TOOTHED ROCKS LEADS TO A LOW OPENING A CLIFF, VISIBLE ONLY AT LOW TIDE...
I'M GETTIN' SICK OF ALL THIS RISK AND WORRY!
IF YOU HAVEN'T GOT NO NERVE, AT LEAST YOU OUGHT TO APPRECIAT THE DOUGH THE BOSS IS PAYIN' YOU!

AND EVENTUALLY TO A SPACIOUS CAVERN WITH SHAFTS LEADING UPWARD!
YOU MAY GO RIGHT UP!
THINK OF IT, BEN—WE GOT A RESPECTABLE FRONT, AND EVERYTHING!
I'M THINKIN' OF IT!

MINUTES LATER...
PRETTY NICE, EH, BOSS?
IT'S A SHAME TO LET RADER HAVE THEM FOR $50,000—BUT I SUPPOSE A BARGAIN IS A BARGAIN!

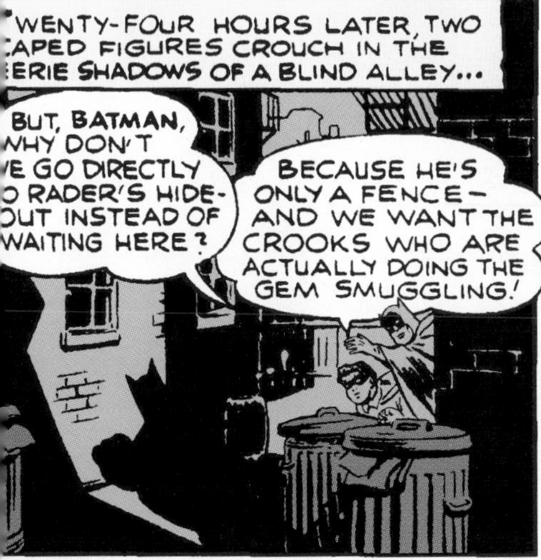
TWENTY-FOUR HOURS LATER, TWO CAPED FIGURES CROUCH IN THE EERIE SHADOWS OF A BLIND ALLEY...
BUT, BATMAN, WHY DON'T WE GO DIRECTLY TO RADER'S HIDE-OUT INSTEAD OF WAITING HERE?
BECAUSE HE'S ONLY A FENCE— AND WE WANT THE CROOKS WHO ARE ACTUALLY DOING THE GEM SMUGGLING!

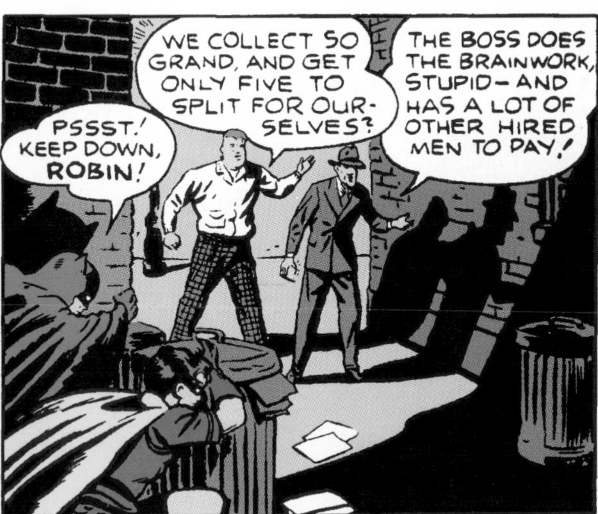
PSSST! KEEP DOWN, ROBIN!
WE COLLECT 50 GRAND, AND GET ONLY FIVE TO SPLIT FOR OUR-SELVES?
THE BOSS DOES THE BRAINWORK, STUPID— AND HAS A LOT OF OTHER HIRED MEN TO PAY!

THEY'RE HEADING STRAIGHT FOR RADER'S PLACE IN THE LOFT OF THAT OLD CARRIAGE HOUSE!
AND THAT MEANS THEY'RE HEADING FOR TROUBLE!

IN THE CARRIAGE-HOUSE LOFT...
KNOCK KNOCK-KNOCK KNOCK-KNOCK-KNOCK
THE SIGNAL! IT WILL BE THEM!

HMM— THEY ARE NOT AS FINE AS I WAS LED TO THINK! AND $50,000 IS A LOT OF MONEY!
LISTEN, RADER, THE BOSS SAYS 50 GRAND— AND WE'RE GETTING THAT MUCH, OR ELSE!

COUNT IT TO MAKE SURE IT'S RIGHT!
YOU'RE TELLING ME!
MAKE IT FAST! I FEEL LIKE SOME-BODY'S WATCHIN' US!
3

SUDDENLY...
RELAX, EVERYBODY! WE'RE TAKING OVER!
BATMAN AND ROBIN!
WE'RE SUNK!
I'LL FIX 'EM!... OH-H-H!
PEOPLE WITH GLASS JAWS SHOULDN'T THROW SLUGS!
UGH!
SO YOU WANT TO GO TO JAIL THE HARD WAY!
ONE OF THEM'S GETTING AWAY!
CAN'T HELP IT! THIS ONE ISN'T, ANYWAY!
SPEAK UP! WHO'S THE BOSS OF YOUR SMUGGLING GANG AND WHERE DOES HE HANG OUT?
GIMME A BREAK, BATMAN! I'LL TALK IF YOU'LL TURN ME LOOSE!
BUT, DESPITE HIS HURRIED EXIT, JORUM HAS NOT DEPARTED FROM THE SCENE!
YOU'RE GOING TO JAIL WHETHER YOU TALK OR NOT— BUT YOU CAN HELP YOURSELF BY TURNING STATE'S EVIDENCE!
ALL RIGHT, ALL RIGHT. THE MOB NEVER TREATED ME RIGHT, ANYHOW!
SO HE THINKS HE'LL RAT ON US, DOES HE?

HE NEXT INSTANT...
SO LONG, SQUEALER!
WHAT–!

TAKE CARE OF HIM, ROBIN! I'LL GO AFTER THAT SKUNK!
WATCH YOURSELF!

HE GUNMAN'S FLIGHT INTO THE HADOWS IS SWIFT, HOWEVER, AND–
E WENT DOWN THE RAINPIPE LIKE GREASED GHTNING–WORSE LUCK! D USE CHASING M IN THE RK!

GOT ME!.. LOOK FOR– BOSS– CROW'S NEST– AAA-AA-A-A...
WHAT'S THAT? CROW'S NEST?..

RESENTLY, WHEN THE LICE HAVE TAKEN ARGE OF RADER D THE DEAD MAN...
ERE IT IS – OW'S NEST– LONELY POINT ROCK TWENTY LES UP THE AST! I'VE EN IT FROM ATS ON FISHING TRIPS!
SO FAR, SO GOOD– BUT WHAT DO WE LOOK FOR WHEN WE GET THERE?
WE LOOK FOR SMUGGLERS! IF I REMEMBER RIGHTLY, A VERY NOTORIOUS ONE LIVED THERE TWENTY YEARS AGO, IN A STRANGE OLD HOUSE WITH A TOWER!
MAYBE HIS GHOST IS INSPIRING THE MAN WE'RE AFTER!

HIS GHOST HAS PROBABLY INSPIRED ONE MAN, ANYWAY! REGINALD SCOFIELD, THE FAMOUS WRITER OF ADVENTURE AND MYSTERY STORIES, LIVES IN THE HOUSE NOW!
I'VE READ SOME OF HIS BOOKS– REAL THRILLERS!
5

MEANWHILE, JORUM CONFERS WITH HIS MYSTERIOUS CHIEF...
WHY DIDN'T YOU SHOOT BATMAN INSTEAD OF BEN? HOW DO YOU KNOW BEN DIDN'T TALK, EVEN WITH A BULLET IN HIM?
GUESS I WAS TOO MAD TO THINK STRAIGHT, BOSS!
WE'LL HAVE TO LOOK OUT FOR BATMAN. HE MUSTN'T EVER REACH THIS PLACE!
HE WON'T! LEAVE IT TO ME!
BESIDE A LONELY ROAD THAT FOLLOWS THE COAST...
HERE'S WHERE WE START WALKING!
CROWS NEST
I'LL CUT THAT ROPE NEARLY THROUGH, AND THEIR WEIGHT'LL DO THE REST! THEY'LL HAVE A HUNDRED-FOOT DROP TO THE ROCKS BELOW!
THIS DOESN'T LOOK TOO SOLID, BATMAN!
PEOPLE HAVE EVIDENTLY BEEN USING IT! IF IT SUPPORTED THEM, IT OUGHT TO HOLD TO-GETHER FOR US!
QUICK, ROBIN! GRAB THE GUARD ROPES!
YOU'RE TELLING ME!
MADE IT— WITHOUT AN INCH TO SPARE!

AS BATMAN UNWINDS HIS LIGHT SILKEN ROPE FROM BENEATH HIS BELT...
I'LL HAVE YOU ACROSS IN A JIFFY, ROBIN!
IT CAN'T BE TOO SOON TO SUIT ME!
THEY'RE NOT SO EASY TO GET RID OF BUT I GOT TO KEEP TRYING!
BULLETS! NOW I'M SURE THE COLLAPSE OF THE BRIDGE WAS NO ACCIDENT!
WE'LL BE OUT OF SIGHT IF WE GET AMONG THOSE DWARFED TREES!
THAT MUST BE SCOFIELD'S HOUSE! WE'LL FIND SHELTER THERE!
OR SOME-THING!
THE LIBRARY OF
IE BIG OLD HOUSE,
MAN WEAVES
NCIFUL TALES OF
YSTERY AND MENACE...
ET ME SEE...
BOVE THE MOAN OF
E WIND, ANOTHER
UND CREPT INTO THE
OOM. WHIRLING
WARD A
NDOW, THE
N BLANCHED
S —"
BATMAN AND ROBIN!
I HOPE WE'RE NOT BUTTING INTO A MASTERPIECE!
WELCOME TO CROW'S NEST! AFTER DREAMING UP SO MANY IMAGINARY MYSTERIES, IT'S A PLEA-SURE TO MEET PEOPLE WHO DEAL WITH THE REAL THING!
YOUR IMAGINARY ONES ARE PLENTY EXCITING!
AND I WOULDN'T BE SURPRISED IF YOU HAVE A GENUINE ONE RIGHT AROUND HOME!
7

HOW DID YOU GUESS? RECENTLY MY SAFE WAS LOOTED, ALTHOUGH IT WAS SECURELY LOCKED, AND ONLY A FEW MINUTES AGO I FANCIED I HEARD SHOOTING!
YOU HEARD RIGHT!
I'VE SEEN STRANGE MEN PROWLING ABOUT, TOO, AND— WHY, DIGGES! WHAT'S WRONG?
IT IS MY SAD DUTY, SIR, TO INFORM YOU THAT—
—A CRIMINAL OF SOME SORT IS CALLING, SIR!
STICK 'EM UP, EVERY-BODY!
WE'D BETTER FOLLOW ORDERS, ROBIN.
MAKE THE ROPES TIGHT, TOO, IF YOU DON'T WANT TO START PUSHING UP DAISIES!
Y-YES, SIR!
YOU WON'T GET AWAY WITH THIS!
NOW TELL YOUR MAN THE COMBINATION OF THE SAFE, SCOFIELD! I WANT IT OPEN RIGHT AWAY!
I HAVEN'T KEPT ANYTHING IN IT SINCE IT WAS ROBBED —BUT THE COMBIN-ATION IS 11 RIGHT, 6 DOUBLE LEFT, 3 RIGHT—
A B-BIT SLOWER, SIR, IF YOU P-PLEASE!
THERE YOU ARE - AND IT'S EMPTY, JUST AS HE SAID!
IT WON'T BE VERY LONG!
YOU RAT! IF YOU'RE PLANNING TO PUT SCOFIELD IN THERE TO SMOTHER—
I'M NOT, BATMAN. I'M ONLY CURIOUS ABOUT—
GOT HIM!
NICE WORK, DIGGES!
ALMOST TOO EASY!
SLAM

'LL CALL
IE POLICE!
WAIT! WHAT'S THE MATTER WITH UNTYING US FIRST?
THAT CROOK MAY HAVE PALS OUTSIDE!
THE NEXT INSTANT...
A TOMMY GUN! GET DOWN ON THE FLOOR, ROBIN!
I'M TRYING!
NE OF
HE
LLETS
T THESE
OPES!
WHEN WE CATCH THAT SNEAKING KILLER, WE'LL THANK HIM FOR THE FAVOR!
KEEP OUT OF THE WAY OF THE WINDOW, ROBIN! AND SEE IF YOU CAN REMEMBER THE COMBINATION OF THE SAFE!
HMM... 11 RIGHT, 6 DOUBLE LEFT...
EMPTY! BUT- BUT-
EXACTLY! NOW IF YOU'LL CLOSE THE DOOR AS SOON AS I GET INSIDE, AND THEN SEE IF YOU CAN REVIVE SCOFIELD, MAYBE WE'LL START GETTING SOMEWHERE!
O MINUTES LATER...
MY HEAD! WHAT HAPPENED?... I REMEMBER... BUT WHERE'S BATMAN?
HE GOT IN THE SAFE! DON'T ASK ME WHY!
WHAT DO YOU MEAN, IN THE SAFE? ARE YOU TRYING TO PLAY SOME KIND OF JOKE?
YOU OUGHT TO KNOW AS MUCH AS I DO ABOUT IT! IT'S YOUR SAFE!
9

WHAT HAS HAPPENED TO BATMAN? IT'S ALL VERY SIMPLE...
THERE'LL BE A SPRING OR A BUTTON SOMEWHERE, IF ONLY I CAN FIND IT!... AH!
A SECRET PASSAGE THROUGH THE WALLS AND DOWN INTO THE EARTH AS I SUSPECTED!
AN UNDERGROUND CACHE - AND ANOTHER LADDER GOING UP THROUGH A SHAFT!
A HOLLOW TREE, OF ALL THINGS! A HIDING PLACE, LOOKOUT POST AND SECRET EXIT, ALL IN ONE!
HERE'S THE TOMMY GUN THAT WAS USED ON US! IT WAS FIRED THROUGH THE WINDOW FROM THIS HOLE!
AT THIS POINT BATMAN KNOWS MOST OF THE ANSWERS TO THE MYSTERY OF THE SMUGGLED GEMS - BUT HIS TROUBLES ARE BY NO MEANS OVER!
AM I BATTY, OR IS THAT BATMAN? THIS TIME I GOT TO BUMP HIM OFF - BUT GOOD - OR WE'RE FINISHED!
THAT DID IT! I KNEW HIS LUCK COULDN'T LAST FOREVER! THE BOSS OUGHT TO GIVE ME A BONUS!
ZING!

SUCH IS THE FAME OF THE GREAT CRIME-FIGHTER THAT, EVEN THOUGH HE LIES SPRAWLED AND STILL, THE GUNMAN APPROACHES HIM IN FEAR AND TREMBLING!
I AIN'T TAKING NO CHANCES! ONE FLICKER OF AN EYELID AND MY HEATER STARTS BLASTING!
AND WELL HE MAY!
YI!!!!
TOUCHÉ — AS WE SAY IN FRANCE!
AAA-AA-A-A..
SO YOU THOUGHT I WAS DONE FOR, JUST BECAUSE ONE OF YOUR SLUGS CREASED MY SCALP!
IN THE MEANTIME, ROBIN IS ALSO FACING A PROBLEM!
PARDON ME IF I'M WRONG — BUT SOMETHING TELLS ME YOU'RE THE SECRET BOSS OF THIS GANG! THAT WALLOP YOUR HIRED MAN GAVE YOU WAS JUST TO TURN SUSPICION AWAY FROM YOU, IN CASE BATMAN AND I ESCAPED!
YOU'RE PARDONED, BECAUSE MENTIONING MY HIRED MAN HAS JUST EXPLAINED SOMETHING THAT HAS PUZZLED ME FOR A LONG TIME! THE REAL CRIMINAL HERE IS—
DIGGES!
RIGHT, SCOFIELD! IT'S UNFORTUNATE THAT YOU SHOULD HAVE GUESSED SO CLEVERLY, AFTER ALL MY PRECAUTIONS!
NO WONDER YOU WOULDN'T UNTIE BATMAN AND ME!
I WORKED WITH SMUGGLERS WHO USED THIS HOUSE YEARS AGO! IT WAS AN IDEAL SPOT, WITH ITS SECRET PASSAGES AND THAT TRICK SAFE! SO WHEN I HEARD YOU'D RENTED IT, I GOT A JOB AS YOUR SERVANT—
BETTER PUT YOUR PISTOL DOWN AND SURRENDER, DIGGES!
11

SUDDENLY...
SO NOW YOU DIE!... EH-?
BATMAN!
NO MORE KILL-ING IF YOU PLEASE! THIS IS THE LAST CHAPTER OF THIS MYSTERY STORY!
I'LL SUPPLY THE PERIOD! HOW'S MY PUNCH-UATION, BATMAN?
BETTER THAN YOU PUN-CTUATIO I MUST ADMIT!
YOU THOUGHT WORK-ING FOR A RESPECTABLE AUTHOR WAS TOO GOOD A BIT OF CAMOUFLAGE TO PASS UP, DIDN'T YOU, DIGGES?
YES... I WOULDN'T HAVE TRIED TO KILL SCOFIELD IF HE HADN'T GUESSED THE TRUTH! I'D HAVE LET JORUM TAKE THE BLAME FOR KILLING YOU, AND TRANSFERRED HIM TO MY ORGANIZATION ABROAD!
I SUPPOSE THAT CHEST OF RECORDS IN THE TUNNEL BELOW WILL TELL US ABOUT THAT ORGAN-IZATION?
YES! MY BIGGEST MISTAKE WAS HAVING JORUM USE THAT SECRET EXIT THROUG THE SAFE, TRYING TO MAKE IT SEEM I WAS ON THE RIGHT SIDE, IN CASE SCOFIELD REGAINED CONSCIOUS-NESS UNEXPECTEDLY.
WRONG! YOUR BIGGEST MISTAKE WAS TURNING CROOKED IN THE BEGINNING!
I'VE BEEN RACKING MY BRAIN FOR A PLOT FOR MY NEXT MYSTERY NOVEL, BATMAN-AND HERE YOU AND ROBIN HAVE HANDED ME ONE READY-MADE!
AS LONG AS IT TEACHES THAT CRIME DOES NOT PAY, I'M FOR IT!
SOME WEEKS LATER, IN THE BRUCE WAYNE HOME...
NOW THAT THE AUTH-ORITIES HAVE FURNISHED THE ENDING, DICK, I SUPPOSE SCOFIELD WILL BE STARTING HIS NEW BOOK!
WHAT MAKES YOU THINK HE'S BEEN WAITING?
GEM SMUGGLERS SENTENCED
IT WAS PUBLISHED YESTER-DAY, AND IT'S DEDICATED TO BATMAN AND ROBIN!
JEWELS OF DEATH by REGINALD SCOFIELD
I HOPE HE'S SENDING SOME PRESENTATION COPIES TO THE PRISON LIBRARY!
The End.

No.101
JULY...TEN CENTS
A SUPERMAN DC PUBLICATION
BATMAN
Detective
COMICS
OKAY, ALFRED, Y'TRACKED ME DOWN! I'LL CONFESS — I DID IT!
DID WHAT, OLD BOY?!? I ONLY WANTED TO URGE YOU TO BACK THE 7TH WAR LOAN!

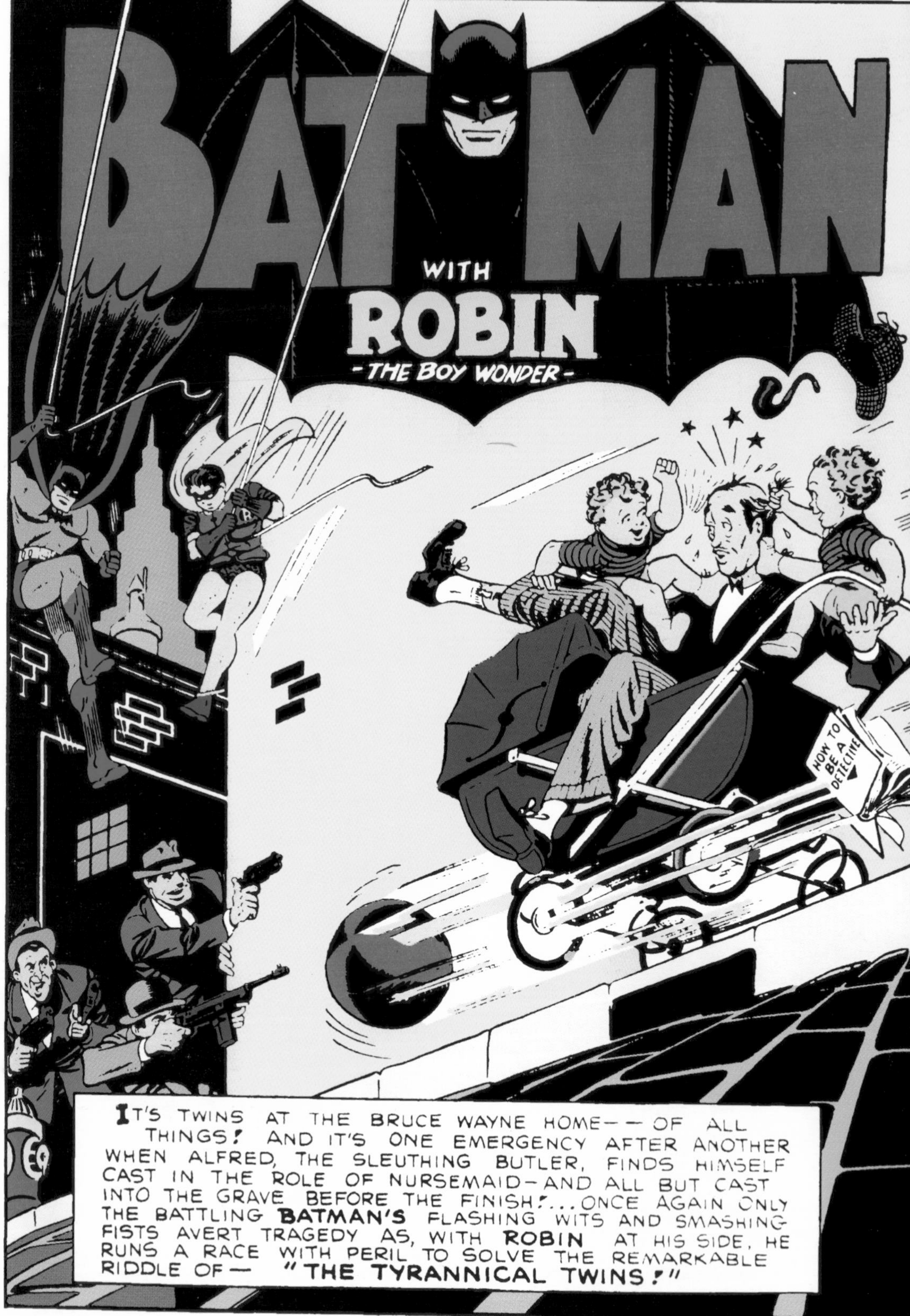
BATMAN
WITH
ROBIN
-THE BOY WONDER-
HOW TO BE A DETECTIVE
IT'S TWINS AT THE BRUCE WAYNE HOME-- OF ALL THINGS! AND IT'S ONE EMERGENCY AFTER ANOTHER WHEN ALFRED, THE SLEUTHING BUTLER, FINDS HIMSELF CAST IN THE ROLE OF NURSEMAID-AND ALL BUT CAST INTO THE GRAVE BEFORE THE FINISH!... ONCE AGAIN ONLY THE BATTLING BATMAN'S FLASHING WITS AND SMASHING FISTS AVERT TRAGEDY AS, WITH ROBIN AT HIS SIDE, HE RUNS A RACE WITH PERIL TO SOLVE THE REMARKABLE RIDDLE OF- "THE TYRANNICAL TWINS!"

BRUCE WAYNE AND DICK GRAYSON ARE LOOKING FORWARD TO AN UNEVENTFUL DAY— WHICH PROVES HOW WRONG THEY CAN BE!
WUXTREE! CLERK RRESTED IN BIG EWELRY OBBERY!
THAT'S ONE CRIME BATMAN AND ROBIN WON'T HAVE TO WORRY ABOUT, EH, BRUCE?
THE POLICE SEEM SURE OF THEIR MAN! HE SERVED TIME ONCE BEFORE FOR GRAND LARCENY!

WANT TO COME IN WHILE I PICK OUT SOME SHIRTS, DICK?
NO, THANKS! I'LL WAIT HERE AND LOOK IN WINDOWS!

I WONDER IF OU'D WATCH Y TWINS WHILE GO INTO THE TORE? I'LL BE RIGHT OUT!
I'LL BE GLAD TO! HUSKY PAIR OF YOUNGSTER, AREN'T THEY?

IN FACT, THE EXCITEMENT HAS ALREADY BEGUN!
WHAT DO I DO NOW? MAYBE THIS BALL WILL HELP!
WHAT'S THE IDEA? STARTING A DAY NURSERY?
WAA-AA-AH!

UICK-TOSS ME HE BALL! THAT EEMS TO MUSE THEM! HERE DID OU FIND THEM?
THEIR MOTHER ASKED ME TO WATCH THEM WHILE SHE WENT INTO THE STORE, JUST FOR A MINUTE!

AN HOUR LATER...
WHEW! IF SHE LEFT THE STORE RIGHT AWAY, AS SHE SAID SHE WOULD, IT MUST HAVE BEEN BY ANOTHER DOOR!
MAYBE YOU'VE GOT SOMETHING THERE, FELLA! THERE'S A NOTE I DIDN'T NOTICE BEFORE—AND IT'S ADDRESSED TO BRUCE WAYNE!

Dear Mr. Wayne:
You can earn a mother's eternal gratitude by caring for these babies for a few days. Forgive me... I'll explain whe I call for them. Meanwhile, here are directions for their car and feeding.

2

LOOKS AS IF WE'VE GOT A FAMILY, DICK! WONDER WHAT THE NEIGHBORS WILL SAY!
THE MOTHER SEEMED NICE! I'M SURPRISED SHE'D TRUST LITTLE TYKES TO STRANGERS!

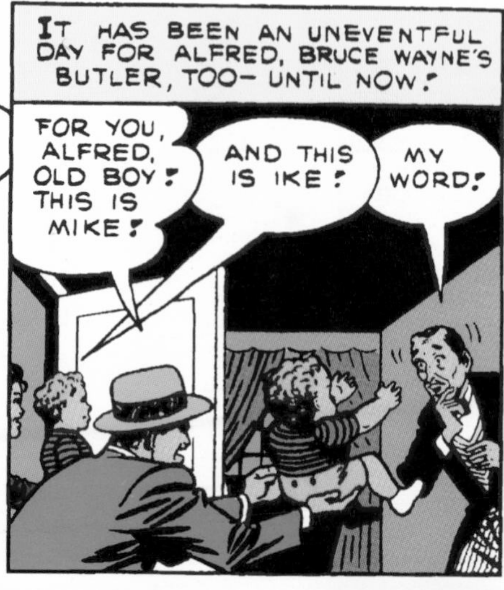
IT HAS BEEN AN UNEVENTFUL DAY FOR ALFRED, BRUCE WAYNE'S BUTLER, TOO– UNTIL NOW!
FOR YOU, ALFRED, OLD BOY! THIS IS MIKE!
AND THIS IS IKE!
MY WORD!

HERE'S A SET OF DIRECTIONS! I'LL READ IT TO YOU!
BUT, I SAY, WHAT AM I GOING TO DO WITH THEM?
WAAH
I'LL GET THEIR BALL! MAYBE IT WILL STOP THEIR BAWLING AGAIN!

NEVER BEFORE HAS LIFE IN THE WAYNE HOME BEEN LIKE THIS!
A TOUCHING SCENE, ISN'T IT?
MAYBE WE SHOULD GET ALFRED A NURSE'S UNIFORM!
LAUGH IF YOU MUST, SIRS! BUT REMEMBER– I'M DOING THIS UNDER PROTEST!
DA-DA!
GOO-OO!

BUGGHUK!
ANYWAY, THEY'RE CUTE LITTLE- OUCH!
HO, HO! STRONG-ARM STUFF!
BRUCE- LOOK!

DIAMONDS, RUBIES AND EMERALDS! REAL ONES!
I'LL BET THEY'RE PART OF THE LOOT FROM THAT JEWELRY STORE ROBBERY!

PRESENTLY...
ARE YOU GOING TO LEAVE ME ALL ALONE WITH THE TWO OF THEM, SIRS!
SORRY, ALFRED– BUT THIS MAY TURN INTO AN IMPORTANT CASE!
YOU CAN HOLD YOUR OWN WITH THEM IF YOU'LL ONLY TRY!
WAAAAAA!!

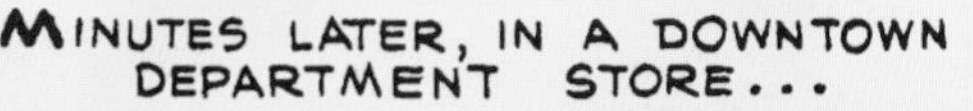
MINUTES LATER, IN A DOWNTOWN DEPARTMENT STORE...
THERE YOU ARE, BATMAN! THE NAME AND ADDRESS OF THE CUSTOMER WHO BOUGHT THE TWIN BABY CARRIAGE WITH THE SERIAL NUMBER YOU GAVE ME!
MRS. STELLA RANIER! THE WIFE OF THE JEWELRY STORE CLERK THE POLICE ARE HOLDING!
MANAGER

BUT IF THOSE TWINS BELONG TO RANIER, AND SOME OF THE STOLEN JEWELS WERE INSIDE THEIR RATTLES, DOESN'T THAT PROVE HE'S GUILTY?
NOT NECESSARILY, ROBIN! AND THERE'S NO SENSE IN GUESSING TILL WE FIND OUT WHAT MRS. RANIER CAN TELL US!
Furs

AT THAT MOMENT, WITHIN THE RANIER HOME...
COME ON! TELL US WHERE THE KIDS ARE AND YOU WON'T GET HURT!
THEY AREN'T HERE! THAT'S ALL I CAN SAY!

SUDDENLY...
THREE ARMED MEN AGAINST ONE WOMAN! IS THAT FAIR?
HUH?... BATMAN!
AN' ROBIN!
THANK GOODNESS!

THE LEAST I CAN DO IS CUT DOWN THE ODDS A LITTLE!

TAKE A DEEP BOW, CHUM!
NICE GOING, ROBIN!
I'LL FIX 'EM!
4

ALL RIGHT, BOYS! BEAT IT WHILE YOU CAN!
HEY!
NOW FOR THE LAST OF THE LOT!.. OOPS!

OH-H-H! ARE YOU HURT?
BE ALL RIGHT IN A MINUTE, WHEN MY HEAD STOPS SPINNING!
ANYWAY, WE'VE GOT A CLEAR HANDPRINT OF ONE OF THEM— BLACK AS INK!

YOU'LL HELP MY HUSBAND AND ME, WON'T YOU? I'M SURE YOU CAN PROVE HIS INNOCENCE IF YOU'LL TRY!
IT MAY NOT BE SO EASY! THIS ISN'T THE FIRST TIME HE'S BEEN IN TROUBLE WITH THE LAW!

I KNOW HE BORROWED MONEY WITHOUT PERMISSION FROM A BANK WHERE HE WORKED, AND WENT TO PRISON— BUT THAT WAS YEARS AGO! HE EXPECTED TO DOUBLE THE MONEY IN INVESTMENTS! SINCE THEN HE HAS PAID BACK EVERY PENNY!
HMMM...

WE'LL PAY A VISIT TO YOUR HUSBAND, MRS. RANIER!
ROGER AND I WILL ALWAYS BE GRATEFUL!

IN THE CELL BLOCK AT POLICE HEADQUARTERS...
VISITORS, RANIER!
STELLA! I WAS JUST THINKING ABOUT YOU!
I'VE BROUGHT BATMAN AND ROBIN WITH ME! THEY'RE GOING TO TRY TO HELP YOU, ROGER!
5

YESTERDAY EVENING I TOOK THE TWINS OUT AND MET JOE BART, WHO RUNS THE PRINTING SHOP NEXT TO THE JEWELRY STORE... WE TALKED FOR A FEW MINUTES, THEN SEPARATED!
HE WAS THE ONLY ONE WHO SAW YOU, EH?

YES—EXCEPT FOR A MASKED MAN WHO SLUGGED ME A LITTLE FARTHER ON! I CAME TO HALF AN HOUR LATER, FELT IN MY POCKET FOR MY STORE KEYS—AND FOUND SOME VALUABLE JEWELS INSTEAD!
AND RECOGNIZED THEM AS COMING FROM YOUR STORE?

RIGHT, ROBIN!... I TOOK THE TWINS HOME, AND FOUND THE POLICE WAITING! SOMEONE HAD MADE AN ANONYMOUS PHONE CALL TO THEM, SAYING I HAD ROBBED THE STORE!
THAT PHONE CALL IN ITSELF MAKES ME THINK YOU'RE PROBABLY INNOCENT, RANIER!

I CAN ADD SOMETHING! EARLY THIS MORNING, I HEARD A NOISE IN THE NURSERY AND FOUND A MAN—ONE OF THE THREE WHO CAME BACK LATER—PROWLING THERE! I SCREAMED AND HE RAN!

I WAS FRANTIC WITH FEAR FOR THE BABIES' SAFETY! I REMEMBERED READING IN THE PAPERS THAT BRUCE WAYNE LIKED CHILDREN AND HAD GIVEN LARGE SUMS TO ORPHANAGES!
AHA—A LIGHT BEGINS TO DAWN!

SO I LEFT THEM WITH HIM—OR, RATHER, A YOUNG BOY WHO WAS WITH HIM—WITHOUT HIS PERMISSION! PERHAPS THAT WAS WRONG, BUT I WAS SO WORRIED...
I'M SURE THEY'LL HAVE THE BEST OF CARE, MRS. RANIER!
6

I'M AFRAID I HAVEN'T BEEN OF MUCH HELP TO YOU OR MYSELF!

ON THE CONTRARY, YOU'VE GIVEN US A FIRST-CLASS CLUE! SHALL WE RUN IT DOWN, **ROBIN?**

YOU RUN, AND I'LL TAG ALONG! I DON'T GET IT YET!

MEANWHILE, A CURIOUS THREESOME STROLLS, NOT FAR AWAY, IN BLISSFUL—IF TEMPORARY—SERENITY!

NOT BAD LITTLE BLIGHTERS, AT THAT! QUEER HOW THAT COLORED BALL SEEMS TO BE THE ONLY THING TO KEEP 'EM PEACEFUL!

WHAT LOVELY TWINS!

ISN'T HE A LUCKY MAN?

EH? THERE GOES THE BALL! MY WORD—THIS IS INDEED A CRISIS!

AH-H-H-H-H!

WA-AA-A-AH-H-H!

BAW-W-W!

I MUST RETRIEVE IT AT ALL COSTS! BUT I CAWN'T LEAVE THE CARRIAGE HERE ON THE SLOPE!

IMAGINE, AFTER ALL OUR TROUBLE, IT COMES BOUNCIN' RIGHT INTA OUR LAPS!
GOT IT!

A WINDED FIGURE WITNESSES THE CAPTURE OF THE RUNAWAY TOY!
WHAT'S THIS? YONDER GENTLEMEN SEEM TO HAVE RECOVERED THE BALL FOR ME!

I SAY, THANKS OR STOPPING MY BALL, MY GOOD MAN!
WHADDYA MEAN, YOUR BALL?
DON'T ARGUE WITH HIM, HUGGINS!

SUCH MANNERS— BUTTIN' IN WHEN WE AIN'T BEEN INTRODUCED!
WHA—? HELP! POLICE!

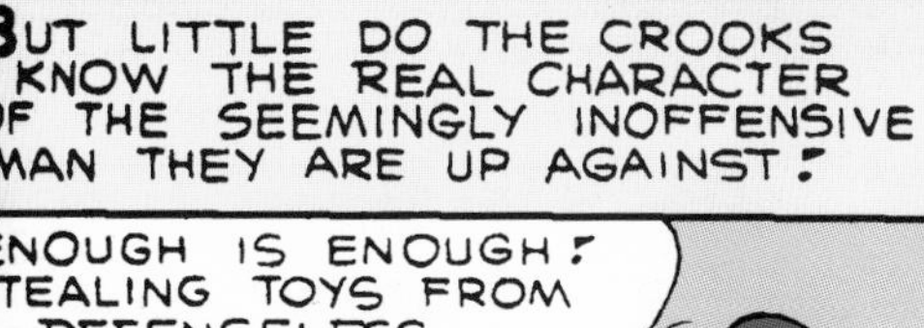
UT LITTLE DO THE CROOKS KNOW THE REAL CHARACTER F THE SEEMINGLY INOFFENSIVE MAN THEY ARE UP AGAINST!

NOUGH IS ENOUGH! TEALING TOYS FROM DEFENSELESS HILDREN! I'LL RACK DOWN THOSE RUFFIANS IF IT'S HE LAWST ACT OF Y DISTINGUISHED CAREER!

NOT FOR NOTHING HAVE THE MAWSTERS DUBBED ME THE BUTTLING BLOODHOUND! I'LL DON MY MANHUNTING DISGUISE, BORROW THAT BICYCLE, AND...
8

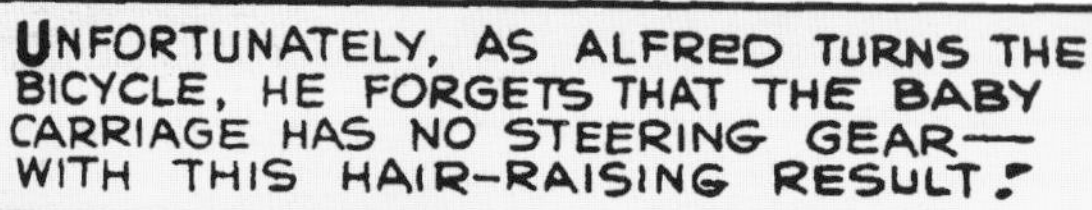
UNFORTUNATELY, AS ALFRED TURNS THE BICYCLE, HE FORGETS THAT THE BABY CARRIAGE HAS NO STEERING GEAR— WITH THIS HAIR-RAISING RESULT!

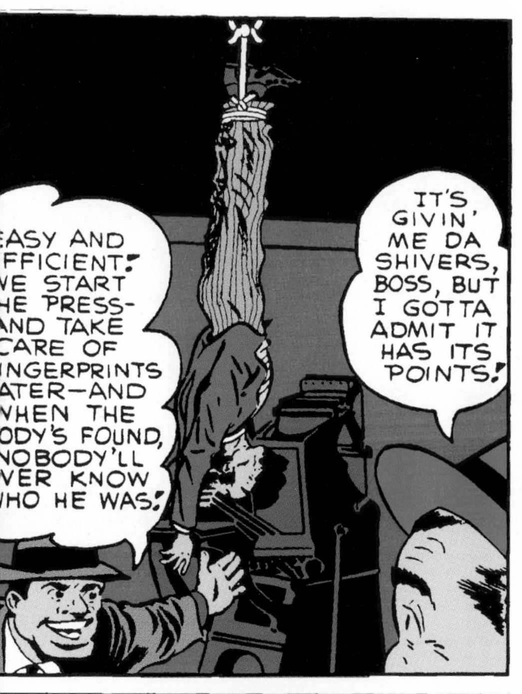

INGERPRINTS

ODY'S FOUND,
NOBODY'LL

IT'S GIVIN' ME DA SHIVERS, BOSS, BUT I GOTTA ADMIT IT HAS ITS POINTS!

A GRAVE AND GRUESOME SITUATION, THIS, WITH NO TIME TO WASTE IF ALFRED IS TO BE SAVED FROM A HORRIBLE FATE! AND—ALTHOUGH THEY ARE UNAWARE OF THEIR MAJOR-DOMO'S PREDICAMENT, **BATMAN** AND **ROBIN** ARE WASTING NO TIME!

WHAT'S THE IDEA OF HEADING STRAIGHT FOR THE JEWELRY SHOP THAT WAS ROBBED, BATMAN? THE THIEF WON'T STILL BE HANGING AROUND!
HOW DO YOU KNOW?

ND NOW— THE TERRIBLE MOMENT ARRIVES!
BETTER GET IT OVER WITH BEFORE HE COMES TO!
I DON'T MIND PLAIN KILLIN'—BUT I CAN'T WATCH DIS!

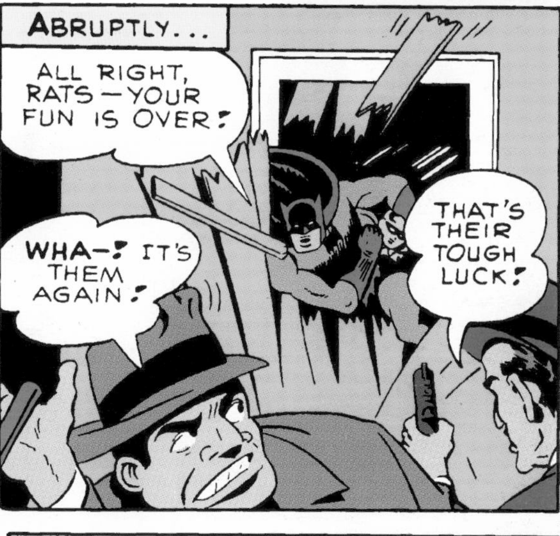

ABRUPTLY...
ALL RIGHT, RATS — YOUR FUN IS OVER!
WHA-! IT'S THEM AGAIN!
THAT'S THEIR TOUGH LUCK!

DON'T LET HIM GET ME!

DON'T FORGET TO WASH BEHIND YOUR EARS WHEN YOU WAKE UP!
QUITE AN INK-SLINGER, ISN'T HE?
IT'S TIME I TOOK A HAND IN THIS!
INK
10

BUT THE NEXT SECOND...

REACH WHILE YOU'RE ABLE, MEDDLERS!

WHERE DID THAT COME FROM?

A TOMMY GUN!

CONSCIOUSNESS RETURNS TO THE DANGLING ALFRED — AND HIGH TIME, TOO!

BUMPING OFF **BATMAN** AND **ROBIN** WILL BE ONE OF THE HAPPIEST CHORES OF MY LIFE!

AND ONE OF THE LAS BEFORE YO WARM UP TH ELECTRIC CHAIR!

WH-WHAT—? WH-WHERE—?.. SO HELP ME, IT' **BATMAN** AND **ROBIN** —AT THE POINT OF DEATH

WHAT HO! YOU CAWN'T DO THAT, YOU KNOW!

HERE IT COMES-! **WHA—!**

GOOD OLD ALFRED! IN THE NICK OF TIME!

THE END OF THE ROAD FOR JOE BART, PRINTER, THIEF AND KILLER

EEL
KE
MING
EAN
ART?
WHY NOT? YOU'VE GOT ME! I USED THIS SHOP TO PRINT FAKE STOCK CERTIFICATES, BUT BUSINESS WAS SLOW, AND I WANTED TO MAKE A BIG HAUL SOMEWHERE AND GET OUT!

I NOTICED RANIER OPENING UP THE JEWELRY STORE, SO I KNEW HE HAD THE KEYS! I KNEW HE WAS AN EX-CON, TOO, AND WOULD BE SUSPECTED IF ANYTHING WENT WRONG!
SO YOU ROUNDED UP SOME GANGSTER PALS TO HELP AND PUT THE FINGER ON HIM YESTERDAY!

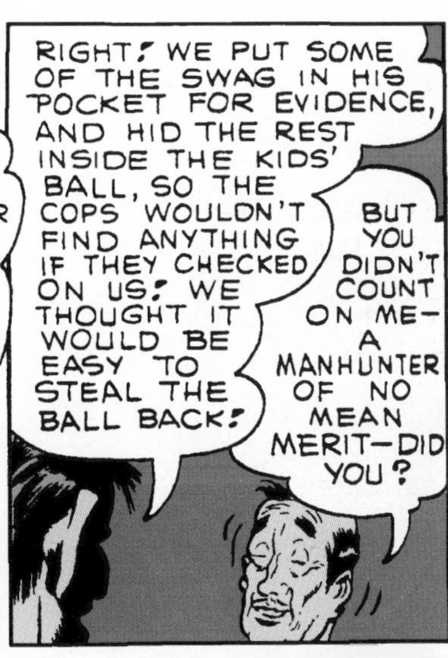
RIGHT! WE PUT SOME OF THE SWAG IN HIS POCKET FOR EVIDENCE, AND HID THE REST INSIDE THE KIDS' BALL, SO THE COPS WOULDN'T FIND ANYTHING IF THEY CHECKED ON US! WE THOUGHT IT WOULD BE EASY TO STEAL THE BALL BACK!
BUT YOU DIDN'T COUNT ON ME— A MANHUNTER OF NO MEAN MERIT—DID YOU?

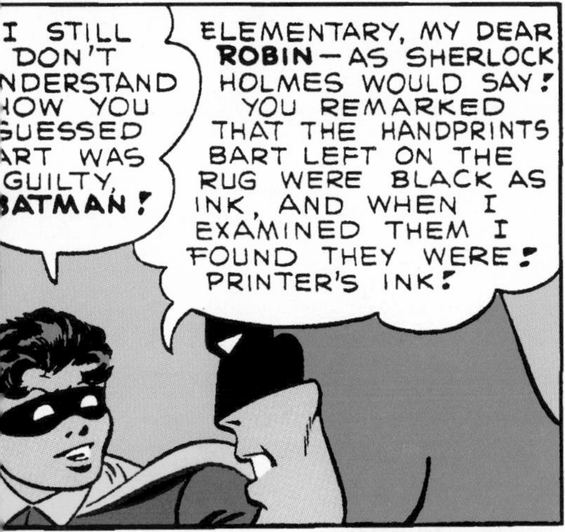
I STILL DON'T NDERSTAND IOW YOU UESSED ART WAS GUILTY, BATMAN!
ELEMENTARY, MY DEAR ROBIN—AS SHERLOCK HOLMES WOULD SAY! YOU REMARKED THAT THE HANDPRINTS BART LEFT ON THE RUG WERE BLACK AS INK, AND WHEN I EXAMINED THEM I FOUND THEY WERE! PRINTER'S INK!

WHEN RANIER TOLD OF MEETING THE OWNER OF THE PRINTING SHOP NEXT DOOR JUST BEFORE HE WAS SLUGGED—
I GET IT!

ATER, WHEN THE THIEVES HAVE BEEN JAILED AND RANIER RELEASED...
OW CAN I VER THANK OU FOR TAKING ARE OF HEM, MR. WAYNE!
DON'T TRY, MRS. RANIER! IT WAS A PLEASURE!
A PLEASURE, HE SAYS!
HERE, MADAM, ARE THE LITTLE -ER- DARLINGS!

AND I'M GLAD TO KNOW THAT YOUR NAME IS CLEARED, RANIER!
I HAVE BATMAN AND ROBIN TO THANK FOR THAT— BUT I DON'T SUPPOSE I'LL EVER SEE THEM AGAIN TO EXPRESS MY GRATITUDE!
IF WE SEE THEM, WE'LL TELL THEM!
THE END

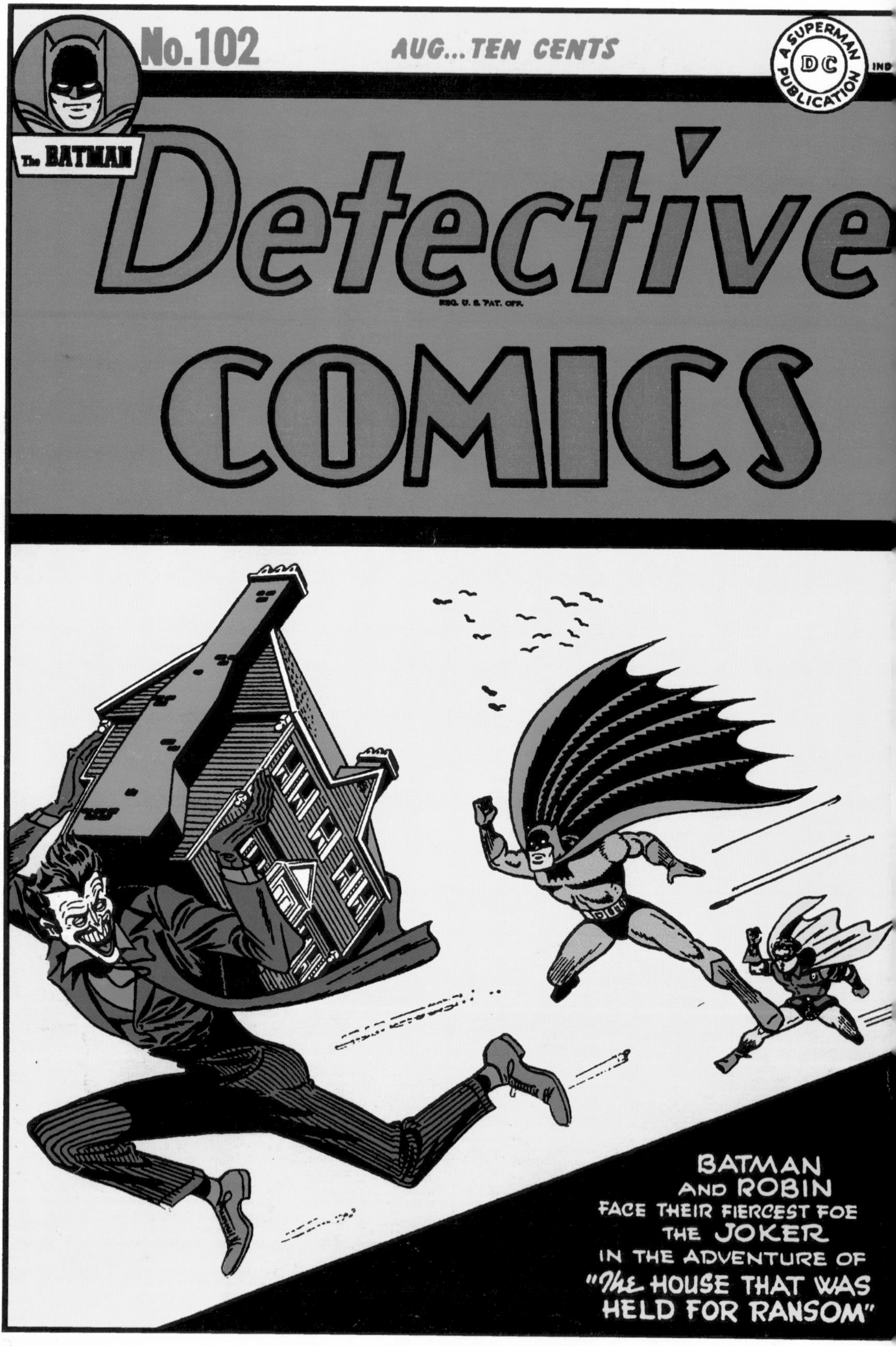

BATMAN
AND ROBIN
FACE THEIR FIERCEST FOE
THE JOKER
IN THE ADVENTURE OF
"The HOUSE THAT WAS
HELD FOR RANSOM"

BATMAN
WITH
ROBIN
-THE BOY WONDER-
LEAVE IT TO THAT MOCKING MASTER OF MENACE, THE JOKER, TO ADD A NEW WRINKLE TO AN OLD RACKET IN ONE OF THE STRANGEST KIDNAPPINGS OF ALL TIME! THE LAUGHING LARCENIST MAKES A BIG MISTAKE, THOUGH, WHEN HE TRIES TO CHANGE A LIVE BATMAN INTO A DEAD PIGEON! AND BIRDS OF A FEATHER GO TO JAIL TOGETHER WHEN A FIGHTING ROBIN JOINS HIS EMBATTLED COMRADE IN A THRILL-PACKED HUNT FOR..."THE HOUSE THAT WAS HELD FOR RANSOM!"
BOB KANE

TWENTY MILES NORTH OF GOTHAM, ON THE EAST BANK OF THE KIDDIWAH RIVER, STANDS A HISTORIC OLD MANSION.

UNDER ITS ANCIENT EAVES, SEVEN GENERATIONS OF STICKNEYS HAVE LIVED AND DIED...

ITS PRESENT OWNER, WEALTHY J. BULLION STICKNEY, IS DEEPLY ATTACHED TO THE HOUSE THAT HOLDS SO MANY MEMORIES...

RARELY VENTURING OFF HIS BELOVED GROUNDS, THE LAST OF THE STICKNEYS PASSES THE TIME TENDING HIS DOVECOTES...

OUR STORY BEGINS WITH A LETTER PICKED UP ONE MORNING BY DODDER, OLD STICKNEY'S ONLY SERVANT...

A LETTER FOR MASTER STICKNEY! MAIL IS A RARE THING IN THIS HOUSE! I HOPE ITS NOT BAD NEWS!

HARUMPH... CAN'T IMAGINE WHO WOULD WRITE TO ME! WELL, LET'S HAVE A LOOK!

POSSIBLY A CIRCULAR, SIR!

Dear Sir:
As a fellow pigeon fancier, you may be interested in some excellent birds I must sell before leaving the city. I shall be staying at the Gotham Hotel Tuesday night. If you can possibly come into town, I am sure it will be worth your while.
Reginald P. Parker

REGGIE PARKER! WHY, HE'S THE GREATEST PIGEON FANCIER IN THE EAST! DODDER, PACK THE OVER-NIGHT BAGS! WE'RE LEAVING FOR GOTHAM CITY THIS AFTERNOON!

GOTHAM CITY! BUT, SIR- YOU HAVEN'T BEEN THAT FAR FROM THE HOUSE IN YEARS!

2

TRUE, DODDER, TRUE BUT YOU KNOW HOW INTERESTED I AM IN PIGEONS! I'M QUITE PREPARED TO ENDURE A NIGHT IN TOWN TO OBTAIN SOME CHOICE SPECIMENS!

UT THAT EVENING, AS STICKNEY ND DODDER ARRIVE AT THE OTHAM HOTEL, AN UNPLEASANT SURPRISE AWAITS THEM...
EGINALD PARKER? HE'S NOT EGISTERED HERE!
WHAT! NOT REGISTERED? BUT THIS IS OUTRAGEOUS!
AMAZING! TRULY AMAZING!
IN ANY CASE, SIR, WE'LL HAVE TO SPEND THE NIGHT! THERE'S NO TRAIN FOR HOME UNTIL MORNING!
I CAN'T UNDERSTAND IT! IF THAT LETTER WAS A HOAX, WHAT WAS THE REASON FOR IT? A QUEER JOKE, I MUST SAY!
A QUEER JOKE INDEED! AND A GRIM ONE, MR. STICKNEY-- AS YOU SHALL SOON DISCOVER!!
HE NEXT MORNING...
OME AT LAST! MAY I NEVER AVE TO SPEND ANOTHER NIGHT TOWN! AH, WHAT A FINE DAY! PPOSE WE WALK TO THE HOUSE!
AN EXCELLENT SUGGESTION, SIR!
VELL, I ECLARE--WE UST HAVE OME THE RONG WAY! DON'T EE THE HOUSE!
WE COULDN'T HAVE THE WRONG PATH! THIS IS VERY STRANGE!
CAN'T BE TRUE! BELOVED HOME! E ONE SOLACE MY DECLINING EARS! HAVE E BOTH ONE AD?
MR. STICKNEY, SIR--A NOTE PINNED ON THIS POST!
SUDDENLY, THE TWO MEN COME UPON AN AMAZING, A FANTASTIC, A TRULY INCREDIBLE SIGHT!
MR. STICKNEY! ARE MY EYES PLAYING TRICKS? THE HOUSE-- IT-- IT'S GONE!
GONE! YES! I SEE, BUT I DON'T BELIEVE IT!
YES, MR. STICKNEY, YOUR PRECIOUS MANSION IS REALLY GONE! WE HAVE MOVED IT TO A SAFE PLACE WHERE WE ARE HOLDING IT FOR RANSOM! AN ORIGINAL IDEA, DON'T YOU THINK? BE SURE TO WATCH THE CLASSIFIED ADS FOR FURTHER INSTRUCTIONS... --THE JOKER
3

KIDNAPPED! A WHOLE HOUSE KIDNAPPED! THAT'S WHY WE WERE LURED TO GOTHAM CITY! ALAS- I'D GLADLY PART WITH MY ENTIRE FORTUNE TO HAVE THE OLD PLACE BACK!
AMAZING! AND WHO IS THE JOKER?

ONLY A RECLUSE WOULD NOT KNOW THE JOKER, THAT PRINCE OF PRANKSTERS, THAT FIENDISH FUNSTER WHOSE DIABOLICAL CRIMES HAVE SPREAD HIS EVIL FAME ACROSS A CONTINENT AND MADE HIM THE ARCHENEMY OF THE MIGHTY **BATMAN!** INDEED, WHAT OTHER BALEFUL BRAIN COULD PLAN SO BOLD A SCHEME AS THIS?

NEWS OF THE STARTLING CRIM
TRAVELS SWIFTLY- AND INTERRUPTS THE VACATION OF BRUCE WAYNE AND DICK GRAYSO

WE SHOULD REACH THE SITE OF THE HOUSE IN ANOTHER THREE HOURS!

I CAN'T UNDERSTAND HOW IT WAS MOVED WITHOU LEAVING TRACK WE'RE GOING TO HAVE OUR HANDS FULL!

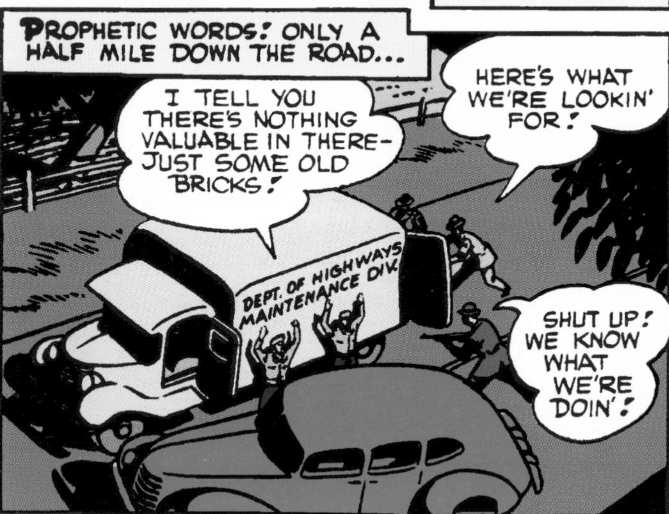

PROPHETIC WORDS! ONLY A HALF MILE DOWN THE ROAD...
I TELL YOU THERE'S NOTHING VALUABLE IN THERE- JUST SOME OLD BRICKS!
HERE'S WHAT WE'RE LOOKIN' FOR!
DEPT. OF HIGHWAYS MAINTENANCE DIV.
SHUT UP! WE KNOW WHAT WE'RE DOIN'!

WHAT'RE WE STOPPING FOR?
TAKE A LOOK UP AHEAD! IF THAT DOESN'T LOOK LIKE A HOLDUP-!

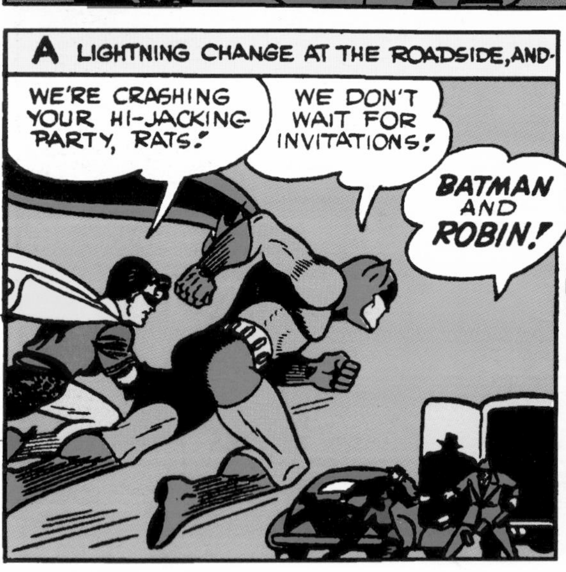

A LIGHTNING CHANGE AT THE ROADSIDE, AND-
WE'RE CRASHING YOUR HI-JACKING PARTY, RATS!
WE DON'T WAIT FOR INVITATIONS!
BATMAN AND ROBIN!

PARDON MY IMPETUOSITY! I'M IN A HURRY!

OOF!

CHIN UP FELLA!
HERE'S A BRICKBAT FOR THE BRAT!

PASS INTERCEPTED!

NOW IT'S MY TURN TO HEAVE ONE!
THEY'RE GETTING AWAY!

ANKS, BATMAN! BUT I N'T IMAGINE WHY THOSE ROOKS WERE AFTER SOME D BRICKS WE CLEARED F THE ANFORD REEK RIDGE!

IS THAT ALL THEY WANTED?

DEPAR
MAINTE

YOU SAY YOU FOUND A HEAP OF THESE ON THE BRIDGE WHILE MAKING AN INSPECTION TOUR? HMM... MAYBE I'D BETTER TAKE A COUPLE ALONG AND CHECK THEM IN MY LABORATORY! THEY MUST HAVE SOME KIND OF VALUE...

ALL THESE BRICKS HAVE SOOT MARKS ON ONE SIDE! MAYBE THEY CAME FROM A FIREPLACE!
THAT DOESN'T EXPLAIN THEIR VALUE TO THOSE THUGS! MEANWHILE, THOUGH, WE'VE GOT TO WORRY ABOUT THE JOKER, NOT BRICKS!
5

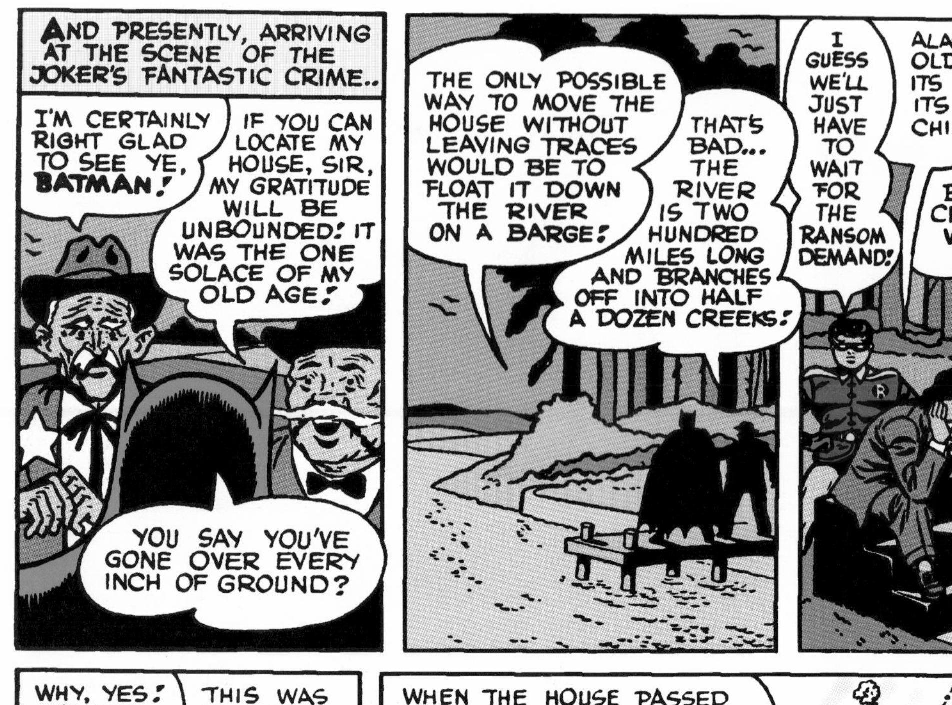
AND PRESENTLY, ARRIVING AT THE SCENE OF THE JOKER'S FANTASTIC CRIME..
I'M CERTAINLY RIGHT GLAD TO SEE YE, BATMAN!
IF YOU CAN LOCATE MY HOUSE, SIR, MY GRATITUDE WILL BE UNBOUNDED! IT WAS THE ONE SOLACE OF MY OLD AGE!
YOU SAY YOU'VE GONE OVER EVERY INCH OF GROUND?
THE ONLY POSSIBLE WAY TO MOVE THE HOUSE WITHOUT LEAVING TRACES WOULD BE TO FLOAT IT DOWN THE RIVER ON A BARGE!
THAT'S BAD... THE RIVER IS TWO HUNDRED MILES LONG AND BRANCHES OFF INTO HALF A DOZEN CREEKS!
I GUESS WE'LL JUST HAVE TO WAIT FOR THE RANSOM DEMAND!
ALAS- MY LOVELY OLD HOUSE WITH ITS OAK RAFTERS ITS BRICK CHIMNEYS-
BRICK CHIMNEYS! WAIT!

WHY, YES! IT'S THE SAME TYPE OF BRICK AS MY CHIMNEYS! BUT WHY DO YOU ASK?
THIS WAS FOUND ON THE STANFORD CREEK BRIDGE! QUICK, SOMEONE GET ME A MAP OF THE RIVER!

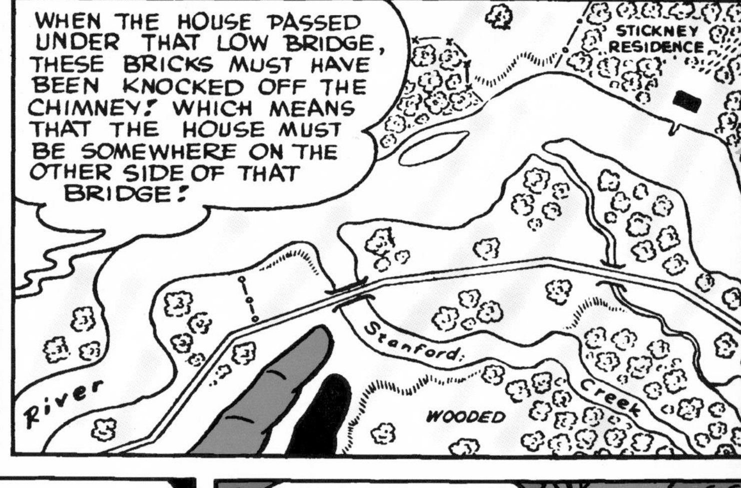
WHEN THE HOUSE PASSED UNDER THAT LOW BRIDGE, THESE BRICKS MUST HAVE BEEN KNOCKED OFF THE CHIMNEY! WHICH MEANS THAT THE HOUSE MUST BE SOMEWHERE ON THE OTHER SIDE OF THAT BRIDGE!
STICKNEY RESIDENCE
Stanford Creek
River
WOODED

WHAT'S MORE—ON THIS MAP THE CREEK IS NOT NAVIGABLE FOR MORE THAN A THOUSAND YARDS PAST THE BRIDGE! THAT'S WHY THOSE CROOKS WANTED THE BRICKS! THEY WERE A TIP-OFF TO THE HIDING PLACE!

IF THE HOUSE IS THERE, WE SHOULD BE ABLE TO SPOT IT FROM THE AIR, ROBIN!
SO IT'S US FOR THE BATPLANE. THIS TIME WE'VE GOT THE JOKER WHERE WE WANT HIM!

LATE THAT AFTERNOON...
NO SIGN OF ANYTHING YET! I'M AFRAID THE JOKER HAS THE HOUSE CAREFULLY CAMOUFLAGED!
WE'VE GOT TO KEEP TRYING, BATMAN!

MEANWHILE, IN THE VERY ROOM WHERE OLD STICKNEY USED TO SIT WITH HIS HALLOWED MEMORIES...

HA-HA! SO THE BATMAN GOT THE BRICKS! HA-HA! HAW!
BUT, JOKER-WHAT'S SO FUNNY?
THE BATMAN MIGHT BUST IN ANY MINUTE, AN' HE SITS THERE AN' LAUGHS!

WHY, YOU MUTTON-HEADS, IT'S A SET-UP! THIS IS OUR ONE CHANCE TO GET RID OF THE BATMAN FOR GOOD! THEN IT'LL BE A CINCH TO COLLECT THE RANSOM! SNOOZER, YOU AND THE BOYS GET THE DOVECOTE DOWN FROM THE ROOF!

OKAY, JOKER! YOU MUST KNOW WHAT YE'RE DOIN'!

SO THE BATMAN MIGHT DROP IN ON US, EH? WELL, WE'LL JUST MAKE IT A LITTLE EASIER FOR HIM TO FIND US! HA-HA!

WHAT DEVILISH DEVICE IS THIS SIMPERING SATAN PLANNING NOW? WHAT SINISTER SIGNIFICANCE LURKS BEHIND THE JOKER'S GRIM GUFFAWS

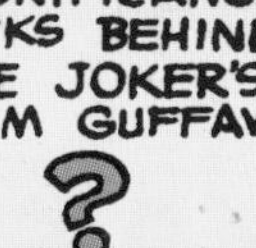

AS THE SUN SINKS IN THE WESTERN SKY...

WELL, ROBIN, IT'S BEGINNING TO LOOK RATHER HOPELESS...

NOTHING BUT TREES LINING THE BANKS ON BOTH SIDES! BUT WAIT—THOSE PIGEONS FLYING ABOUT DOWN THERE!

PIGEONS—OF COURSE! THE HOUSE MAY BE DIRECTLY BELOW! LOWER THE ROPE LADDER!

GUESS THE JOKER DIDN'T EXPECT HIS CAMOUFLAGE TO GO FOWL!

I STILL CAN'T MAKE OUT THE HOUSE..
IF IT WEREN'T FOR THOSE PIGEONS...

7

THAT'S FUNNY— THE HOUSE ISN'T HERE!
THAT DOVECOTE! IT MUST HAVE BEEN CARRIED FROM THE HOUSE! ROBIN— THIS LOOKS LIKE A TRAP!

WE'D BETTER GET OUT OF HERE BEFORE— OOF!
A CONK ON DA HEAD PUTS DA BATMAN TO BED!
THE JOKER! UGH!

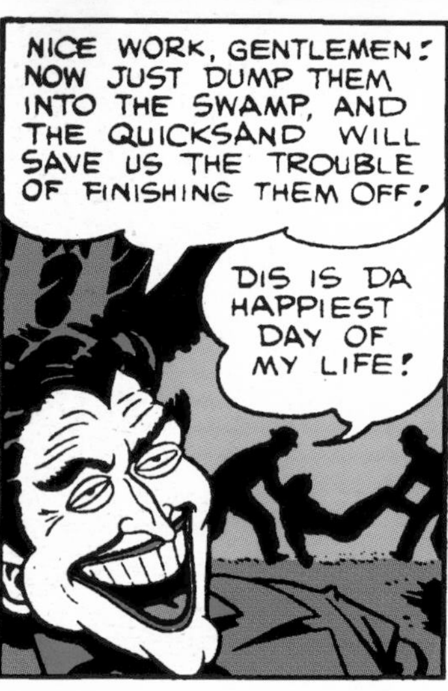
NICE WORK, GENTLEMEN! NOW JUST DUMP THEM INTO THE SWAMP, AND THE QUICKSAND WILL SAVE US THE TROUBLE OF FINISHING THEM OFF!
DIS IS DA HAPPIEST DAY OF MY LIFE!

PERFECT! IN A SHORT WHILE, THERE WON'T BE A TRACE LEFT OF THEM! JUST THE QUIET OOZING QUICKSAND AND THE CROAKING FROGS! HA-HA-HA! NOW LET'S GET THE DOVECOTE BACK TO THE HOUSE!

GIT INSIDE, BOIDIES! YOUSE IS GOIN' HOME! OOPS— I SLAMMED THE DOOR ON DIS ONE'S WING!

GEE, JOKER, I HOIT ONE OF DEM! MAYBE I BETTER CARRY DE POOR LITTLE T'ING IN MY ARMS...
THIS IS A FINE TIME TO GET SENTIMENTAL! LEAVE IT THERE! ONE PIGEON MORE OR LESS DOESN'T MATTER!

CHEE...DA POOR LIDDLE PIGEON... LEFT ALL ALONE IN DA FOREST WID A BUSTED WING! WELL, DAT'S LIFE!
8

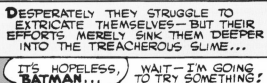

AND BACK AT THE SWAMP...
WHA-! QUICKSAND! AND WE'RE SINKING FAST! ROBIN!
MM... HUH?

DESPERATELY THEY STRUGGLE TO EXTRICATE THEMSELVES—BUT THEIR EFFORTS MERELY SINK THEM DEEPER INTO THE TREACHEROUS SLIME...
IT'S HOPELESS, BATMAN...
WAIT—I'M GOING TO TRY SOMETHING!

EVERISHLY BATMAN RIPS THE LINING OF HIS PE INTO NARROW STRIPS AND KNOTS THEM TO A MAKESHIFT ROPE—BUT...
MAYBE IF YOU TIE THIS ON... IT'S A PIECE OF BRICK FROM THE STICKNEY CHIMNEY! I HAD IT IN MY POCKET...
IT'S NO USE—THIS CLOTH IS TOO LIGHT TO CARRY THAT FAR...

IF THIS DOESN'T WORK, WE'RE LOST!

STEEL MUSCLES STRAIN AT THE CRUDE ROPE... SLOWLY, RELUCTANTLY, THE SWAMP GIVES UP ITS VICTIMS...

EXHAUSTED, THE VALIANT PAIR PAUSE BRIEFLY TO REST—THEN...
9

THE HOUSE COULD BE ANYWHERE ALONG THE CREEK BANK FOR A THOUSAND YARDS! IT'LL TAKE HOURS TO FIND IT— WE'VE GOT TO BE CAREFUL NOT TO WALK INTO ANOTHER TRAP...
SAY— WHAT'S THAT COOING NOISE?

WHY, IT'S A PIGEON! AND ITS WING IS BROKEN!
MUST BE ONE OF STICKNEY'S BIRDS! LET'S HAVE A LOOK!

HMM... THIS WING ISN'T BROKEN, JUST DISLOCATED MAYBE I CAN SNAP IT BACK INTO PLACE!

THERE, THAT'S BETTER! AND IT GIVES ME AN IDEA! THE FIRST PLACE THAT PIGEON WILL HEAD FOR IS HOME—
SO IT CAN LEAD US STRAIGHT TO THE HOUSE! BUT HOW ARE WE GOING TO FOLLOW IT?

ITS WING ISN'T IN GOOD ENOUGH SHAPE FOR ANY REAL FLYING! SEE HOW IT'S HEDGEHOPPING? LET'S GO!
WHAT A JOKE ON THE JOKER! HE TRAPPED US WITH PIGEONS, AND NOW WE'LL TRAP HIM THE SAME WAY!

AND ONLY MINUTES LATER...
THE HOUSE! COVERED WITH A CAMOUFLAGE NET SO WE COULDN'T SPOT IT FROM THE AIR!
AND STILL ON THE ROLLERS THEY USED TO BRING IT UP FROM THE CREEK BANK!

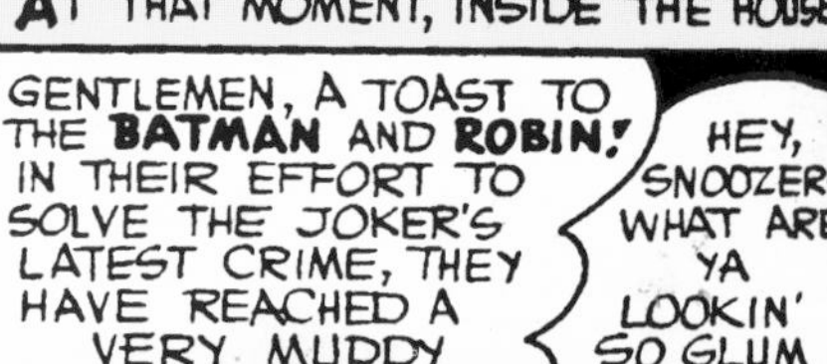
AT THAT MOMENT, INSIDE THE HOUSE.

GENTLEMEN, A TOAST TO THE BATMAN AND ROBIN! IN THEIR EFFORT TO SOLVE THE JOKER'S LATEST CRIME, THEY HAVE REACHED A VERY MUDDY CONCLUSION! HA-HA!
HEY, SNOOZER- WHAT ARE YA LOOKIN' SO GLUM ABOUT?
10

I WUZ JUS'
NKIN' OF DAT
OOR LITTLE
IGEON! IT
AKES ME FEEL
KE A HEEL!
WE'RE GOING TO MAKE YOU FEEL A LOT WORSE!
GHOSTS !!
DON'T YOU TWO EVER STAY DEAD?
OW- I WISH I WUZ SAFE IN JAIL!
BOK!
THIS IS AN OLD
AG, BUT I CAN'T
E CHOOSY AT A
IME LIKE THIS!
YOUR HOUSE-NAPPING DAYS WILL SOON BE OVER!
NEVER COUNT YOUR JAIL-BIRDS BEFORE THEY'RE CAUGHT! HA-HA!
NCE MORE, THE JOKER IS ON TOP...
YOU'LL NOT ESCAPE THIS TIME!
BUT ONLY TEMPORARILY...!
A RAT WITHOUT A GAT IS JUST A MOUSE!
OWW!
11

YOU HAVEN'T GOT ME YET!
WHO KNOWS? MAYBE IT'LL WORK AGAIN!
YOW!
TSK-TSK—TO THINK YOU'D FALL FOR SUCH AN OLD GAG!
AND NOW—AS I WAS SAYING ABOUT PUTTING YOU AWAY—!
AND HERE'S SOME MORE MISERY TO KEEP YOU COMPANY!
QUICK, BOSS! DO SOMETHIN'!
HE'S GOING TO DO SOMETHING! AND SO WILL ALL OF YOU — ABOUT TWENTY YEARS!
THAT'S WHAT YOU THINK, BATMAN! YOU JUST WAIT AND SEE!
12
SEVERAL DAYS LATER...
WE MADE THE OLD MAN HAPPY AND THE JOKER SAD—WHICH IS AS IT SHOULD BE!
THERE'S THE HOUSE THAT WAS HELD FOR RANSOM, BACK WHERE IT BELONGS—AND STICKNEY WAVING A GREETING AT US!
THE END

HARDIN "JACK" BURNLEY

Working for King Features Syndicate in 1929, an 18-year-old Jack Burnley became the youngest artist at the time ever to have a syndicated feature. Turning freelance in 1938, he soon received assignments for single-page sports fillers from DC Comics. One of his earliest published DC assignments was the cover of NEW YORK WORLD'S FAIR 1940. Burnley also developed Starman and became DC's top ghost artist, handling the main characters and best titles. He pencilled over 100 covers and worked on many stories as well as the *Batman and Robin* and *Superman* newspaper strips. Burnley left DC in August 1947 to return to sports cartooning. He now lives in Virginia.

DON CAMERON

Don Cameron was born December 21, 1905 in Detroit. He worked in newspapers, moved to New York in 1934 and began writing pulp fiction in 1935. The first of several mystery novels appeared in 1939 (*Murder's Coming*, Henry Holt). During September 1941, he began working for DC Comics, his chief source of income for over six years. Among others, he handled scripts for Batman, Superman, Johnny Quick and nearly all of Superboy's initial appearances in MORE FUN COMICS. Cameron evidently left comics in November 1947, although his inventoried scripts continued to appear. He returned to newpaper work and was working on a book about occultism when he died of cancer in New York City on November 17, 1954.

BILL FINGER

Born February 8, 1914, Bill Finger met cartoonist Bob Kane at a party in 1938. They subsequently collaborated on several adventure strips including Batman. Finger made several significant suggestions, including a cowl and gloves, and wrote Batman's first two adventures for DETECTIVE COMICS. His fondness for pulp fiction and movies heavily influenced his plots and writing style for comic books. Although notoriously tardy with submissions, Finger was a gifted and prodigious author, working on numerous DC characters as well as writing for Quality Comics, Fawcett and Timely. His TV credits include *Hawaiian Eye* and a two-part Clock King episode for the *Batman* TV series. He died in Manhattan on January 24, 1974.

PAT GORDON

Born in 1914, Lora A. Sprang sometimes worked pseudonymously as Pat Gordon. She was married to Dick Sprang when he began illustrating Batman. Sprang taught Gordon how to letter comics and, except for his earliest efforts, Gordon lettered many of his Batman stories, coloring a number of them as well. She also freelanced as a photographer for *Film Fun* magazine, hand-lettered titles for industrial films, worked on title photography and art for Navy training films during World War II and did theater posters for 20th Century-Fox. Gordon continued to work for DC Comics throughout the 1950s, lettering numerous stories for Batman, Superman, Superboy and others. She left DC about 1961.

JOSEPH GREENE

Joseph Greene was born August 1, 1914. His tenure at DC Comics began in 1942 on the All-American line with his final DC efforts appearing around 1946. Greene wrote for Aquaman, Boy Commandos, Green Arrow, Hawkman, Superman, and Wonder Woman among others. During the 1940s and 1950s, he also worked for Fawcett, Hillman, Holyoke, Ken Crossen, Lev Gleason, Timely and Whitman. He was a writer of science fiction and mystery books, short stories and non-fiction as well as radio and TV. He worked at Grosset and Dunlap from 1964 to 1973 and is believed to be deceased. (Some information courtesy of Jerry Bails's *Who's Who of American Comic Books*.)

EDMOND HAMILTON

Considered one of the major pioneers in science fiction pulps and a protagonist of U.S. space opera beginning in 1928, Edmond Hamilton's stories of interplanetary conflicts and universe-spanning adventures eventually earned him the nicknames "World-Saver Hamilton" and "The World Wrecker." Hamilton wrote the first Batman/Superman team-up story from SUPERMAN #76 (1952), as well as many of the subsequent team-ups appearing in WORLD'S FINEST COMICS. He also introduced Kathy Kane as the first Batwoman in 1956. Hamilton wrote numerous scripts for various Superman Family titles and is held in high esteem for his work on the Legion of Super-Heroes. He continued to write novels until 1968, and collections of his work appeared into the 1970s. Hamilton died February 1, 1977.

BOB KANE

In 1936, Bob Kane pencilled and inked his first comic-book work, Hiram Hick. By 1938, he was selling humorous filler stories to DC Comics. Kane met writer Bill Finger that same year, and they soon were collaborating on comic-book submissions, Batman being their most famous effort. Kane kept up the pace of Batman's success by adding assistants and dropping non-Batman assignments. He discontinued comic-book efforts in mid-1943 to pencil the daily *Batman and Robin* newspaper strip. After the strip's 1946 demise, Kane returned to comics, and with the help of several ghosts remained involved with Batman until retiring in 1968. Kane has been featured in various one-man art shows by galleries and museums nationwide, and he served as a consultant on the Warner Bros. *Batman* feature films from the last ten years. The autobiographical *Batman and Me* was published in 1989.

ED KRESSY

Former Associated Press illustrator Ed Kressy linked up with fellow artists Dick Sprang and Norm Fallon in 1936, freelancing commercial art from a New York loft office. Kressy's by-line appeared on King Features' *The Lone Ranger* Sunday syndicated newspaper strip from its September 11, 1938 inception through March 5, 1939. He worked on dailies from September 12, 1938 through January 28, 1939. Several Power Nelson stories in *Prize Comics* followed. Sprang recalls that Kressy did rough pencil layouts for probably three of Sprang's earliest Batman stories, which Sprang then pencilled and inked. Kressy died at age 84 in 1986.

BIOGRAPHIES

CHARLES PARIS

Born in 1911, Charles Paris moved to New York in 1934. He met Jack Lehti in spring 1941 and shortly was inking and lettering Lehti's Crimson Avenger for DETECTIVE COMICS. Paris soon obtained a job in the DC bullpen inking Airwave, later working on Vigilante and Johnny Quick among others. He inked most of the 1943-1946 *Batman and Robin* newspaper strip and then became the regular inker on numerous Batman comic-book stories and covers until 1964. His last regular DC assignment was the 1960s METAMORPHO. Between the late 1940s and mid-1950s, Paris produced a variety of artwork outside of comics including Western genre paintings. Paris died March 19, 1994 due to complications from an auto accident.

JERRY ROBINSON

It was around October 1939 when a 17-year-old Jerry Robinson began assisting Bob Kane. Within three years, Robinson was completely pencilling, lettering, inking and coloring stories and covers for BATMAN and DETECTIVE COMICS. Robinson's numerous and diverse credits include illustration and advertising work as well as comic-book art. He created and illustrated various syndicated newspaper features and has taught and lectured on graphic journalism at the School of Visual Arts and The New School in New York. Robinson is the only past president of both the Association of American Editorial Cartoonists and the National Cartoonists Society, having also been awarded three Reubens. He has written several books and illustrated over 30 others. He is the President and Editorial Director of Cartoonists & Writers Syndicate.

GEORGE ROUSSOS

George Roussos was hired by Jerry Robinson to assist on Batman by lettering and inking backgrounds. His first work in this capacity appeared in BATMAN #2 (Summer 1940) and he was a mainstay until 1944 when he went freelance. Roussos pencilled, inked and colored Airwave, as well as inking Superman, Johnny Quick, Star Spangled Kid, Vigilante and other DC characters and titles. From the late 1940s into the 1950s, he worked freelance for a number of comic-book publishers, including Harvey, Hillman, Avon, Ziff-Davis, Fiction House, EC, Timely, Prize and Pines. In 1963, Roussos began inking stories for Marvel, including X-Men, Fantastic Four, Captain America and many others. He left DC around 1970 to work full-time for Marvel and soon became cover colorist. His career in the comic-book field spans over a half century, and his contributions are numerous.

ALVIN SCHWARTZ

Alvin Schwartz was born in New York City in 1916. He sold several comic-book scripts to Street and Smith Publications around 1941, subsequently writing for All-American Comics and Fawcett, then joining DC in 1944. He wrote for the *Superman* and *Batman and Robin* newspaper strips, and worked on numerous DC characters, including the first in a series of Superman/Batman team-up stories (WORLD'S FINEST COMICS #71, July-August 1954). He left DC in 1958 and set up his own consulting firm, later working in advertising and at the National Film Board of Canada. His literary efforts outside of comics include *The Blowtop* (Dial Press, 1948) and a novel, *No Such Mirrors* (Montreal, 1973). His most recent book, An *Unlikely Prophet* (Divina) was released in 1998.

DICK SPRANG

Born in 1915, Dick Sprang moved to New York City in 1936, freelancing art as well as writing and illustrating pulp stories. Editor Whitney Ellsworth assigned Sprang's first Batman story in 1941, but concerns about the potential drafting of Bob Kane resulted in Sprang's material being inventoried until 1943. Sprang principally illustrated Batman stories and covers; however, from 1955 through 1963, he also pencilled Superman/Batman team-up stories for WORLD'S FINEST COMICS. He departed comics in 1963. His stories were first reprinted in 1961, and nearly all subsequent Batman collections have contained at least one of his efforts. He began recreating comic-book material in 1984 and finally returned to comics in 1987 with occasional assignments.

MORT WEISINGER

Mort Weisinger was born April 25, 1915. He became an editor at Standard Magazines in 1936, moving to DC Comics in 1940. Weisinger created Aquaman, Green Arrow, Johnny Quick and Vigilante, while also writing for other characters. He served in the Army from 1943 until late in 1945 and, upon returning, acquired editorial duties for all Superman titles. He plotted numerous stories, introduced new villains and characters and was responsible for the Fortress of Solitude among other significant elements of Superman mythology. Weisinger served as story editor on the 1950s *Superman* TV series, and ultimately departed DC in 1970. He also wrote several hundred articles and three books. Weisinger died May 7, 1978.

Biographical material researched and written by Joe Desris.